John Watkins Pitchford

The Morning Song

A ninefold praise of love

John Watkins Pitchford

The Morning Song
A ninefold praise of love

ISBN/EAN: 9783744775618

Printed in Europe, USA, Canada, Australia, Japan

Cover: Foto ©Thomas Meinert / pixelio.de

More available books at **www.hansebooks.com**

THE
MORNING SONG

A Ninefold Praise of Love

BY

JOHN WATKINS PITCHFORD

LONDON: ELLIOT STOCK
1883

CONTENTS.

BOOK	PAGE
I. The Song of Earth's Beauty	1
II. The Song of Life	39
III. The Song of Sorrow	77
IV. The Song of Human Life	113
V. The Song of the Past	155
VI. The Song of Incarnate Love	185
VII. The Song of Love's Triumph	221
VIII. The Song of the Militant Host	273
IX. The Requiem Song	319

BOOK THE FIRST

THE SONG OF EARTH'S BEAUTY

THE ARGUMENT.

Object of the work set forth—Invocation—Love the language of the beautiful—Beauty everywhere—View from the southern downs described—Joy of existence prompting the inquiry—Difficulties of the subject—Beauty of the night—A moonlight scene—Changes of light and shade—Each clime its own loveliness—Woodlands in spring—View of the sea from the downs in summer—Storm in the Atlantic—Moonrise in tropical seas—Beauty of the human form—Meaning of the earth's beauty—Why this order, symmetry, grace?—Variety—The seasons—Spring—The festival of flowers—The hay-field—Dusk in the harvest-field—Golden September—Afternoon in the orchard—Approach of winter—Frost work—The wintry landscape—Nature full of instruction—Human life mirrored—The flush of the dawn—Early morning village scene—Morning of life—The pause of noon—Life's solemn noon—Approach of evening—The shadowed fields, hushed village, darkened churchyard—Life's night—Whisperings of nature—The cadence of life.

BOOK THE FIRST.

THE SONG OF EARTH'S BEAUTY.

F Love I sing, the pure celestial stream,
Fountain of natural love, the fount of life;
The loveliest of the graces, sovereign, chief,
Throned in the mystery of divinity;
Crown of all attributes, encrowned in God;
The fairest jewel of philosophy,
Enshrined in natural things, in providence,
In human life; with purest lustre seen
In One, pre-eminently Son of Man,
Yet Son of God, whose love's constraining power
Has ruled the centuries; and of that time
When the King's daughter glorious shall return
Th' accepted bride, in garments redolent
Of myrrh and cassia, heaven's high festival.
Majestic theme! best fitted to the best,
Fitly adventured by angelic powers,
Sung by the brightest seraph, yet unsung,

That passes understanding, heights and depths
Beyond the plummet as beyond the wing
Of loftiest reason, or ambition high :
Unworthy and inapt, yet with a heart
Attuned by gratitude, by impulse led,
Attraction irresistible of love,
I sing. Great effluence of the Father's love,
Thyself essential love, to Thee I turn,
And Thee invoke, not in dumb platitude
Of customary verse, but with desire,
And prayer sincere ; and Thee, O Spirit blest!
Since 'tis Thy function to diffuse that love
Whose praise I now would sing, Thine aid bestow
Instruct, uphold, direct the aspiring thought,
And with Thy blessing sanctify the end.

   The language of the beautiful is love.
Not in far distant worlds, systems remote,
Need proof demonstrative of love be sought.
Here is it found on our familiar earth ;
Nor here alone in choice peculiar scenes,
Landscapes whose loveliness is world renowned ;
The snowy mountain range that piercing heaven
Wears for its mantle heaven's imperial blue ;
Or the high summits of the silver clouds ;
Cliffs towering high, mirrored in clear blue lakes,
The silvery cataract, the peaceful glade ;
Pacific coral reefs, 'mid purple seas,
Edged with white wavy lines of endless surf ;
Rivers that wind through woods their shining streams
Or golden oceans in the flood of noon ;
But everywhere are its rich treasures spread ;

Few glimpses in the natural world but yield
That which we seek, the evidence of love.
 No audible voice in this bright pleasant hour
Comes through the breezy silence to the ear.
The golden day, the all-embracing light
That curtains yon blue hills, the cadence full
Of varying and innumerable tones
In the great anthem of created life,
Whisper their message to the listening mind.
The eye looks forth from these steep grassy downs
Whose thymy slopes roll towards the cultured plain
That westward stretches to the Severn's flood
And the Atlantic, rich, well wooded, full
Of centuries of labour and of love;
A landscape broad, well peopled, gardened well.
Floating o'erhead in summer's dazzling blue,
Majestical, as stately argosies
Upon calm southern seas, glide mounded clouds,
Towering like Alpine cliffs precipitous,
Snow-flanked, or icebergs in their southward drift,
Met by the gentle winds that breathe around
Bermuda, or the Azores, the warmer waves
Lapping their gelid flanks till masses fall
Dislodged, and vanish in blue ocean depths.
How grand a roof for this fair summer scene!
Like heaven's own dome it seems, the vestibule
Sublime of the great palace of heaven's King.
Miles wide, extending to the horizon's edge
Where distant hills round off the fading view,
The peaceful landscape lies. Here, at the foot
Of these broad grassy bastions, harvest fields

Unfold their golden treasures to the sun,
A sea of red ripe corn on which the eye
Rests with delight; the rich brown billows sway
And whisper, as the wind breathes fitfully,
Throwing the laughing ripples o'er the field.
Like birds at play, o'er the broad cloth of gold
Cloud shadows chase each other, till once more
Unbroken sunshine slumbers on the grain.
Bordered with ragged and uneven elms
Fields beyond fields, orchards and groves are seen,
With glimpses of bright green among the woods
Mellowed by distance; cornfields interspersed;
Homesteads 'mid bowering foliage; cottage smoke,
Rising in light blue columns through the trees,
Or film that floats above the far-off town;
And thickening woodlands in the bluish haze
Of distance; dotted here and there, far off,
Gray towers of ancient village churches rise;
The fitful breeze coyly reveals the scene,
Then hides its beauties, as the drifting clouds
Pass and repass, and on the landscape throw
Islands of golden light. The summer wind
Blows softly o'er a thousand scenes like this,
Peaceful and bright, in our well-ordered land.

 The peewit's call, the crow of farmyard cock
Far off upon the downs, scarce audible,
The low faint swish as sweeps the vagrant wind
Among the bents and clover blossoms near,
The sheep-bell's tinkle from the rambling flock
Are heard; then, all is still. The silence quakes.
An arm's length round yields wealth of flowers abloom

Ungardened in wild simple loveliness,
And unobtrusive; cinquefoil, eyebright meek,
Or wild thyme clustered in its mimic groves,
Where the exploring ants run to and fro,
A fragrant world! The orange tawny bee
Comes by on busy way with surly hum,
Fluttering the tremulous harebells in his path;
The shining swallow in its rapid flight
Skimming the bents, shoots down the steep hillside,
And with its twitter startles from the corn,
The lark, who springs on high, drops a few notes,
And straight is still. The silent grassy mounds,
Earthworks with their forgotten history,
Are near, thrown up in anxious perilous times,
When breathless scout or spy told of the foe,
And set a thousand willing arms to work,
Building these ramparts. All deserted now!
Nor bugle's call, nor sentry's challenge sounds,
Left to the foraging bee or clambering sheep.
  The breeze that fans the brow, tossing the plumes
Of meadow grass, whispers its secret, peace.
A feeling of instinctive joy, pleased sense
Of living fills the breast; of mere delight
To be in this bright hour, in this, God's world,
One of His creatures, sheltered by His care.
The mind is proud to know, to recognise
And give expression to the natural joy
Of being; prouder far to look abroad
And by our rational intelligence,
The gift distinctive of our race, to pay
Its homage to the Intelligence Supreme.

Come forth, O longing heart, pining to know
Life's true felicity, that fain would learn
How the Almighty is disposed to man,
And how to thee; momentous question! asked
Instinctively by thousands; whose reply
Decides grave issues; brings perplexity,
That drops the anchor in the quicksands deep
Of endless doubt, there to abide the storm;
Or, bright and happy hours of sunny love,
Of confidence divine, far-reaching thoughts
And lasting satisfaction, gratitude
That makes each hour a shrine, a sacrifice
Each good possessed, yea, even life itself
Ceaseless oblation. Blest reply! faint heard,
Or, with conviction's deeper tones, borne in
Upon the mind, sweet memories thee await;
Days filled with cheerful labours, peaceful nights,
Sorrow's submissive smile, a heart at rest,
Firm anchorage of the soul, conviction sure
Of an o'er-ruling Hand that safely guides
Our frail and lonely bark o'er life's rough sea.
Adventure forth and yield thee to the dream,
If dream it be, o'er which earth's best have mused,
Whose potency has nursed the strength sublime
Of martyrdom, and lit the face of saints
With calm, celestial light. No vision dim,
But glorious certainty, oft realised;
Embodied in earth's ever-changing forms
Of natural loveliness, or sweetly sung
By voices countless as the ocean waves
Blending harmoniously; a strain unheard,

Unheeded, in the thickening din; a good,
Like other excellencies of this life,
Disparaged, since approachable and near,
Oft dimly veiled by trivialities,
By dull familiarities and cares,
Yet life's best things, through lack of earnestness,
And resolution of the thoughtful mind,
Excluded, to th' impoverishment of life.
   Much to perplex awaits the inquiring mind,
In this wide scene, much that must still remain
For the clear light of heaven's eternal day:
Yet, though with broken harmonies full oft,
And discords pitiful, that wake the soul
To echoes sympathetic, undefined
And desolate yearnings, hauntings drear of doubt,
Still may'st thou hear the grand harmonious psalm
Of nature, rising 'neath the azure vault;
May'st hear, perchance, if that to thee be given
The keener spiritual sense that apprehends
Things spiritual, the inward harmony,
And blending of things natural with those
Of heavenly origin: thus welcoming peace,
The mild majestic sovereign of the heart.
   As flows the evening light from tint to tint,
Quivering and tremulous through an endless scale,
Colour's gradations infinite, so flows
The tide of beauty, filling every nook,
Crevice, and cranny of this varied world.
The purple night unveils the starry sky,
Sublime, astonishing magnificence!
The moon in mild tranquillity serene

Riding alone the blue unclouded heavens,
Bathes with soft radiance hamlet, field, and wood,
Plain, hill, or shining river seen afar ;
Hushed is the silent world, save when the bark
Of distant house-dog borne upon the wind,
Or brawl of pebbly brook the silence breaks.
Night's starry concave wheels its grand array
All silently, from the dim shutting up
Of dewy eve, what time the noiseless bat
Flits 'mid the darkening trees on velvet wing,
Till the fair innocent face of morning smile,
Crowned with baptismal dew ; worlds upon worlds,
Each orb with rich appurtenance of life,
Worlds upon worlds scattered throughout the void !
Far distant nebulæ, resolvable
To suns and systems, planets numberless ;
Prodigious distances ungrasped by thought.
Here silent stand ! here think how grandly roofed
Is this familiar earth, this threshold dim
Of the star-paved infinity ! this speck
And unconsidered mote, amid the array
Of powdered star-dust, and unnumbered worlds.
Here from the open tent look forth ; hence gaze
Up boundless vistas, down the awful depths.
The confident mind trips forth, but soon is balked
Amid the infinite darkness, formless void,
Unstirred by pregnant ray, unmoved by voice
Creative, where dazed sense drops like a stone.
What explorations for the adventurous soul
Remain, when from the body freed, access
To these remoter spheres perchance is given,

With powers renewed, excursive and reflective,
With ampler knowledge stored, hope fondly dreams.
   The azure concave arching this wide earth
Seems like an ocean, where light's refluent tides
Flush the abyss. The darkly purple depths
Of night, star-shot, with luminous threads, as 't were
The woof of heaven's imperial robe, wide flung
Around the throne, give place to wonders new,
When the day dawns and the illumined clouds
Appear, like towers or campaniles, spires,
And fretted chantries, streaming sanguine hues,
Glimpses, 't would seem, of some celestial fane;
Or rise black thunder-clouds like fortresses
Deep bastioned, charged with heaven's sulphurean fires;
Or with light flecks, like Cytherea's doves,
Skimming the innocent blue; aerial films
Trailed o'er the sky, cast by the hurrying wind
Round its imperious bosom; light and shade,
Blending in numberless effects, produce
Endless magnificence in endless change.
   Amid the wastes of desolate northern climes,
Icefields all mantled with untrodden snow,
Or towering icebergs glistening in the sun,
Ermined and capped, in regal state, and throned
Amid the frosty silence, even here,
In her severe and virgin purity,
The spirit of beauty dwells. The tasselled woods,
With odours resinous, the pleasant glades
Blue foliage of pines, the misty spires
Of heather tipped with purple bloom; rivers
Submissive, 'neath the castled crag that sweep,

Where through the quivering drowsy afternoons
The purple shadows sleep on golden hills,
And vineyards bask in the sun, by waters calm,
Calm, but when plash of slow and dripping oar
Wrinkles the shadows; sunny southern shores,
Past where the pillars of Hercules renowned,
Iberian Calpe stands and Abyla,
Blue bays dotted with sails, far headlands dim
That fade in golden mists o'er golden seas,
White towers faint glimmering 'mid the orange groves,
That blow their fragrant perfumes far to sea,
Citron and jasmine from the Italian shores;
These are her haunts; or where 'neath tropic skies
The breeze fresh blowing o'er the margined foam
Lifts the fair tresses of the whispering palm,
When crimson western skies all deep suffused
Die o'er the darkening jungle depths to night.
 The woodland scene invites forgetfulness
Of life, with all its cares. How calm, how still
These silent woodpaths, shadowy aisles of peace!
Patches of sunlight on the mossy ground,
And quivering poplars with their sparkling leaves,
And oaks and laurels glistening in the sun,
And whispering trees that throw a spray of sound
Upon the balmy silence, then are still,
Allure the lingering not unwilling step.
The rabbit listening stops, but darts from view
Amid the adder-haunted fern; now comes
The blackbird's startled challenge from the hedge;
The frisking squirrel hears the passing step,
Squats on his bushy tail, with glistening eye

Peers round, and with well simulated fright
Climbs the smooth beech tree's bark, and refuge takes
'Mid the thick leaves. Wild pigeons softly coo,
Till startled from their love-song by the foot
Of the invader rustling in the fern,
With rapid and directed flight escape.
Needless alarm! ye timid ones. The world
Is wide enough for all. No thoughtless act,
No sound of violence shall break the charm
Of nature's quietude. I would not hurt
One hair, ruffle one feather, or excite
One fear within your breasts. Will ye not give
Admission to your gentle company
Awhile? Will ye not suffer us to watch
Your sweet wild innocent ways, or pause to hear
Your innocent songs? Ye are God's creatures, fair,
Unfallen, not as man. Man well might seek
Silence and refuge in the wood's green light
To pour his heart's full song, his penitence,
The sorrow and the mystery of his life,
Feelings too deep for tears, thoughts beyond words,
And hopes too big for utterance; or might learn
With unpremeditated gratitude,
To sing God's praises from a loving heart.

    How lovely are the woods when spring first clothes
Their barrenness with beauty! How the eye
Rests on the clouds of faint anemones
That flutter in the wind, or the steep banks
Blurred with a gauzy blue, where hyacinths breathe
Strong odours to the opening buds now glowing
In their first lustre. Through the emerald boughs,

Latticing the neighbouring fields, the sunbeams strike
Athwart the misty gloom like bars of gold,
Gilding the mimic wavelets of the brook,
That chatters as it goes. The coo of doves
Murmurs the whole day long, a sound of peace,
Of deep contentment burdened with its joy;
A twinkling light of wings, a speck of blue
From the tipped feathers of the swift-winged jay,
That sweeps into the further cloistered gloom,
Crosses the view; and then the querulous brook
Takes up its liquid melancholy tale,
And there's a gentle hush that dwells among
The million green-veined leaves; one seems to hear,
Breathless, the very heart of nature beat.
The mossy-smelling wood-paths seem all filled
With faint fresh-growing odours from the trees;
The grass with its innumerable spires
Seems listening, as the errant wind unfolds
The leafy portals, for the clover scent
Nimbly to trip with fragrant sandals down
The green arcades. Lakes of blue sky o'erhead,
Among the tree-tops, beautiful and bright,
Tell of the overspreading care of Heaven.
The sunshine, and the movement, and the peace,
Contentment breathe, breathe undisturbed repose.
My God! In this dim grove I worship Thee,
This natural temple with its leafy aisles
Pillared around, as with cathedral columns
Sprung by no human hand. All redolent
With incense sweet is this Thy presence-chamber;
Thy servitors vested to wait on Thee,

Discharge their several functions with delight;
Spending brief life in duty; while the song,
The loveliness, the fragrance all are Thine!
   The sea-shore has its beauty, with its fringe
Of creamy foam, creeping o'er yellow sands.
The southern downs with white and glimmering cliffs
Far visible o'er the waves, broadly unfold
Their thymy undulations to the breeze.
Reclining on the slope, whose cushion soft,
Woven with golden moss, yields to the form
Recumbent, with the peaceful hour well pleased,
The eye, ranges the ocean's vast expanse;
The ever-broadening blue and level floor
Looks like a part of heaven, a shining plain,
Where, in the distance, sky and ocean meet,
In the wide belt of dreamy haze. Silent
And stately go the shipping by. A sail,
Like some white bird that lingering to alight
Drops on the wave with its upslanted wings,
With white reflection tapering to a point
Detains the eye. On the horizon's edge,
All ghostlike, vanishing amid the haze,
Some noble Indiaman, with canvas spread,
Catches the loitering breeze, appearing now
But a faint spectral shadow of her bulk.
Th' unclouded sun burns on the sapphire plain,
As if approachable by track of gold,
Molten and burnished like a heavenly street,
The hook-winged sea-gull mounts aslant, then sinks
Behind the cliff. How sabbath-like the calm!
How absolute, as if the whole world slept.

Pleasant the pure free air, pleasant the hour;
The rain of light upon the whispering sea,
And the soft plunge of ocean's creamy marge;
The slumb'rous surge wakens as from a dream,
Hurries the chattering shingle on the beach,
Then dozes in the sun. The restful air
Breathes forth a gentle inarticulate sigh,
As if of satisfaction deep, and skims
The sea, sweeping with flickering quivering lines,
As 't were in play, while colours come and go,
Violet and purple, amethystine blue,
Till ocean seems a vast mosaic, wrought
Of divers colours cunningly inlaid.

    Such in her calmer moods; but when the storm
Blows its defiance from the rifted clouds
The deep assumes a yet sublimer form
Of beauty, and majestic in its wrath
Destruction challenges. The yelling gale
Coursing o'er tortured leagues of hissing foam,
Summons gigantic forces from the abyss
To rise and struggle for the mastery.
How grand the billows in their onward sweep
Daring th' attack; repulsed, in hissing foam,
Retreating, but to reinforce their strength.
Curling aloft, the pale green oily wave
Again advancing, crowned with cresting foam,
Thunders against the cliff as if to reach
Its yawning caves for sanctuary from the gale
That lashes it to madness. Inky black,
Dark heaven shuts in with wall impassable,
Th' brine-swept bark forlorn that staggers on,

And plunges in the trough as if it sought
Its grave. Now from the pitchy gloom darts forth
The lightning's shaft, as if the tempest's sting;
While bursts majestical the thunder's roar,
O'ertopping all the clamour of the waves;
A cry of agony, or wrath, it seems,
Or disappointed vengeance, muttering far
In long reverberations o'er the foam.
Grandly sublime, the beauty of the storm
Tells of omnipotence, before whose might
Man's power is dwarfed to insignificance.

Moonrise at sea! Night that obscures, reveals;
Drapes the immediate neighbourhood with gloom
But opes the vistas of infinity.
Never does ocean wear a lovelier charm
Than when in southern latitudes the night
Spangles both sea and sky. O glorious sight!
The ship, small fragment of man's busy world,
Seems hung suspended 'twixt two jewelled heavens.
Shot o'er the waters dark a tremulous ray
Attention wakes. With silvery lines the waves
Are tipped, as, slowly rising from the deep,
The moon's broad disc serene, undimmed by cloud,
Grandly appears, and mounts the silent heaven
To sit as queen. Her full-orbed splendour sheds
A wide effulgent pathway o'er the wave,
Silvering the masts, and sails, and spars with sheen,
Throwing the shadows to remoter shades
Of ebon blackness. From the bulwark's edge
The eye discovers in the ocean depths
A phosphorescent world, a mimic sky

All sown with living light. Far as the eye
May pierce, innumerable sparks of life
Shine in the nether depths. Here thought may range,
Upward amidst a wilderness of stars
Unnumbered, or, may downward seek the abyss
Of ocean, peopled to its farthest depths,
Yet find new beauties lavished all around.

    Nor is the spirit of beauty to be sought
Alone in woodland scenes, o'er silvered waves.
Through Nature's works, through all her mighty web
The thread of gold appears; in man God's hand
Has set its signet; for the human frame,
Built wondrously, attests at once His power
And His benevolence. How skilfully
Have been concealed beneath the polished skin,
The smooth exterior, arteries and veins,
The valves, and ducts, canals, and ligaments,
And all the intricate machinery
Of this our physical frame. Nor this alone,
To matchless symmetry of parts, He adds
Peculiar graces that affect the soul;
The witchery of form; the nameless charm
That in the expression lurks; the beaming eyes,
Where now love dwells, now sweetly pensive thoughts;
The damask cheek where blushes come and go,
As their chaste mistress modesty commands;
The coral lips, sweet portals rosy red;
Dimples and smiles the heraldry of love;
And the firm mouth where resolution dwells.
That beauty oft betrays, alas! the world
Has learned too well; too often has it proved

To its possessor, as to those most charmed,
A fatal gift; yet is it but the sign
Of physical excellence, the expression due
Of healthful life, perfection, buoyant youth,
Of strength, sweetness of soul, of truth, of love;
From these dissevered beauty but betrays,
Entraps the unwary, and at length becomes
The minister of lust, the slave of sin.
 Fished from the deep Atlantic's oozy bed,
Dark wastes unvisited by straggling ray
Of daylight, comes the tiny shell, finished
To exquisite perfection, as designed
For man's intelligence; hid in the fields
The rich red purple of the pheasant's eye,
Flower of Adonis, lurks among the corn
Or clover, 'mid the wealth of wild-flower bloom
An unconsidered thing; coral that drifts
Upon the gulf-weed spray far out at sea,
Changeling of ocean, plaything of the waves;
The fritillary on the sweet-pea bloom;
The tiny beetle hastening through the dust,
Shielded and panoplied with lustrous mail
As warrior never was, all testify
To Nature's loveliness. Thought cannot range
Where beauty is not found. Placed 'neath the lens
The pimpernel plucked from amidst the corn,
Or bindweed's blossoms, veined with delicate pink,
Or roadside weed, marvels of beauty seem,
Built of translucent cells, all nectar-laden,
And tinged with pigments of intensest dyes,
But whence derived, how made, or how applied,

Science conjectures, but she cannot tell.
Even in the heart of dense and solid rock
Quarried deep down and by the hammer split
Wonders are seen ; compacted to the eye
Are lustrous particles, crystal arcades
Pervious mayhap to beings now unknown
To man, who, in these mimic halls, a world
In its own light, spacious and fair, enjoy.
Nay, in the caves of nothingness, new forms
Of beauty, by the optic lens, are seen ;
Far as the horizon of th' assisted sight
New types of beauteous life being still revealed.
    Had chance the marshalling of these molecules
Beauty would rise but at rare intervals.
Dread chaos waits conceivably around.
Why should the wheel of life new forms evolve
Yet all endowed with beauty ? Whence are cast,
Where hidden lie, the monstrous and misshaped,
By Nature's plastic hand rejected, forms
Unfit to meet the gaze intelligent ?
If Nature's loom throw only certain shapes,
And pictured patterns all of symmetry,
Then chance has had no part in this great work ;
Like to Amphion's lute, by which the stones
Were stirred to life and Thebes' city built
Intelligence has ruled with its quick force,
Has framed earth's exquisite machinery,
Fixed its due bounds and times, endowed with power
Of reproduction, given initial force,
And still sustains. Go tell the credulous
That chance in all its changes only makes

The beautiful, nor brings abortions forth :
Seems it not wilful blindness to deny
The Hand that works thus visibly around ;
To cheat with wretched trickery of words
Distinctions of causation, or the thread
Fine-spun of sequence or coincidence,
The expectant mind of its great heritage,
Making the ample fields of God's rich world
A dreary desert for th' inquiring mind.
Open around us is the treasure-house
Of Nature's wealth ; before us lies outspread
Creation's page, filled with its heavenly lore,
With heavenly lore all filled, and heavenly love.
Science, mayhap, will yet lift up her voice
Indignant, for her heart is reverent,
And, recognising the informing Mind
That in these natural scenes her wonder stirs,
Will yet protest against the attempt to exclude
Intelligent design from natural things.
 Obedient to original command
The world of ordered life emerged at first,
Bearing the impress of primordial forms
Of beauty ; yet not rigidly enchained
But that development to higher modes
Were possible. But why such lavish wealth,
Bounty profuse, that he who would escape
Its soft allurements, must betake himself
To man's blank world, scant thoughts, utility,
In narrowest range of uniformity ?
Beauty would seem correlative to life,
To life percipient, if not rational life ;

The mute expression of a fixed regard,
Thoughtful consideration for the wants
Of man's brief state, else too monotonous :
Mute witness of a kindliness divine,
The beauty of the universe appeals
To man's intelligence, a mute appeal
Yet eloquent ; a ladder to the skies ;
Heaven's golden pathway, as by Plato dreamed,
Once nobly dreamed, earth's beauty leading man
To the supreme, divinely Beautiful.
Few are the archetypal forms of beauty
But these in endless variation wrought
Develop ever changing, ever new,
All-varying shapes.   Mark the variety
In form, dimensions, colour, number, time.
Modes of existence change and interchange
Incessantly ; the ebb and flow, full tide
Now poised a while, then flowing to dead neap ;
Procession and succession to strict law
Subordinate, and preparation sprung
Out of fruition's heart ; thus moves the world,
Yielding new pleasures in its ceaseless flow ;
Thus weaves for ever in its mighty loom
A varied pattern.   Flashing in the sun,
The snow's pure crystals change to summer showers,
That from the awned grass and hedgerows drip,
And deck the drinking fields with broidered hues,
Kindle the fragrant flame of flowers, or make
The wood's grand canopy, or harvests brown.
   Were time prolonged duration, nothing more,
Though fair, how dull would prove the unvaried hour :

But from the cradle to the grave, from May
To flowery May again, from the dim dawn
Till eve, the ever-changing hour presents
New pleasures, gilds the fading past and decks
Th' oncoming hour with hope. The spring-time comes,
The fragrant, sweet, and acceptable spring,
And smiles relax the face of sullen death.
Coyly at first, the early blossoms come,
And timidly, scarce daring to unfold
Their shivering petals on the nipping air.
Forth from its grave the shrouded snowdrop comes,
First waked in Nature's resurrection fair,
While the bold crocus with its golden spear
Cleaves the hard sod, as if to ope the path,
Whence the fair sisterhood of flowers may pass
In glad procession on their odorous way.
With lengthening days 'neath balmier skies steals forth
The perfume of the violet, to waylay
The unconscious sense with its sweet violence;
Fair plunderer! that gives more than it takes;
The tender primrose too, with pensive eye
Looks for your recognition, from the hedge;
The young birds twitter on the soft spring air.
Day blends with day. Cowslips are in the fields
With freckled blossoms, bunched and breathing sweet,
As a child's kiss. There the lark nestles; thence
Upsprings from out the gold green meadow grass,
Startled with his own joy, his speckled breast
Dew-wet, but tremulous, and fills the sky
With sweet shrill quivering strains that call the thoughts
To mount aloft the golden sunbeam stairs

With their sweet music, grateful love and praise.
   Then comes all-blossoming May. The lilacs stand
Fragrant with clustering spires; laburnums droop
Their golden cascades o'er the dusty road;
Orchards and hedges, decked in bridal white,
Are dressed as for a marriage festival.
By slow degrees and gently blending change
Scarce visible, spring into summer grows.
The cuckoo's shout echoes from grove to grove,
As if itself an echo, nothing more.
Meadows of mowing grass shine in the sun
And billow in the breeze, with sorrel red,
With glistening buttercups and meadow-sweet,
White clover bolls, and winged shepherd's clocks.
Now is the very festival of flowers.
Spiked lilies, roses blushing in their pride,
Quaint fluted columbine, with antique grace,
Pinks, stocks all built of fragrance, pansies meek,
Carnations pure that crowd and bask i' the sun.
From many a hedge where June's wild roses blush,
The clamb'ring woodbine hangs, flirts with each breeze,
And tells the passer-by how sweet it is.
   In sultrier days the whetting of the scythe,
And its swift whistling rush through the deep grass
Are heard around. Warm breathes the hayfield broad
Full of the fragrance of the new-mown hay,
Strewn with fresh swaths, where the swart villagers
All kerchiefed from the sun, with pleasant chat,
And call that comes and goes upon the wind,
Cheer sweltering labour, till they leave at night
The glimmering meadow to the corn-crake's voice.

Sickle on arm the sunburnt reapers pass,
Their faces goldened by the early sun,
Half-hidden in the rich brown umber corn,
That rustles in the August sun ; there toil
From the cool dawn till noon brings short repose.
Stretched 'mid the sheaves they watch the balanced hawk
Hovering aloft, and poised on moveless wing,
Fixing his quarry.   So wears by their day,
Till from the churchyard elms the clock tells out
The evening hour, and in the fading light
The wearied labourers turn towards their homes ;
The partridge calls ; flickers the restless bat ;
The drowsy beetle heavily goes by
On buzzing wing ; the glow-worm lights his lamp,
While o'er the shoulder of the eastern hills
Rises the broad and ruddy harvest moon ;
Noiseless the white owl down the hedgerow flits ;
The last note of the busy day has dropped ;
Silent the world ; the toilers hushed to rest.
  Then autumn comes with calm and misty airs,
Dreamlike and still ; bare stubble-fields festooned
By gossamer, beaded with hoary dew,
Where sniffs the pointer, and the sportsman's gun
Wakens the shattering echoes in the hills ;
With shortening days and slumb'rous afternoons,
Spellbound, the land sleeps in its golden haze.
Pleasant the orchards, red with dropping fruit,
Where the crooked mossy apple-trees stand forth,
As offering up with grateful hands to Heaven
The produce of the labours of the year,
Ere yet they strew it on the sward below.

The swallows twitter, on the lichened barns
Collected, garrulous perchance of flight
Impending, or of southern climes more fair,
Escaping from the swollen muddy streams,
Of dark November's chill and foggy days.
 Slowly gray murky skies and empty fields
Usher old winter on the stage once more.
The tide of life ebbs fast. To secret cells,
Deep catacombs and crevices and nooks,
The million pensioners of summer life
Betake themselves, and safe protection find,
Beneath the mighty pent-house of the earth.
All muffled in its winding-sheet of snow
Blind, silent, shrouded, cold, the dead earth lies.
Misty the woodlands; on the roadside banks,
Folded with smooth o'erhanging creamy edge,
Lie the soft-handed drifts; vaporous the breath;
Silent the footfalls; from the belfry's tower
Come brooding echoes on the frosty air.
Now gleams the sunshine of our English homes,
The crackling fire, while innocent mirth defies
Winter's keen whistling winds and driving snows.
Yet beautiful, still beautiful the world,
In all its spotless loveliness arrayed;
The fretted icicle, the snowdrift smooth,
All sown with diamonds glistening in the sun,
And soft as virgin breast of innocence;
The hoarfrost's delicate lacework on the trees,
When the twigs crackled in the midnight frost,
As if some frisky sprites had decked the boughs
In honour of some natural festival.

So grandly shift these ever-changing scenes,
All varied and all beautiful; with storms
And calms, glimpses of sunshine, veiling fogs,
Clear skies, or drenching rains; few days alike;
Save when the summer broods with fervid ray,
And through the sultry hours a cloudless sky
Records no changes but the ebb and flow
Of daylight. Even then the eye discerns
Each day's progression slowly registered
In deeper tones of brown maturity.
Rigid with frost the winter oft will bind
Successive days in uniformity:
Dull cheerless scenes, bleak dreary wastes of snow
Where withered bents shake in the icy wind,
Or in deep rural lanes buried in drifts,
Where the tamed blackbird scratches in the hedge,
And on the frosty air the piteous bleat
Of sheep half-famished, borne in muffled tones,
Is heard. Each day bears its distinctive marks,
Cloudy and gloomy, cheerful, calm, and bright;
Days of sweet quiet, days with tempest rent,
And buffeting winds, and pitiless drenching rains;
Life's counterpart, with all its hopes and joys,
Despair and grief, perplexity and pain.

If not from love, from kindliness to man,
Whence can this principle of beauty rise?
Why should the eye be pleased, why note the change,
The shifting, the succession, and the grace
Of nature, and in noting find delight,
As of some gift conferred? Why should the ear
Find pleasure in the sweetly-blending strains

Of music, dropping as the honeycomb?
The thought entranced, lingering upon the sound,
Or awestruck, listening to the echoes vague
That from the inward depths responsive come,
Is pleased, nor asks the cause. There here exists
A correlation to man's rational life,
A nice adjustment suiting ill with chance,
Fortuitous development, or drift;
But well with harmony and plain intent;
For how this were accomplished matters not;
Whether at first man's nature were so framed
And moulded to the original make of things,
Or fitted by long processes, research,
And apprehension of the intelligent mind,
Taught to find pleasure in the symmetry
And beauty of the world. The fact remains.

Nor does variety alone delight,
Breaking the currents of familiar thought,
Grown languid, and by stimulus of hope
Quickening the pulses, but instruction too
This vast and ever-changing scene conveys.
Happy who hearkens thus to Nature's voice,
Unheard but by the patient listening soul,
Receives her accents grave, and does her will.

Would we behold an image of man's life,
Its brevity, its opportunities
Priceless, if used, t' ensure our future good;
And large adventures with their large reward?
Or, would we learn the dangers that surround,
The perilous drifts of circumstance, that lock
Their commonness in the character, clay built,

Where marble was designed ; the onward flow,
The need for vigorous and large-hearted strain,
And the quick rendering forth of manliness,
Modest withal, yet earnest to attain
The height of honour, and to give account
Of our existence, not in words, but deeds,
Self-registered in kindliness and truth,
Spotless integrity, and loyalty
To all that truly makes us man :
Or would we in mute eloquent pictures see
The sad pathetic spending of our powers
And laws of irresistible decay ?
Look on the passing hours ; there we behold
In miniature our life ; in sweetest strains
The tale is told us, if we will but hear.

    Fair is the dawning of the natural day.
Gently it comes, as if it feared to wake
The world's great family, curtained in sleep ;
The swallows twitter faintly in the eaves,
And then are still : now throb the eastern heavens
With tremulous liquid haze, soft innocent tints,
Which come and go, and modulate and merge,
Till bolder rays flash to the zenith, tinging
The crimson edges of the dappled clouds,
The harbingers of the bright king of day.
The splendid pageant moves. With amber, gold,
And saffron dyes, the new-crowned morn is robed.
As at some secret herald trumpet blast,
Night's barbican its dark portcullis lifts
To give admission to the king of day.
Mark him approach amid his bannered pomp,

THE MORNING SONG.

How Nature curtsies to him, bending low,
The dew-washed daisies twinkling in his glance.
The birds are mad for joy the night is past,
And with melodious welcome make the woods
Re-echo to their glee.   The grass blades tipped
With diamond drops seem trembling with delight.
   Now rest upon the ivied village tower
The sun's first rays, gilding the glittering vane.
Ere from the cottage chimneys faint blue smoke
Upcurls among the elms, the thrush begins ;
While from the mowing grass, drooping with dew,
Comes up the cuckoo's note.   The barnyard cock,
With shrill and lusty crow, wakens the echoes.
Now the first signs of human life appear.
Clicking the latch the labourer leaves his home,
Curtained and still, shouldering his scythe ;
Along the dusty road the teamster goes,
With jingling harness glistening in the sun,
Whistling afield ; while in the orchard stand,
With wide-distended udders, patient cows,
Their sweet breath hanging on the morning air,
Waiting the fresh-cheeked milkmaid at the gate
With clinking pail.   The forge is lit, and soon
The anvil rings ; the millwheel is at work ;
Voices of children sound ; the village wakes ;
The morning sun shines broad o'er all the land,
And labour's busy hands have grasped their work.
   Sweet hour ! so bright, so calm, so fresh, so full
Of pleasant memories and nimble hopes,
That from the dewy hilltops of the past
Kissed the smooth brow of promised happiness,

Now thou hast won a fresh and magic power,
And whisperest from the sepulchre of night
Of larger hopes and ampler fields for love,
When o'er the darker night of death shall steal
The growing brightness of eternal morn,
And from the drowsy grave, with powers renewed,
The soul shall rise to an immortal day.
Morn is the hour for prayer : the soul draws near,
And to the Mind Supreme obeisance pays,
Not grudgingly, but with a grateful heart,
Blessing the Life-Giver for life renewed ;
Brings the fair tribute of its earliest thoughts,
High purposes, affections high, and waits
The benison divine, while the firm will
Braces its girdle for the coming fight.

Fair morning of our life ! what words can tell
The brightness of thy promised happiness ?
Just as the streamlet from the mountain crags
Spurns with its silver foot high solitudes,
Where screams the eagle, and the chamois leaps,
Gray rocks, and mists that brood among the pines,
Seeking below the friendship of the sun,
The company of flowers, the whispering grass,
And bending trees that crowd its fertile banks,
So leaped the brave young life to run its course ;
So love drew forth the energy of life ;
Hope with its magic pencil touched each scene,
Gilding the day ! How pleasant were the fields !
The commonest flowers, the simplest pleasures wore
A magic charm, which time has filched long since.
The soul, as if with music dimly heard,

Was lured into existence; pleasures thick
Lay strewn on every hand. 'Twas joy to live,
To feel the bounding pulse, th' untroubled mind,
And all the kindling energies of youth
Exultant. Happy they who wisely use
Life's earliest hours preparing for life's work;
Who make the loveliness and joy of youth
To be the prelude of life's glorious psalm.
Happy who recognise the dignity
Of living well, and early make their choice;
Who consecrate life's morn to life's great end;
Choose for their lasting good, the Good supreme,
And in that choice find endless joy and peace.
    By slow gradations, imperceptibly,
The day wears on to noon. The shadows move
Coincident, the bents upon the hills,
Poplars and elms, tell that the sun has neared
His southern throne. Now breathes a deeper peace,
Stillness profound brooding o'er all the land.
The quivering landscape blurred with hazy lines,
Pants 'neath the sun, nor cool retreat appears,
Save shaded hills, green woodland depths, or streams,
Where, 'neath the willows, the sweet-scented rush,
Or brooklime blooms. The cattle, fetlock deep,
Stand in the brook, dreaming with half-closed eyes,
Whisking the pestering flies from off their flanks,
And ruminating with complete content;
The glistening scythe rests on the deep-cut swath;
Fresh smell of new-mown grass and meadow-sweet
Is on the air, while from remoter parts
The tedded heaps a deeper fragrance yield.

Snatching a short repose, the mowers lie
Beneath the oak, that, like a patriarch,
Spreads his broad arms umbrageous, 'midst the field,
The corn-crake's note, the grasshopper's faint trill
Have dropped : the drowsy world seems fallen asleep
  So steal, by slow degrees, the hours of youth,
Till, mounting to the sky of noon, our sun
Reaches, all unaware, meridian height!
Life being half-spent while yet we count us young,
Boast our to-morrows, and with kindling fire
Adventures great prepare, befooling self,
Again befooled, with oft-repeated pledge,
To redeem the promise of the morn of youth,
Playing the child, and paltering with our time;
Till bitterly the imperious will demands
The reason of existence ? not content
With the dull beat mechanical of toil;
To eat, to drink, to sleep, to pay the round
Of petty courtesy, to smile, and lisp
The scandal prattle of the passing day;
On simpering folly wait, or dog the steps
Of mammon, while it shames one's secret self;
But hungering to acquit some manlier deeds :
Play left, to stretch the unaccustomed thews
Of resolution, act youth's noble dreams,
Embalm the earnest sweetness of our life,
In seeking to advance the common good,
By throwing on some darkened path one ray,
Though transient, and by wholesome influence,
True words, or, truer deeds life's quit-rent pay;

THE MORNING SONG.

Lest shamed of death, we slink into the grave,
As to a debtor's prison, self-condemned.
    Now is life's hour of noon. As with full flood,
The shining tide rocks in the noonday sun,
So manhood's strength, in mounting to its height,
Has summoned all life's concentrated force
Till the full mark of possibility
Is reached : now comes a pause. The sobered mind
Looks to the future, where time's refluent tide
Will sweep life's force. O solemn hour of noon!
Life's midway height, whence the reflective mind
Turns to behold th' irrevocable past,
Knows it for ever past, then onward looks!
Though mists and darkness o'er the future hang,
Happy, if years before, the precious seeds
Of diligence, thrift, temperance, piety,
That best of husbandry, in furrowed youth,
Had with a lavish hand been scattered wide.
Rich harvest will await, plenteous and full ;
The peaceful outcome of the good man's life ;
The field, where long we laboured, standing full
Of grain that whispers for the reaper's arms ;
Sense of accomplished work, of duty done,
Calm reminiscence, gentle thoughts of life,
Respect and kindly offices of love,
Gentle descent towards death, and cheerful hope,
And grateful friendliness to mother earth.
    What heart, O peaceful evening! welcomes not
Thy soft approach, when from the western sky,
Fragrant with sweetbrier, or the clambering bine,
With deepening hush, and gentle duskiness,

And dewy freshness, round thy graceful steps,
Gathering thine airy robes and breathing peace,
Thou com'st to still the clamours of the day.
All things rejoice, hailing thy glad approach;
The trodden camomile, amid the dust,
Hears thy light footfall, to thy dewy kiss
Lifts its bruised head; the birds renew their song,
All silent through the drowsy afternoon;
High in the air the whistling swallows dive,
The sparrows chirp, the lagging crow goes by;
The lengthening shadows on the golden grass
Die in the twilight o'er the level fields.
The calm white pool is lying ghostly, still,
In silent wonderment beneath the sky,
Moveless, save where the leaping fish make rings
Scarce visible, or clouds of dancing gnats
Brush the smooth surface. Now the water-hen
Leads warily her chicks among the grass;
The beetle is abroad. The woodland's edge
Stirs with wild rabbits frisking in their glee,
Their white tails glimmering in the growing dusk.
O'er darkening coppice, o'er the silent fields,
The murmurous hum of drowsy day dies off;
Voices of village children at their play
Fade as in dreams. Lights twinkle here and there
In cottage windows; wreaths of pale blue smoke
From cottage chimneys tell of evening fires:
Within, kissing the child upon his knee,
The tired labourer sits, his bright-faced wife
Busily spreading forth the evening meal.
The cottage hollyhocks are wet with dew;

Where the spiked lavender betrays itself,
Near by the garden hedge, with murmurs low,
The lingering bees come home. Now fade from view
Familiar scenes to indistincter gloom.
The trees seem black, and in the soft warm sky
And reddening haze shines with its quivering gold,
Scarce visible, the evening star. Now fall
Fast deepening shadows o'er the glimmering scene.
Darkness and quiet on the churchyard rest,
Night's thickening veil concealing from the view
The last low resting-places of the dead.
   So whispers nature to the listening soul,
Rendering the lesson with sweet eloquence,
Of death's great cadence, and the winding up
Of this familiar, pleasing, painful life :
Which with avidity is seized at first,
Then held by right as indefeasible ;
Though solemnly admonished by grim death,
The unwelcome admonition oft ignored,
With clinging rootlets lingering to the last ;
Until old age accepts the time of day,
And bears its faded graces to the tomb
Regretfully, yet wise to match the hour,
And with composure deck and gratitude.
Ripe wisdom from dear-bought experience culled,
Noble submission that so well befits
The mind acknowledging a will supreme,
Blend their sweet music in the cadence grand
Closing the anthem of a well-spent life.
   Nor fear we thee, O solemn night of death,
Though thy concomitants appal the mind,

Thy menacing darkness, thy all-quenching cold,
Dreadful corruption, and the silent grave,
The aching gloom, home of the conquering worm.
With each recurring eve the great world dies;
The day with its glad beauty, waving woods,
Blue sky and blossoming flowers, are buried deep
In the dark grave of night; extinct all seem
And dead, till the fair morning comes, when all
Emerge again with fresher, brighter tints.
Bereft of bright free life, and faces dear,
And visible companionship, taught well
By Him who has unlocked thy fast-barred gate,
Hope looks within death's ebon garden walls
For paradise, refreshment and repose,
The cloudless blue of an unfading day;
And well may bear ungrudgingly to toil
The last few weary miles of life's long road.

 Such is the varied world we call our home.
Man finds himself the proud inhabitant
Of earth's most royal palace, whence the mind
Discursive, down the starry colonnades
May walk, and commerce with sublimest things;
Divine relations form, purged of the taint
Of sin. Mark this great temple, built of God;
What stones are here, how framed, how polished fair!
Richly endowed and sumptuously adorned
Is this most noble fane, this wondrous world,
Built by the Hand supreme. Lo! all around,
Graved on heaven's spacious dome in living light,
Or filling this huge element of earth
Woven in its tapestry of living forms

Embroidered in light tracery of cloud,
Flowers odorous, mighty forests bending low,
The choiring voices of the sapphire sea;
Sung on the breeze in every wild bird's note,
With every soft caress of earthly love,
Comes the most welcome lesson, God is love!
Summer with all its flowers hath naught so sweet;
Nor autumn's golden store so rich a fruit.
The eye of gratitude sees endless proofs
And living witnesses of love divine;
The love whence we have come and to whose breast
And everlasting welcome we return.

BOOK THE SECOND

THE SONG OF LIFE

THE ARGUMENT.

The theme a happy one—View of creation—The varied inhabitants of air, earth, and sea—Living care everywhere shown—No trace of chance—The world of flowers—Gratuitous pleasure—Beauty, colour, fragrance, all have a language—The melodies of birds—American forest scene—The morning lark—The blackbird in the hedge—The song of the thrush—The litany of the birds—Fruits in their variety, value, and beauty—Orchards in May—Autumn scene—The feeding of God's innumerable creatures—Nature's harvesting—Acorns, berries, seeds, wild fruits—The rooks going forth—Evening scene—Preservation of species—The joy of living—The child on its mother's knee—Birds in the sunshine—The pulse of nature's life—Care for the young—The golden thread of love—Birds and their nests—The tigress and her young—The love lavished round a child—The mother's love—The family life—What all these speak.

BOOK THE SECOND.

THE SONG OF LIFE.

LOVE Divine, thy genial warmth calls forth
My heart with inexpressible delight
To sing thy praise, and bask in thy bright beams.
As in the summer morn the bees will fly
From flower to flower, headlong to dive and probe
The odorous canopies and painted cells
Where honey lurks, singing with murmurous hum
Of satisfaction deep and pleased delight,
Still revelling in the sweetness that they find,
So would my thoughts, in this the world's broad field,
Fly forth from proof to proof of heavenly love,
Haply some precious sweetness thence to bring,
Some truths of gentleness and tender power,
Which, hived within the honeycomb of song,
May cheer desponding hearts in gloomy hours;
An ample recompense, although not all:

THE MORNING SONG.

The simple joy of singing is my joy,
Though in rude tones, with unaccustomed skill,
Confiding in the melody of truth,
Mayhap unwelcome to fastidious ears,
Yet, if with native pathos rendered, sure
To find the heart's response; pleased beyond words
To sing of the bright sunshine of the soul,
The spiritual fragrance and the inward peace
Of the Lord's garden, paradise restored.
There is a music of the heart, more sweet
Than ever thrilled the high ecstatic lyre,
Or voice e'er sung, heard by the inward ear,
Yet ever yearning to o'erleap the bounds
Of jealous silence, and with wandering strains,
Floating about this dull mechanic world,
To win an audience from the noisy crowds,
Life's fierce and jarring discords to reduce,
And hush its babblings with the ocean tide
Majestical, of God's great harmony.

Now in this silent hour of reverent thought,
Look forth upon the wide and varied scene
Of natural things, harmonious, beautiful,
Strangely impassive, unresponsive, slow,
Lost in its onward way, of busy man
Unmindful, as it seems, yet quick to teach,
And ready to impart its priceless truths
To every patient, humble, listening soul.

Who made, or making, who upholds intact
This mighty structure of the universe;
Balanced these stellar spheres, restrained by check
And counter-check, each in its fixèd place;

Roofed this large world with soft ethereal blue,
Grateful to sense, and filled the world with life?
No wild and aimless scene before us lies,
The theatre of chaos, field of chance ;
Order here rules. How simple, yet how grand
Are all the silent processes of Nature ;
From the ice crystal of the winter night,
To the majestic sweep of suns and stars.
If thou art willing but to learn the truth,
Truth will confront thee wheresoe'er thou look ;
The moving lips of zoophytes shall speak,
The crackling broom, the dandelion seed
That with light wings sails upon every wind,
Bring thee a message of most weighty truth.
The earth is vocal with her glorious psalm,
And by the inward ear, attentive still,
Nature's grand " Benedicite " is heard.
Give ear, and with great Verulam thou'lt hear
" The voice of God revealed in natural facts."
    Why should the sea-bird's breast be clothed with down,
Or why the condor's wing with strength equipped
And amplitude, the monarch of the clouds
Aloft to bear, to scale the windy heights
Of the drear mountain solitude his throne ?
The tiger with lithe form and velvet foot
Glides through the thickest jungle like a snake ;
While wallowing in the turbid river depths,
Armed to the snout with thick impervious hide,
Leviathan will mock at death. Firm fixed,
As anchored to the rocks with toughest steel,
The tiny limpet clings, and safe endures

THE MORNING SONG.

The surge's thundering and redoubled shock,
Secure, as is the frail translucent shell
Glued to the withered bent upon the hill,
That sways in every wind. The small-eyed mole,
Burrowing the dark dense earth to find a home,
The kestrel balanced on the viewless winds,
Or the fleet dolphin clad with burnished mail
That rides the blue and crested waves as steeds,
Live in congenial elements. For thus
God suits His creatures to their modes of life,
Their habitation and their needs ; equips
And arms them for their work ; their feebleness
Defends ; the pensioners of His bounty they,
Wards of omnipotence, are, in His care,
Tenderly kept and fed with open hand.
Behold the work of some far-seeing Mind !
Considerate, generous, condescending too,
In details infinite of friendliness
To these uncounted humble servitors,
These poor dependants. Whether this were wrought
At the first calling forth of ordered life,
Or moulded since by force of circumstance,
The fruit of dearly-bought experience,
Vicarious death of millions that the few
Might live, the nice adjustment is the same :
The individual welfare is secured.

Earth, air, and sea, the various tenements
Of this great globe, have their inhabitants,
Tenants distinctive ; none unpeopled left.
The ocean's heaving and disordered waste,
Abounds with varied, ever-active life.

Beneath the waves, glistening in light, as clad
With silver sheen, unnumbered myriads glide,
Dive to the azure depths profound, and sweep
Through glassy caverns, grottoes, cells, weed-tressed ;
Not of one pattern all ; the ponderous whale
Whose spoutings and unwieldy gambols oft
Attract the mariner's eye ; the ashy shark
With villainous glance, that like a sheeted ghost
Darts through the dusk abyss ; the flying fish
Escaping from the fierce bonito's jaws,
That from the smooth green wave springs forth to drop
On quickly-drying wing ; all creatures strange,
Uncouth, and quaint, with eyes protuberant,
Restless antennæ, frills, and scales, and shells,
Folds sinuous involved. With faint sweet tints
Bloom sea-anemones, as living flowers,
Orange and pink, flesh-coloured, throwing forth
Their wavy ever-moving filaments
In the transparent depths ; there seaweeds spread
Their crimson leafage, or with darker fronds
In mimic forests rise, and shelter give
To tiny nations. In the nether depths
Unreached by plummet, undisturbed, unlit
By straggling ray from this bright upper world,
What creatures herd, dragons or serpents huge
Wallow in darkness, and in deadly strife
Lock their gigantic strength amid the slime,
Science may yet discover, and reveal
Wonders undreamed : far as her light extends
Beneficent, she shows the work of God.
 The vaster ocean of the upper air

Has its inhabitants. Birds of all form,
Colour, and song; some for the mountain height,
Broad-pinioned, with a quick and piercing eye
That like a diamond burns, and power far off
To scent their quarry; some with jewelled wings
To hover o'er the breast of tropic flowers;
Some for the ocean's melancholy waste,
The lonely albatross, that sleeps on wing,
Or petrel, harbinger of coming storm;
Some dive the foam, or poised upon the gale,
Toss their white wings against the gathering gloom,
Exulting 'mid the turmoil and the din
Of elemental strife. Marshes and swamps,
The sedgy waste, with black forbidding pools,
And water-paths amid the peaty ooze,
Where nods the bulrush, and the desolate flag
Chatters upon the wind, have visitants.
Trailing aloft the melancholy crane,
Or bustard in remote recess, wild ducks
Heard by the reddening fires on winter eves,
Far overhead on their migrations dark,
When the wild goose's cry sounds faint far off,
High in the night; or by the mountain tarn
Drenching their plumage, as the silvery drops
Sparkle like diamonds in the noonday sun;
Or from the bright and ample fields of air,
The heaven of blossoming hawthorn, or dark copse,
Flinging abroad their pure delicious strains,
That pensive memory loves, and echo too,
Clasping them till the ravishing silence casts

To dull oblivion's vast and envious depths.
  Here too a deft and loving Hand has shaped
The creature to its lot; given it content;
Endowed it with instinctive knowledge fit
To its capacity; the circle marked
Of its small nest, which snugly lined with down,
Or moss, in nook of gray and lichened rock,
Hid in moist bank where early violets come,
And burly humble bees buzz in the grass,
Hammocked in whispering bents 'mid nodding flowers,
Or, anchored safe amid the swaying boughs,
Is home and cradle of its helpless young.
  Mountain or plain, woodland or desert sands,
Each finds its own inhabitant, each range
Affords glad life, delightful occupation,
Scope for the exercise of natural powers.
The timid hare that crouches in the grass
With eye askance; the branchèd stag that laves
Its heated flanks in the clear mountain pool;
Or antelope, swift as the driving wind
To scour the plain; the camel petulant
That finds endurable the burning sand,
And braves the dread simoom; the elephant,
That crushes with loud trumpetings the jungle,
Uttering its boisterous joy; or 'mid the rocks
The tawny lion with his playful cubs;
Each creature is adapted to its lot,
Widely diverse, each finds contentment there.
  He who is earnest, as the theme demands,
Solicitous with fixed concern to know
How God regards the creatures of His Hand,

Their welfare, and their future happiness,
Will mark this natural language, hear the voice,
As if of many waters, from the sea
Of wide existence, the significance
Of adaptation note, prescient of need,
Contingent, in God's creatures manifold.
Far as the eye can trace the particles
That build the living structure, tiniest points,
The dust life of the physical frame, is seen
This care provisional, beneficent.
He who piles up the protoplastic cells
In blade, or leaf, or animal fibre, shows
A living care. No trace of chance appears,
Caprice, or negligence in Nature's works.
All share a common love, a common care.
The happiness of everything that breathes
His love secures. Nor is the margin great.
For happiness from many factors springs,
Co-operate, converging to one end,
The culminating point, ultimate outcome,
Balance and crown of widely-varying powers.
Were He who formed man's frame indifferent
To human happiness, or negligent
To tune the varying strings whose concord makes
The harmony of life, or physical
Or mental, or the deeper chords profound
Of moral being, how vast His power to cloud
The life with pain! How soon could He o'ertop
High clambering ambition, ruffle quick
The calm placidity that else would sleep
Beneath the shadow of the natural laws,

Seeking forbidden joys. Man's happiness
Is found where God has placed it : nowhere else.
  The world of flowers invites the willing thoughts
To linger 'mid their loveliness, and cull
Diviner blooms, thoughts of God's kindliness,
Suggestions fragrant to the inner sense.
Whence comes the sweetness of the floral world ?
The nodding clover blossom blurred with dew,
The fragrant cyclamen on lifted wing,
Germander speedwell of the hedgerow side,
The white fringed daisy of the meadow, seem
All weighted with the tenderest thoughts of God.
Why should these graceful forms of loveliness
Encamp in sheltering nook, or nestle round
The homes of men, with more than regal pomp
And spotless virgin innocency clad ?
Why should the Unseen Hand scatter abroad
The freckled cowslip in the April fields,
Or purple heather o'er the breezy moor ?
We strew fresh blossoms on the churchyard path,
To meet the bride, betokening happy thoughts,
Or crown the merry prattling child with flowers,
Nor other meaning have than love and hope.
The primrose, 'midst the oak's brown fallen leaves,
Comes like a thought of cheerfulness and hope
After the winter's dank and dropping days.
Even the poppies in the harvest-field
Seem like its garnishing ; God's generous Hand
Decking His largess. From their wild wood haunts
And lonely solitudes, transplanted near
Human abodes, with blushing gratitude,

And more exuberant loveliness, the flowers
With their sweet gifts repay man's fostering care.
God's works serve many ends. That which delights
His creature man, may happiness confer
On other beings. Who but coldly sees
In these fair works of Nature, graceful forms,
Ravishing odours, tints of rainbow dyes,
Distinctive marks to attract the wandering bee,
And insects numberless, that find their food
In flowers, nor counts it worthy of his thought
That man finds pleasure there, must yet allow
These ends conjoined, a double purpose served,
And wisdom mingled with a larger care.
The fragrance of the honeysuckle borne
Upon the evening dew; fair starry snow
Of jessamine, like modesty's own thoughts;
Syringa bloom, or jonquils' creamy discs;
The bank of lemon thyme, or odorous nook
Where from green campanile of lush leaves,
The lily of the valley shakes its bells;
Or lilac bloom scenting the air of May;
Bushes of hawthorn, hooded violets,
Winking among the leaves, close bonneted,
As fearing lest the fingers of desire
Would filch their sweets; or high and dazzling rose,
That in full sun courts every lingering breeze;
Their mingling odours rise like incense sweet,
In fragrant streams invisible, and fill
This vestibule of earth, and court of heaven.

    Had chance the shaping of these beauteous forms?
Why should the calyx with such elegance

Be rounded off, science in vain divines :
Or why with colours numberless should glow
The silken petals, freckled, fringed, or stained,
Or of one common hue, of spotless white,
Resplendent scarlet, purple, blushing pink.
When first did the adventurous molecules
In dumb succession, motion purposeless,
First leave the track, and from the coffers fetch
Of bounteous Nature, the rich living gold
That crowns the lily ? Whence the pigment bring
That blushes in the rose ? Has chance her hoards
Deep hidden in the dark and colourless earth ?
Distilled in what alembic, in what nook
Preserved, keeps she her jars of essences ?
Hath she invisible stores in the pure light
Around, and hath she taught these fragile forms
By living prayer, from the bright heaven to bring
The loveliness in which they stand arrayed ?
O myriad blossoming spires of May ! your breath
That makes the gadding breeze all redolent
With sweet perfume, a glorious anthem seems
Blending in silent harmonies of praise.

 Colour and fragrance, perfect symmetry,
Thus superadded to th' organic life,
Seem but to speak of kindliness and care.
Plants might have germinated, might have come
To fruitage full, with blossoms colourless,
Or none. If, wandering down trim garden paths,
The eye, well pleased, observe on every hand
All flowers that in successive seasons bloom,
Parterres of dazzling scarlet, innocent blue,

Or bushes clustered o'er the velvet lawn
Covered with bloom, although no form be seen
Bending to dig the earth, to drop the seed,
Or plant the root, to lop, to prune, to stay
With friendly hand the weak and drooping branch,
'Tis known, that, though the agent be unseen,
An agent here has wrought; this beauty comes,
And must have come from labour, from the aim
Intelligent to please. In this wide scene,
The garden of the world, appears design
Pleasure to give, or flowers would have no place.
The casuistic and unwilling mind
May reason as it please: spring's buttercups
Robing the emerald fields with cloth of gold,
The hawthorn hedge drifted with fragrant snow,
And gardens glowing with their living gems,
Will whisper still their gentle lore, and tell
To simple hearts, of God's goodwill to man.

How much the melodies of birds enhance
The sylvan scene, he knows, who in the woods,
The pathless forests of the Western World,
That border on the Mississippi's banks,
Where to the Mexique gulf the turbid flood
Makes devious way, flushing creek, bayou, pool,
Has wandered. Solitude intense! How drear
The pillared columns, ghostlike, dreamy, still,
Diminishing in distance! From the boughs
Hangs, like funereal tresses, drooping moss,
And through the lofty colonnades, forlorn,
The wind's faint sigh wanders as if 'twere lost.
A silence reigns like death; the clattering jay,

Or brush of turkey-buzzard's carrion wings,
The alligator's roar, or croak of frogs,
Rustle of rattlesnake, or dismal splash
That for a moment stirs the mantled pool,
Or drip of paddle from the swift canoe ;
Perchance a crash re-echoing, loud, prolonged,
Reverberating through the sombre aisles,
Telling the downfall of some ancient tree,
The monarch of the forest, brought to death,
By slow decay, alone the silence break.
 What time the level morning sun just tips
The emerald of the growing corn with gold,
Upsprings the speckled dewy-breasted lark,
The merry minstrel of the jocund morn,
On tremulous wing, rising yet higher and higher
Above the mists that trail the warm hillside.
Beloved songster! to our English fields
Sacred by all the ties that bind the soul
To childhood's days. How often stands the boy
Shading with outstretched hand the well-pleased eyes
That losing it amid the dazzling blue,
Catches again the tiny tremulous speck,
Whose trill of ecstasy the echo seems
Of all the gladness in the youthful breast ;
At length, lost to the eye, the song remains
Although the songster's gone. One with bright hours
Of freedom is it, the romance of life,
The nameless charm that lay on flower and bird,
Green lane, and pleasant field and primrose banks,
Fresh morn, the imagined happiness of life,
Th' elastic spring, lost in the rougher years.

THE MORNING SONG.

Ye russet songsters of the fields and woods,
How do we love you, every one, and watch
Your sweet wild ways, your flittings to and fro.
Now o'er the clover-field, the cottage thatch,
The red ploughed furrows, or the hazel wood,
Or breezy hilltop, come your melodies.
The ruddy-breasted robin on the brier,
When hoar-frost glimmers through the ghostly fog,
All the dull winter day, with piercing strains,
Will make the silent snowy landscape live.
For very glee of heart the blackbird sings,
And from his golden bill, amid the hedge,
Fresh budding with the promise of the spring,
Will pour a flood of mellow raptured notes,
The thronging utterance of a soul of love.
Perched on the lichened orchard gate, the thrush
Seen in the green arcade, all interlaced
With golden sunbeams, from his speckled throat,
Warbles with tuneful bill the livelong day,
And revels in the music that he makes.
How cheerful, how inspiriting the sounds
Thus sprinkled on the air around our path;
The ploughman following his team afield
Whistles light-heartedly, he knows not why,
Forgets his hard and ill-requited toil,
The cares that wait him in his cheerless home;
The wayfarer with quickened step renews
His journey; while the satcheled village lad
Loitering to school, sings too for joy of heart.
The Sabbath morning calls through daisied fields
The village folk to worship; from the hills

THE SONG OF LIFE.

Rises the singing of unnumbered larks,
Blending so sweetly with the pealing bells,
The listener scarce can tell the sweeter chime,
The mellow murmurs from the gray old tower,
Or lark songs from the belfry of the sky.

Thus onward, would I trace, O Lord, Thy will
In human happiness, caught by each fringe
And golden gleam, and added ornament
To this substantial frame, this spacious world,
The house for man Thou'st built beneath the sky,
No prison house, our earth, but home, and life
No drudgery, nor slavery enforced,
But the free service of our gracious Lord.

The quick-compelling appetite might find
In mere abundance gross satiety,
Lacking discrimination of the taste.
The elements that build man's physical frame
Exist, perchance, elsewhere than in our food,
Nor need digestion, nor the process slow
That with the lacking part assimilates.
The orchid from the circumambient air
Derives its nutriment, nor contact needs
With the gross soil.   Yet God hath otherwise
Decreed for man, and honoured His decree;
For that which wisdom saw as necessary
Love has made a pleasure of his life.

The downy peach upon some southern wall
Hiding its blushing beauty 'mid the leaves,
And taking on its soft and velvet cheek
The amorous kisses of the August sun;
The burden-bearing vine with clusters rich

Dependent, liquid globes of nectar piled
In pyramids inverted, annual gift
That, like the spies from Eshcol, promise brings
Of inexhaustible and lavish gifts
In Nature's stores ; are these the gifts of chance ?
O rich and generous chance ! friendly and kind ;
That stor'st the barren universe with gifts,
Hiding within the dark unfathomed depths
Earth's treasures, metals, gems, concealing there
The ruined forest ; throwing to the light
Each year the blush of flowers, the bloom of fruit ;
Man hath mis-named thee, or thou hast forgot
Thy native wastefulness, thy heedless whirl.
The pagan nursed 'mid cruelty and blood
Brought the Idæan mother, turret crowned,
The Phrygian Cybele, his votive gifts,
Or Ceres or Pomona, nor could judge
That bounties so acceptable to man
Fortuitous could spring, but that they came
From some unseen but generous donor's hand.
 What sight more lovely 'neath the April sky
Than that which meets the gaze where Vaga winds
Her devious waters through the pleasant woods,
And deep-grassed fields, past granges, cottage homes,
By Tintern's pile, to meet the surges hoarse
Of Severn's yellow foam. The ramparts blue
Of Cambria's ancient fastnesses look down
Upon the Mercian realm ; a wide champain
Of orchards all abloom, the faint pink snow
Of apple blossoms, as the land had drawn
Its innocent white kerchief o'er its breast,

Blushing as if in maiden modesty :
All fragrant is the still and sunny hour,
And populous with hum of myriad bees,
For them a paradise. When autumn comes ;
How changed the scene ! The landscape now puts on
Serener beauty of maturity.
Gray, crooked, mossy trunks, all gnarled and stained
And yellow lichened, ramify aloft,
And on the mellow autumn air put forth
Their juicy blushing treasures, ample gifts.
Each russet, streaked, or lemon golden globe
Burnished, as if in some clear fountain laved,
Seems witness of a thought considerate,
And eloquent of kindliness to man.

Unnumbered are the gifts the leafy world
Discloses with each slow revolving year ;
Th' enamell'd pomegranate with shining grain,
Or sunny apricot from Eastern lands,
Where Oxus, or Jaxartes rolls its flood,
Or Persian nightingales 'mid roses sing,
Wakening in breasts poetic sweeter songs ;
Golden bananas, on the rocking palm
The milky cocoa-nut, guavas, or pines,
Odorous of foreign marts. The colder north
Carpets with strawberries its forest glades,
And o'er its tree-tops spreads the bloom of plums.
Each country yields its own peculiar fruit ;
The date-palm waves above the arid sand,
Stirred by the dark simoom ; where moderate suns
Sleep on the trellised blue Italian hills,
Or Rhineland, with its mystic charm of song,

And antique fable, cliffs festooned with vines,
Grace with their blushing honours all the land.
Luscious and fragrant, cool, refreshing, sweet,
Clustered or bunched amid the shadowing leaves,
Gemming the ground, or crowning topmost boughs,
Each fruit that forms tells of the Unseen Love!
 Placed in a system intricate and vast,
Of operations numberless, beyond
The ken of reason, by a various host
Surrounded, beings lower in life's scale,
Inferior spirits, incarnated, brought near,
Whose nature and whose future are unknown,
Or subject or opposed to human will,
Wherefore thus placed? Behold the commonest leaf,
How veined, how fringed, how folded with a skill
Divine, where through its labyrinthine cells
Life finds its way. Why placed with this grand scene
Contiguous? But that the human mind
May see the workings of the Hand Divine,
Learn trust, obedience learn, and recognise
Man's high position, and as it beseems,
Yield his glad homage. Flowers bloom, plants thrive,
And in this spacious air winds come and go,
Nor is there found creature superior
To man, who with the offices sublime
Of reason, and of speech endowed, stands forth,
Servant of God, Nature's interpreter!
 How intricate the scheme of Providence!
In operation vast, and in detail
Minute. Myriads of creatures live, and look
To Him who formed them for their daily food;

Nor vainly. From God's full yet open hand
Comes their supply, ample, ungrudged, and free.
Thine eye has wandered o'er the harvest-field
All sickle-ripe, with spires innumerable
Stippling the brown expanse; thine ear has caught
The barley's silken rustling as the wind
Went by, or hush like satisfaction deep
Of whispering billowing corn, but hast thou thought
Of the great harvest-fields untilled by man,
Delved by the frost, God's plough, and broadcast sown
By the swift winds? The selfsame showers that filled
The milky grain, the same warm generous sun
Whose heat matured the harvest-fields for man,
Nourished these casual growths. On moorlands high,
Where come and go the gossiping idle winds.
Heaths, wastes, and barren corners unimproved,
Wild corners where the gadding brambles bloom,
Nettles and burdocks, thistles, shepherd's clocks,
Grow and mature, are Nature's granaries.
The scarlet hip that decks the wild rose brier,
Or clustering berries of the hawthorn hedge
Gleaming like coral in the yellowing leaves,
Or ripening hazel-nuts in autumn's woods,
Where children's voices sound, harsh blackberries,
Or elderberries with their purple juice,
Capsules, and cones, acorns, and winged awns
That fly to meet the hungry: here is spread
Provision ample stored by Unseen Care
Against bleak wintry days, black, biting frosts,
And deep concealing snows. Count, if thou canst,
The Great Provider's guests, whom clear-voiced morn

Invites from out the shivering night to come
Into this fair and well-lit hall of day,
Heaven's banquet chamber ; not the shining ranks
Of life intelligent, angel or man
Godlike, though ruined, or enraptured saint,
But creatures insignificant to view,
Humble dependants on the Father's care,
Dwellers beyond the bourn of visible things,
In crannies, crevices, of this great earth.
 Mark how the birds are fed ; bold trespassers
With saucy eye and ever-restless wing,
Improvident, and with each day's supply
Content. At morn, as at a bugle call,
Like an outspreading fan, they scatter wide.
The clamorous rooks rise from the surging elms
Circling aloft against the morning blue,
Seem like black specks from conflagration vast ;
Then to their feeding grounds pour forth in train,
Divide their forces in the outward track,
To left, to right, and through the day's long hours
Seek provender. Not all plundered from man,
Or filched from scenes of human industry,
The littered barnyard, where the sounding flail
Scatters through crevices or open door
Some casual grains, and where the barndoor cock
With his stout challenge makes the echoes ring,
Waiting with bold bright eye and head askance
The faint far-off reply ; or fresh-ploughed field,
Following the sower's steps ; or cottage door,
Where peasant maidens shake forth table crumbs,
With kindly thoughts for God's small pensioners :

THE SONG OF LIFE.

Larvæ of noxious insects, grubs, and blight,
Rejected unconsidered particles
Flung from the world's full table, which would else
Return to earth's great laboratory, the dust,
Yield food. Finches, and linnets, sparrows pert,
With chirp incessant, flutter 'midst the corn,
Or, in the earlier weeks, hide 'neath the eaves
Or rick thatch, watching opportunity
To filch the bunching cherries, and to take,
As Nature's choristers, first toll of these
Free gifts of Nature, not for man alone.
By unknown means, in unknown ways, the host
Innumerable is fed, as ages since,
The Master taught on Galilee's sacred hill,
Pointing the moral of the uselessness
Of self-corroding care. The evening comes
To bird and beast, and through the growing dusk,
The ashen dusk of gray and silent eve,
The lagging crow on leaden wing sweeps by;
The cricket chirps, the fluttering moth's abroad;
Silvering the dusky grove the rising moon
Looks from the purple balcony of the east,
Upon the dewy landscape, hushed and still.
With twitter scarcely audible, and chirp,
Or tiny rustle in the hedge, their heads
Buried beneath their wings, their wants supplied,
All sleep secure under night's dark concave,
The shade and mystery of brooding night,
As if beneath the all-covering Hand of God!

    O mighty Care! O all-surrounding Hand!
That through the teeming ages of the past,

THE MORNING SONG.

The cataclysms, the rude imperious brunt
Gigantic of conflicting force, hast saved
Earth's frail and delicate forms of loveliness,
How through the stormy sea hast thou convoyed
Their gentle company. Mere power unchecked
Would soon have swept the stage of weaker life,
Leaving no cranny where the frail might hide,
And so find transport : but a gentler hand
Has interposed amid tumultuous change,
Barring dumb force, and claiming a due place
E'en for the weakest. In the strata dense,
Four hundred fathoms deep in the dark earth,
The miner finds th' embedded filament
Of weed, that once had waved in seaside pool,
Now solid stone, fern leaf, or stem, or branch
Coniferous, the counterpart of forms
Existent still. How long within its tomb
The fossil thus has slept, millions of years
By millions multiplied, let science tell.
Faith can take up the parable, and smile,
And trust unfalteringly the care Divine,
That this slight form through centuries past has kept,
In chain of living forms congenerous,
Can trust the soul to ferry o'er the straits
Of death, nor fear profound oblivion.
  Whence, if not from Divine beneficence,
Springs the instinctive happiness of life ?
Existence is not so endowed with bliss,
That creatures claim of right the joy to live.
If the creative power alone had sought
Utility, man were mechanical.

Needless this thrilling frame, more sensitive
Than placid bosom of the mountain lake,
That takes the flaw that ruffles its smooth wave,
Or soft impinging shadows, rock, or pine,
Or antlered monarch of the heathery glen,
Or the steep mountain-side that slopes aloft ;
Needless his sentient and percipient powers ;
Then were the margin of his joy seamed o'er,
And to its narrowest dimensions clipped,
Unconscious, unrecipient, there were left
Nought but the dumb imprisonment of force.
But, as the sun, new-risen on summer morn,
Shines on the myriad spires of meadow grass
And freshened flowers, bedropped with gems of dew,
The benison of night, day's coronal,
Each pearly globe as with a diamond light,
Sparkling and glistening with a blaze suffused ;
The orb of day, source of glad light, beholds
Its image in each drop reflected clear,
Till by th' attraction of its own warm beams
It gathers up its jewels to itself :
So in earth's joyous lives innumerable,
The Life Supreme has multiplied its life,
The Joy Supreme has multiplied its joy,
Taking its tribute of earth's happiness.

  Youth revels in the wine of life. The child
Kicking and crowing on his mother's knee,
Ere reason has awaked, or lively hope
Lured the gay spirit with its pictures bright ;
His innocent glee o'erbrimming from his eyes,
Or voiced in silvery tones, clear laugh, or song,

In every limb, and look, and utterance, seems
O'ermastered with delight; the pattering feet,
Sweet music to the listening ear of love
Parental, echoing in memory still,
And to the vacant eye of brooding age
Bringing new light; sunshine of golden curls,
And musical melodious voice, and ways,
Antics grotesque, yet strangely sweet, all make
The heart a willing captive, and inscribe,
Deep graved, their lasting characters of joy.
   Nor is th' instinctive joy of living found
In man alone, the appanage of reason,
And gift of the Supreme Intelligent
To creatures likest Him; the lure of life,
Grapes of a vintage never to be plucked;
First burden of the memory, the first,
But oft the last. When the spring meadows show
Their earliest green, how frolicsome the lambs,
Leaping and frisking in their cowslip world,
And gamboling in the sun; the lissom hare
Bounds down the hillside o'er the dewy bents;
In the blue noon the pigeons dive and toss,
And sun their snowy feathers, or with curve
Fantastic show their iridescent necks;
When blinks the landscape, in the noontide heat
Of the unutterable summer calm,
Come the low burdened tones of deep content
From wood-dove, hidden 'mid the tasselled pines;
Now the red squirrel peeping through the leaves
Scampers from bough to bough, or diving swings
Upon the branches moving in the wind;

Even the waters swarm with happy life,
In willowed brooklets where the long-tressed weeds
Wave in the threading current, minnows dart
And balance 'gainst the stream their silvery sides ;
Amongst the cool green cress the lamprey hides ;
The water-rat from out the bordering sedge,
Or flowering rushes, leaps into the stream ;
The kingfisher, a streak of living blue
Amid the willows, darts athwart the brook.
The busy dragon-flies course up and down
The hedgerow, on their gauzy crackling wings,
Whose sheen, sun-touched, gleams with unnumbered hues,
'Mid buzz of flies zig-zagging in the sun,
Or murmurous hum of bees about the limes,
Plundering unchecked the fragrance of the spring :
The earth resounds with life, exultant life.
'T would seem it were the world's high festival,
In the bright day, all circled round with night,
And from th' abyss of nothingness God's power
Had called these countless myriads forth to share
In glad existence ; brief the longest span,
Conjoined duration from creation's dawn
To the last spasm of an expiring world,
Nought but the shadow of a passing cloud
Across the azure of infinity.
    The Hand that forged this mighty chain of life
Frames its successive links. Quickly the past
Becomes the present, while the present lays
Foundations deep and broad for future need,
Not on the sea of chance are set afloat

The seeds and germs of life to drift or drown,
But due provision, constant care are shown.
Within the narrow limits of the seed,
The fullest bloom and lustiest life that throbs,
Contracted in death's mighty systole,
Hide their diminished powers, their beauties fair,
Again to expand with fresh and balanced force,
Filling the utmost margin with the tide
Of a determined purpose. Nature e'er
Renews herself, retracts her ebbing strength,
Within the seed its ripened being casts,
And with short check resists the downward flow
To dissolution. In the cornered void
Of thought here stand, here watch the vanishing powers
Round off in death, forging the vital link
That binds each to the other, all to God.
The oak throws forth its sturdy vigour bred
Of wrestling storms that grind its lichened boughs,
Hot suns, and rains, and keen star-twinkling frosts
And, in the acorn dropped upon the sward,
Hides a potential forest. Here, enclosed,
Secure within the firm compacted shell,
Alike impervious to the sun and rain,
Till, buried in the soil, are felt within
The quickening impulses of mother earth,
Slumber imprisoned powers. So sheathed and wrapped
The innumerable germs of varied life,
Reductions of the glory of the past,
Wait with suspended force deliverance.
    Nor care alone is seen but prescience ;
The dormant seed lies in a nutrient bed,

THE SONG OF LIFE.

A tiny cabin stored with sustenance
For the frail voyaging life in its essay
Upon time's stormy sea. What power endued
The dusty butterfly, that flickers round
On primrose-coloured wings among the flowers,
With foresight, in depositing its eggs
To choose both time and place, that when its young
Should stir their torpid faculties, their food
May be at hand? This were no habit formed
Of long continuance, acquisition gained
By the slow increment of tardy years,
And gradual moulding of the generations.
Or, gained, how was the experience transferred;
And, being transferred, in instinct closely locked?
O'er the Egyptian fields the Mighty One
Hissed for the locusts, and their darkening swarms
Came at His call, to circumvent His foes;
An army terrible, invincible.
Each year's decaying and putrescent mass,
Poisoning the springs of life, is quick removed.
Soon as decay, its banners in the grove
Holds forth in sickly tints, or on the air
The deadly gases, of corruption bred,
Bear their swift message, issuing forth appear
Nature's great host to clear and cleanse the stage.
Here instinct finds fit nidus for the swarm,
The progeny of air, next year to dance
Their brief existence in the sultry beam,
And steals the poison, finding wholesome food.

Care for the young, defenceless, and the weak,
Through all the tissue of existence runs

Like a bright golden thread. For this, strong ties
Are rent, like crackling tow before the spark.
Bosomed in blossoming thorn, the mother bird
Sits on her nest, ruffled in murmuring love,
The picture of an absolute content,
And dazed enjoyment; while on neighbouring spray,
Her partner with his thrilling melody
Will make the echoes all applaud his joy.
Why should the russet pair contentedly
Forego the liberty they love so well ;
The ample fields of blue, the wood's green depths,
Sunshine and breeze, and flittings to and fro,
To sit and brood upon the mossy nest,
Guarding its speckled treasure ; thus to spend
Successive days in idleness enforced,
The willing captives of parental love ?
By what strange chance has this high passion come
To enshrine itself within these tiny breasts ?
Or how may we explain the sudden glow
Of love parental, self-denying, pure,
Worthy of creatures of a higher grade ?
Who taught these little architects to choose
Materials fit wherewith to build their nests,
The twigs, and straws, feathers, and thorn-plucked wool
And ligaments that bind their pendent home
Amid the moving boughs ; and these with skill
To interweave and form to fittest shape,
Lining the cradle for their helpless young
With softest down ? Who bid them patiently
Await th' appointed hour, when the faint chirp
Should tell the tiny prisoners set free,

And fill with busier cares their little life?
Who taught to forage far and near, and feed
The yellow bills that upward reach for food?
Can chance design? For here design appears
Pre-eminent. Is chance then merciful,
As well as wise, and powerful to boot?
Can dull reiteration mercy learn?
Wisdom and power conjoin with tenderness
To shield the helpless. All that goes to prove
The being, proves the love of God. No; 't were
But trifling with our reason to suppose
That aught except a Mind intelligent
Could frame intelligent results; or aught
Than tenderness could tenderly contrive
To succour weakness, and to minister
To helpless want; nay, with imperious will
To bend the rudest natures, savage breasts,
To mild access of gentle clemency.
The lion's whelps play with their tawny sire,
Gambol and frolic with his murderous paws;
The merciless tigress lies amid her cubs
Fondling and purring, her ferocity
Forgotten; from her fierce green eyes new light,
Affection's light, now beams. Natures that else
Were timid and unwarlike, win new strength,
Acquire unwonted fierceness, when their young
Demand for their defence severer front.
And all this tenderness this gentle care
Accumulates and culminates in man.
The mother folds her infant in her arms,
Kisses and lulls the little one to sleep.

THE MORNING SONG.

Wakening, the tiny wondering eyes look up
To their first heaven, the gentle smiling face,
Sweet mother face, all mantled o'er with love,
Never so beautiful, as when it looks
With pity on the helplessness it shields.

    Behold the welcome to the new-born babe,
Upon his entrance on this perilous life!
A friend awaits him faithful, loving, true;
A mother's kiss salutes him, sacrament
Of an undying love; and all the depths
Of a fond, loving, woman's heart are his.
Or e'er the mind slow gathers in the mist
Intelligent thought, and consciousness of life,
Love pours around its lavish, costly gifts,
Low gentle words and sunshine of bright looks,
And ceaseless offices of patient care.
To her fond breast the mother clasps her child,
Entrusted to her fond parental care,
To love, to nurture, and to teach to live.
Rough the first steps of life, scanty the strength
Of the young traveller, all unequipped
And ignorant of the road, yet with him goes
Upon his pilgrimage Heaven's chosen guide,
A mother's faithful, self-denying love.

    We sing in mournful elegies the tale
Of man's humiliation wrought by death;
Thence eloquence her sharpest sarcasm brings,
There finds her sorrow for the mighty dead,
Now brought so low. Into the darkness pass
The great, the insignificant alike,
Dastard or brave, the ignorant, the wise;

Death's dread antithesis ever confronts
The boldest most ambitious pride of man.
Yet well we know, that, though the house of clay
Crumble to dust, virtue will yet defy
Destruction, passing from these wintry skies
To a congenial clime. But human pride
Finds man's most abject lowliness in birth,
And helplessness complete; the tiny fist
That yet will grasp the sceptre, wield the sword
Amid war's thunders on the lurid field,
Or stay the helm that struggles with the storm
Upon the yeasty waves, now scarce can grasp
Love's finger; while the proud commanding voice,
Shrill as the winter cricket on the hearth,
Sounds like the cry of weakness audible.
Perfect in helplessness! the senses shut,
Vacant the eye, the ear unskilled to note
The difference of sounds, pithless the limbs:
The child of sorrow makes its faint appeal
To pity, whilst its weakness is its strength;
Its strength all concentrated in its cry.
Reason lies dormant, and the conscious mind
Not yet commercing with the external world
Is wrapped in sleep. Developed in due course
The faculties come forth; nor is the child
Entrusted with himself until the eye
Computing distances shall aid the step,
Or hand that grasps more firmly for support.
Nature supplies its food, warm, pure, and light,
Commingled well by skilful chemistry,
Suited to build the form, tendons, and nerves,

Bones, muscles, sinews, and supply the needs
Of this most curiously compacted frame,
In due proportion all; until the eye
Distinguish substances, the palate tastes,
Or the instructed sense of smell rejects
Obnoxious food. His wants thus slowly learned,
And mode of their supply, the child now stands
Prepared for less dependent life, makes known
His wants to others by articulate speech,
And slowly wakens to the mystery
Of all this varied and perplexing scene.

  The helplessness that touched at first the fount
Of human pity now gives place to love;
Not mutual at first. The months roll by,
And as the daybreak of the summer's morn
Throws o'er the eastern waves its feeble glow,
Its first faint twinkle touching them with gold,
So, o'er the infant's vague and wondering face,
Passes a look of meaning, and the smile
Of recognition breaks, the welcome sign
Of consciousness. Forth from the darkness comes
The sweet young love with its companionship
Immortal. How the mother gently woos
The flickering smile soon lost in vacancy!
How tenderly the nestling is caressed!
How lavish the maternal blandishments!
Nor sight more beautiful, more innocent
On earth, than love thus going forth to meet
The dawning consciousness. To helplessness
Activity succeeds and waywardness,
Yet with its own protection, for the love

It brings kindles a growing love, and casts
A charm, a very sanctity around
The busy prattler's daily words and ways.
Like sunshine in the chamber, like the song,
Pure and delicious in clear melody,
That through the woodland rings, the beaming face,
The silver laugh, bring gladness to the home ;
And when the long and restless day is o'er,
Laid in its quiet bed so strangely still,
And death-like, with deep breathing scarcely heard
Till listened for, how lovingly the eye
Rests on the peaceful face, the white-clad form,
Notes the forsaken playthings, or the dress
Laid by, loved for the wearer's sake. How soon,
How tenderly forgiven are all its faults,
Its foibles, as on the sleeper's brow
Is pressed the kiss, the prayer to Heaven is raised.
With provident thought the gardener plants his flowers
Where they may flourish best, in friendly shade,
Or morning sun that lures their beauties forth,
Giving fit soil and tendence meet ; so God
Has placed the child where best the human plant
May thrive. The centre of a family,
This small community with interests linked,
Seeks for his good ; none could be found his faults
More readily to overlook, or give
More sympathy. An angel by his side
Could scarce more purely love, more patiently
Abide with waywardness, and steadfast seek
His highest good, than does the earthly mother.
  Sweet mother face ! that through the past obscure,

The hardness and the roughness of the years,
Still looks on us, though death long since has hid
The dear reality, still do we turn,
Still cherish thy dear image, and our love
Reaches towards thee through the utter gloom,
With the fond hope that wheresoe'er thou art,
That thou art still, what thou wert long, our friend.
   Will one await the disembodied soul
Upon its entrance to th' eternal world,
To love, to watch, and tenderly to guard,
As here the mother guards her helpless babe?
For thus, O Lord, didst Thou appoint, thus send
True friends to meet us on the path of life,
With treasures in their hands, or wisdom's wealth
Pleasure's sweet cup, or dear companionship.
Those we deemed enemies, at Thy command
Experience taught, or patience, or, perchance,
Stirred to a loftier height our slumbering aim.
All were Thy messengers of love, O Lord,
Thy love, all sent by Thee, our tardy steps
To quicken in returning to our home,
And to Thy beatific presence blest.
   The family exists a microcosm,
A world in little, all the elements
That form the larger family of man
There finding place; old age, enriched by time,
Though robbed of many a grace, maturity,
In the full vigour of its bounding tide
Of earnestness, its tensity of care,
And happy youth all brimming o'er with smiles;
Rough manhood's fire, subdued to softer glow

By woman's self-forgetting tenderness,
And interlocked affections, mutually
Upholding and upheld. The laws that bind
In union close this small community
Developed in the general life, would make
Our world a paradise. Thus tended, watched,
The child grows slowly to maturity.
Love is its guardian. Couldst thou doubt the love
That sheltered thee, the mother's love that beamed
From mild fair eyes upon thine infant face,
The lips of love that on thine infant cheek
Pressed their fond kiss, the arms of love that bore
Thine infant form, and brought thee through life's press
To full possession of thy faculties,
To manhood's strength? Thou couldst not. Canst
    thou doubt
The further love that made the mother love;
The all-embracing charity that flung
Round mother and child its deeper tenderness,
Loved in her loving, in her blessing blessed,
And filled the chalice of the human heart
O'erflowing with the royal wine of heaven?

BOOK THE THIRD

THE SONG OF SORROW

THE ARGUMENT.

The mystery of pain—Difficult to harmonise with Divine benevolence—The shadow of doubt—Revelation's explanation—Perpetuity of life on earth denied—How then shall the stroke fall?—The leveret's skull—Death no injustice—Possibility of happiness may involve possibility of pain—Bells heard amid the city's din—Gratuitous pain nowhere found—Pain the hedge of life—May be in highest degree preservative—Pain as a punishment—God's angel sent to rebuke pride—Its power to mould character—The real wants of man few—The happy life like a woodland brook—Pleasure of labour—The pleasure arising from the exercise of natural gifts—The labourer's evening rest—Pleasure of change—The Alpine landscape—Sleep a gift of God—Its mercifulness—The slumbering king—The vagrant on the barn-straw—The condemned criminal—The judge—The merchant—The sick man's dreams—The maniac lulled—Man's nature tells of kindliness—The king's highway—Reflection's power—Pleasure of memory—The ruined temple by the Nile—Possibilities of human nature—Happiness the end in view.

BOOK THE THIRD.

THE SONG OF SORROW.

YET while I dream of happy faces, smiles,
And fond caresses of parental love,
Low tones, and gentle words, and sunny looks,
Another face presents itself to view ;
The face of pain, all troubled, ashy white,
With quivering lips, and dark and liquid eyes,
Like wells of agony, and mournful gaze
As though it searched the soul, faint querulous voice,
With intermingling sobs, that feebly asks,
" Have I a place in God's great world of love ?
Have I a place amidst the flowers, the songs,
The smiles and blandishments of tenderness ?
Lives there a purpose in affliction's sting ? "
　O mystery of pain ! Enigma dark,
Thou sorrowful eclipse that drift'st across
The landscape bright ; O subterranean stream,
How have earth's wisest sons in vain explored

Thy caverns deep, still hoping where to find
Thy gloomy waters to the sunshine rise
Of an established purpose! Though in vain,
We cast the plummet in thine awful depths,
By faith emboldened, and the sanction high
Of Holy Writ, from a sublimer state
We hope to see thy mysteries explained,
Thy waters brighten, and the purposes
Full justified of the omniscient love.
 Turn where we may, the evidence of pain
Confronts the mind ; nor can we onward pass,
Ignoring with averted eyes the ills
That crowd life's path, engrossed by self, by hope
Unwarranted deceived ; not rare are they,
Alas! tempting the speculative thought :
Too common ; for each nerve, each sense, each limb,
Of this most wondrous fleshly tenement,
May prove an avenue of pain. Not long
We sojourn unassailed. It well may be
That in the initial moment of man's life,
With the first troubled breath of vital air,
Pain claims him as its own ; and through life's course
The shadow is projected on the path,
At intervals, till, by the dying-bed,
Pain takes its last farewell ; or, whisper low
The dreadful thought, ushers the trembling soul
To other scenes, further developments,
And dim but dread contingencies of grief.
Surveying this vast area of woe,
Of human misery, these pallid forms,
And wasted faces on their beds of pain,

The question still will reassert itself,
Wherefore this dread concomitant of life?
Is it original deficiency
In Nature's scheme, a mal-adjustment harsh
Of sentient life to changeless physical law?
Bespeaks it negligence or helplessness,
Confusion in the government of things?
Is order being evolved from chaos still,
Creation yet unfinished? Through the mind,
Like night birds foul, dark thoughts unbidden fly.
   The musing eye rests on the mottled hills,
Where play the shadows of the moving clouds;
The skimming swallow sweeps the velvet fields,
The whispering of the wheat is on the air,
And in the sun a hum of happy life,
As in the fresh and restful silence comes
The dark conjecture of malevolence,
Comes to be negatived on every hand,
By every wind that blows, or flower that blooms,
Or thing that breathes. Reason revulsive turns,
And stern denial gives. All sentient things,
Rejoicing in the gift of life bestowed,
Proclaim their contradiction trumpet-tongued:
"The Ever-Blessed God hath made us well!"
This is His world: He loves what He has formed.
No creature of His hand would He have made
If He had hated it; and how could aught
Continue if it were not by His will?
Pain is none other than the accident,
Not of the substance of our mortal life;
And from the prison-house of pain, full oft

Lies open many a door, before we reach
The evening twilight of all-restful death.
 Can love be Nature's universal law?
Why then the bloody fang, the serpent's sting,
The fierce green tigrish eyes, and murderous paw
That with its victim plays, delays the stroke,
To multiply the agonies of death?
The pyramid of life rises deep-based
Upon the pediment of death. Whole tribes
Live by the death of others; these, in turn,
Become the prey of yet more savage foes;
Till onward through creation seems to roll
The endless ravage of the tide of death.
A system merciless, inexorable,
It seems, crushing the virtuous and the vile
Alike in its blind fury, when its powers
O'erstep the margin of life's narrow round,
And meet us unawares. E'en at its best
Man's life appears but disappointment, want,
Labour, vexation, anguish manifold;
Until a double doubt assails the mind
That God is weak or heedless of man's woes.
 As drifts the shadow of a passing cloud,
Dreary and chill, across broad sunny fields,
Thus o'er the pleasant theme of heavenly love
Drifts the dark shade of death, saddening the mind,
Awakening apprehension and the dread,
Lest, sinking in the unutterable void,
The cherished hope should to oblivion pass
And leave the soul tenfold more desolate.
 To clear the awful mystery of pain,

Trace to its roots in justice absolute
Innocent suffering,—hardest of all tasks!—
Were hopeless, and a problem too complex,
Had we no light but reason. To our aid
Comes revelation with its lucid beam,
Not to disperse, indeed, all lingering doubt,
But for this intricate and endless maze
Affording general reasons, and the clue
To many a mystery, else unsolvable;
Crushing life's dreary discords, like rich grapes,
Into the wine of perfect harmony.
Creation groans; a burden on her lies;
Her sweetest bells are jangled in their peals,
Her beauty fretted, and her lord dethroned.
The curse of sin rests on earth's fairest scenes,
Mildew and rust, and time with moss-grown stains,
Have the fresh beauty of the world defaced.
Corruption foul, of chaos latest born,
And the all-conquering dust that caps man's pride,
And buries in oblivion; these have leaped
The broken hedge, and followed in the train
Of grisly death, and all his lictors dark,
His grim apparitors, sorrow and pain,
Disease of ghastly form and aspect wan,
And all the dismal retinue of woe.
The world is large; the purposes of God,
E'en to our dim and purblind sight appear
T' accomplish many ends, far-reaching, deep,
Remote in their design and their effects,
Involving in their operation oft
Apparent contradiction, yet by man

Not easily to be impugned. Far off,
Beyond our ken, their full results may lie,
And their conjoined and interchanged effects
Cover too wide a field for us to scan ;
For life is brief, and human reason weak ;
This minor strain, discord forlorn and drear
Of death, may yet resolve to harmony,
Majestic, and eternal, and divine.
  To none, not e'en to man, Heaven's choicest work,
Earth's king, similitude, and son of God,
Albeit estranged, is given perpetual life
Below the sun. The world is but the stage
On which men play their brief and hurried parts :
Then comes death's hour ; the actors pass from view ;
Vanish behind the scenes ; leave their gay robes,
And scattering in the blank and rayless night
Are lost in darkness. Life's a troubled flight ;
Youth's pleased awakening ; sorely-burdened trudge ;
Then grief to find the journey's end so near ;
And all is finished ; man, poor whimpering child !
Tired with the day, lies down to sleep : death lulls,
Soothes with its anodyne his sharpest pangs,
Then lays his heated aching head to rest,
Upon the lowly pillow of the dust.
Our transitory home ! Behold 'tis writ
Full large and clear, and loudly trumpeted
On every wind that blows, lest we delay,
Counting this earth our permanent abode.
  And not for man alone is this decree :
The giant pine in Californian vales,
Or tiny spore to unassisted sight

Invisible, to their successors yield.
The mightiest king that e'er the sceptre swayed,
Peopled the world with echoes of his fame,
And sighed beneath the heavy splendid load
Of his own greatness, to the self-same law
Submits as the poor infusoria
Dipped from the turbid pool. All things must die.
How shall the stroke descend? What hand shall bear
The sword executive? who from the field
Remove the cumbering dead, lest earth should prove
A reeking slaughter-house and charnel foul?
 So mused I, as I kicked all unawares
Amid the grass a leveret's tiny skull,
Lying all bleached amid the blossoming thyme
And nodding clover bolls. A group of ants
The cavities explored and eyeless cells,
And busy thought ran o'er the existence brief
Which here had left so mute pathetic trace.
Nibbling the milky corn, or sweet-juiced grass,
All wet with dew, with many a merry frisk
And gambol quaint, scampering in evening's dusk,
When the cold moon rose o'er these silent downs,
Or when the golden morning kissed the hills,
Its innocent life was spent. The keen-eyed hawk,
With fur upon his beak and bloody spur
Stood on the quivering form; weasel or stoat,
Or fire-eyed ferret, in relentless chase
Attacked, and life was finished; nought remained,
When Nature's scavengers had done their work,
But this poor glistening bone amid the grass.
 Life is a boon full lavishly bestowed,

Millions of creatures struggle into life,
Sip the sweet nectar of existence, then
Withdraw in turn, and fall from out the view,
Yielding to new competitors to drink
With joy of life's bright stream. Why should we count
Duration necessary point of bliss?
The insect dancing in the May-day sun
A few short hours, may find intensity
Of bliss, an exquisite delight, unknown
To him, before whose glazing eyes have passed
A hundred summers in their painted pride.
No charge against Divine benevolence
Have we, nor accusation, should it choose
To share its bounties, calling from the depths
New pensioners. Hath life perpetual fee?
Or is it claimed that where life once is given
Death were injustice? Narrowness of thought!
Shall we then count as matter of complaint
The misdirection of the appetite?
Is this a fierce economy that arms
With mandibles and stings? Or does the pang,
The agony of quick and violent death,
Outweigh the natural sufferings which disease,
Or feebleness of age entail? The hour
Of separation, oft embittered sore
With pain, cannot annul past hours of joy
And healthy life, though in the dreadful gulf
Remembrance perishes. The joy of life
Is in the living, not in consciousness
Of having lived. Who gave the spark of life
Whene'er He will, withdraws the boon unblamed.

Earth is no paradise. When man stood forth
In the bright light of present Deity
Immaculate, unfallen, in Eden placed,
No thorns were there, nor pains, nor weaknesses,
Nor sullen death. But now gloom falls athwart
The sunshine, pain intrudes and drops its gall
E'en in the sweetest cup; fierce passions rage,
Contend with reason, and too oft o'erthrow
Deep-seated purposes and great resolves.
Fears goad man to despair, and wild despair
Wails o'er his ruined hopes. For Nature armed
Takes sharp reprisals of her recreant son,
Nor suffers unavenged her broken laws,
While the severest stroke comes from her hand.
   Perchance the very possibility
Of happiness, the possibility
Of pain involves. The fine-strung chords that yield,
If finely touched, divinest harmony,
Yield discord loosely strung or badly struck.
We in our imperfection prove but poor,
Unskilled musicians; ours are broken thoughts,
Glimpses inadequate of this great world,
And all its inner harmony; unknown
Our very selves, the limits of our powers;
What best conduces to our happiness;
How best to spend the energies of life;
Poor captives to the semblances of things.
   As one who walks the noisy peopled streets
Of some great capital, whose ceaseless din
Bewilders, harsh discordant cries, the roar
Of world-wide traffic, rumbling vehicles,

And prancing hoofs down echoing streets, perchance
May come anear some vast cathedral's pile,
And hear all unaware, or think he hear,
Strange sounds commingling of a sweeter sort,
Resolved at length out of the noise confused
To peals of bells in regular cadences ;
Till, nearer drawn, the full-toned organ hears,
And pure sweet singing of the clear-voiced choir ;
Smiles as he finds the uproar to enfold
Diviner thoughts and hidden harmony :
So 'neath the problem and perplexity
Of human suffering, the sweet surprise
Of many an explanation may await,
The unfolding clear of many a mystery.
 Wherefore should happiness contingent rest
On pain ; or why so near at hand should lie
The instruments of mischief ? Why is man
Unformed and weak, to peril thus exposed,
And heavily weighted in the race of life ?
Conjectures, airy speculations all !
Two or three links we weave ; the chain then drops
From clumsy fingers ; far beyond our powers
The explanation lies. Yet, though afloat
Like mariners upon the pathless wave,
Seeking some distant shore remote, unseen,
Weeks pass, nor glimpse of distant land appears,
Mountain, nor promontory, towering peak,
Cloud-veiled, as Pico in the western main,
Or Teneriffe ; nor marks to tell how fare
The voyagers, but lengthening days or skies
More torrid grown : the needle points their way :

So, guided by some general truths, we steer
Across the dark, mysterious, sea of life,
Content to know the Judge of all the earth,
Despite our ignorance, will e'er do right.
    Humanity hath fallen off from God,
Like some fair branch that withers on the ground,
Torn from its parent stem, weeping its life.
Man's sorrows have their deep significance,
Their noble origin. Yet even here
Goodwill is seen : the fallen are not lost ;
For He hath hedged the sinner's path with thorns,
Embittered the false cup of sinful joy,
And interposed to check the swift descent
To evil, lest that man should there find rest :
Surrounded life with pangs, restraints, and checks,
Making sin difficult ; ordaining too,
That when the soul 'gainst evil takes up arms
In blessed conflict, shall arise blest ends,
Noblest of virtues, sprung from death of self,
Determination of the will on truth,
Free choice of good, resolve, and high contempt
Of sin's gross pleasures that ensnare the soul,
Patience, obedience, loyalty, and love.
    Within the natural world gratuitous pain
Nowhere appears, though opportunities
Stand all around ; for every moment's life
Is hedged by changeless laws inexorable,
Whose operation and accomplishment
Demand the balancing of particles
Minute beyond our thought, adjustment nice,
And delicate commingling. E'en the air,

Most salutary, whence supplies are drawn
Of fuel for the hidden fires of life,
If but few atoms more or less be mixed,
Becomes mephitic, and death's messenger.
Science reveals that man, poor, feeble man,
With all his pride and boasted sovereignty,
Lies at the mercy of a molecule!
  Pain is the hedge of life; the sentinel
Whose quick alarm wakens the garrison
To rally for the citadel's defence,
While hope remains: its function is discharged
If hope to save th' organic structure fail.
The lethal injury that crushes through
The outworks of sensation, overleaps
The bounds of feeling. Is not here a glimpse
Of mercy in the ordinance of pain?
Danger were armed with power ten-thousandfold
Had we not this resistance, and this frame,
This curiously-compacted tenement
Of clay, would open lie to many a stroke,
And, unexpected, yield to sable death,
At the first summons of its dreadful trump.
  If in the physical frame preservative,
Highest ulterior moral ends are wrought
By human suffering. To save from loss,
From detriment, and depravation slow
Of higher spiritual powers, more wisely feared
Than injury to this material frame,
Howe'er severe, t' induce the love of truth,
And upward seeking of the mind that spurns
Short-lived advantages, may justify

THE SONG OF SORROW.

The stern decree of pain. By Herod's throne
The unseen angel stood, and smote in wrath
The towering superstructure of his pride.
So pain, God's servitor of darkened face,
Unwelcome visitor, humbles the proud,
Lifts glory's splendid pall to show beneath
The crawling worm, the dusty ways of death.
The strong man whimpers as a girl; the proud
Now groans as though he mocked his misery,
Forgets his full-blown vanities wherewith
He skimmed the deep before the prosperous gale,
Now derelict, stripped to bare poles and driven,
Lashed and accursed across the wintry foam,
Laughed at by every echo, and reduced
To the strait limits of the common lot.
Is it not well to disenchant the dupe,
Fortune's poor fool, the visionary led
By the deluding semblances of things?
If the next life resemble this, no need;
But if that man would know himself in truth,
Not walk in dreams but 'mid realities,
With life's all-potent facts concern himself,
The hand that tears the mask aside and shows
The truth of things, is still a friendly hand.

Pain is full oft the punishment of sin,
Mute retribution; distant the offence,
Forgotten, or foreshortened in the past,
The misty background of our vanishing years.
In darkness of oblivion man would hide
His now rejected and corrupting dead;
Dead sins, once loved, but now disowned and loathed.

'Tis written, in the plainest characters,
That God must punish sin ; no frigid, blind,
Indifferent Deity is He, a God
Of truth and holiness, too good to spare
Th' unpurged, to tolerate iniquity.
Hence sends He sorrow on its dreaded path ;
Slow-footed Nemesis, laggard in youth,
Trips the swift fugitive, the fleetest runner
Balks, and in grip of pain the culprit feels
His self-wrought bitterness. Into his bones,
Shattering the physical frame, the vengeance goes,
And in the echoes dread the sinner hears,
All tremblingly, the doom retributive,
Unpurged transgression punished, punishing.
The handmaid of repentance, when it brings
Consideration just, contrition deep,
And upward turning thoughts to Him who bare
The bruise of our transgression, pain becomes
No longer pain but welcome suffering.
Life's duties left undone, the debtor quakes,
Fearing the solemn audit, the arrest
By stern, gray bailiff time, who claims man's goods,
His all, and will eject him in the night,
Death's bitter night, homeless and penniless.
    Pain, like the sculptor's chisel, shapes the soul
To nobler form and fairer destinies.
Were it not thus, that by the pricks and stings,
Nettles and thorns, hidden entangling briers,
And numberless perplexities of life,
Our drowsy lagging purposes were galled,
Our earnestness were roused, loitering along

Life's road should we be found, too well content
With present satisfaction e'er to lift
The eye to future good, till life's brief day
Should darken ere our journey was half done.
The hand that from the growing sapling tears
The strangling parasite, acts to best ends;
The knife, keen-edged, alas! too keen, that lops
The rank exuberance of too lusty life,
And the maimed stock or the scarred branches decks
With richer clusters, is but edged with love.
When time has bruised its poppies o'er our wounds,
And lulled the sorrow of the grieving heart,
Even in the darkness of our pain we see
Tender consideration of our God.
Too well He loves the creatures He has formed,
Too carefully He gardens these fair plants
That grow within His paradise, to give
One pang of suffering gratuitous.
To prove, to hinder, to reform, such ends
Our sorrows serve, working our highest good.
Not stigmatising those who grieve, as marks
Of wrath divine: but are they gifts of love.
'Tis mercy all, though dimly seen, though hard
To be received; the hand that mars our joy
Will yet be seen to be a hand of love.

The love compulsive that through suffering seeks
Man's good, and makes the evils manifold
And sharp that bristle round life's path conduce
To highest ends, designs our happiness.
Pleasure abounds on earth, if rightly sought,
And Nature's manifest intentions marked;

Lies level to the common run of men,
Though sought in high romance ; for happiness
From duty springs, simplicity of life,
From virtue, source prolific ! thought and deed
Conjoined, to all accessible and free :
Not like the exotic, beautiful but frail,
Safe shielded from the common blasts that blow
Through this rough world, with shivering petals fair,
Nursed 'mid conventionalities and taught
To lean on every help, 'mid luxuries
Impatient, with its own dissatisfied,
Craving for that which lies beyond its reach.

 Few are the real essential wants of man :
Plain, wholesome food, and vigorous exercise ;
The open air ; rest after honest toil ;
The free possession of our faculties,
Unhampered by disease ; to look upon
The open face of Nature in her smiles,
And feel her calming and subduing power ;
Oft from the noisy world to turn aside
To the indulgence of sweet silent thoughts,
Commerce with beauty, and all holy things ;
Nor vintage like the sweet thyme-scented air
Upon the hills, bright sunshine, restful peace,
Whereof deep draughts the thirsty spirit drinks ;
The earnest diligence of active life ;
The temperate enjoyment of the good
That lies within the reach of every hour ;
These give the scope he seeks ; the strength he needs ;
Kind thoughts, kind deeds for others : thus speeds by
The happy life, that, like a hidden brook

Among the woods, singing a constant song
That with the pleasant forest echoes blends,
Where blooms the violet, and soft spring rains
Whisper their music in the growing grass;
Refreshment brings through all its varied course.
Faithful to present duty, nourishing thoughts
Noblest and most ambitious, kindling hopes,
Celestial aspirations, larger aims
Of which the world knows not; with things divine
Humbly familiar, though with chastened awe
And reverence profound; upheld by grace,
And the disposing of entrusted powers,
Faithful expenditure of talents given,
So with composure he can watch the light
Slow fading in his peaceful western sky,
Watch the oncoming of death's solemn night.

    Labour, man's primal curse, may blessing prove;
Set to due limits, and by thoughts redeemed
Of higher destinies and nobler ends;
Its coronal of sweat, and aching limbs,
Tired thews, and weariness, and rub of use,
Wrestlings incessant with the stubborn soil,
Or passionate ocean with its treacherous strength,
Work ends beneficent, enriching life.
Inaction brings its punishment; the powers
Unbraced by conflict or endeavour keen,
Unpurged by exercise, will lose their force,
And waste their energy; till, like the stream
That from its banks wanders in miry wastes,
Finding base sluggishness, corruption, death,
The croaking marsh, polluted waters foul,

Home of all slimy and unsightly things,
The life of sloth will contradict its end.
Man owes the world his toil : forming a part
Of this great scheme, the labouring winds, rain-clouds,
That trail their hair-like tresses o'er the fields,
The hurrying streams, or delving frosts, or dews
All copious 'neath the mantling drowsy night,
The secret ministry of light and heat,
The quick prolific agency that strikes
Through the dull womb of earth these sparks of life,
Upward to meet the sun with flowers and fruit.
Claims he to take his place at Nature's board,
To quaff the sparkling cup of joy, and feel
The farthest fibre of his frame to thrill
With joy of being ? Nature claims his strength,
And calls him to take part in this great scheme
Of glad activity, earnest to fetch
The fee of life, Heaven's usury, from his toil ;
To fill unthinkingly the passing hour,
Pour from the deep recesses of his soul
The refluent tide of energy, that moulds
To profitable ends of fruitful thought
Or honest labour. Nature scrupulous
Repays the sluggard in his own base coin
Of sluggishness, starves him 'mid plenty's hoard,
And to the weevils and the maggots gives
The store of earth's abundance it denies
To avarice. Pleasure on labour waits.
The brisk and perfumed hours of morn, with flowers
All redolent, that from night's dewy cells
Have brought new fragrance, melodies of birds

Ringing from hedgerows, coppices, and woods,
Red tilth, or cowslip fields, or orchards white,
In re-attempted songs, as hopeful yet
To reach the culminating point of joy,
The glow of life, the sense of peace and strength,
And all the morning's fresh and fragrant bloom,
With song of lark and glitter of the dew,
And acquiescence in the ordinance
Of Nature, these are his who early spurns
The couch luxurious, and the dull suspense
Of powers bemused in sleep's uncertain world,
And goes with gladness forth to welcome toil,
Devising, or with vigorous resolve
Effecting what th' inventive mind commands.
The labourer girt to work, finds buoyancy
And relish of exertion, he knows not,
Society's domestic, who has toiled
The livelong night in the gay ballroom's glare,
To find enjoyment in the giddy dance,
And found it not. Work, honourable toil,
Moves the machinery of the physical frame,
Clears the phlegmatic humours from each sluice,
Drives from the sky of care its gathered clouds;
The flaccid muscle soon regains its tone,
The nerves lost vigour, while through ducts, canals,
Innumerable, that irrigate the field
Of physical life, now swifter currents flow,
Bearing due sustenance to every part,
And lending to the whole free, vigorous power,
Gracing the action of th' informing life.
Blessed be God who hath created toil!

THE MORNING SONG.

There is a pleasure in mere exercise
Of natural gifts, strength physical, or power
Creative, shrined in mystery of life,
That hails exultingly the dawning thought,
And moulds it to completion's perfect shape ;
To build aloft some glorious fane of song
To shape a nation's ends ; or deep imprint
Upon the mind and memory of the race
Thoughts luminous, prolific of high deeds,
Deeds of stern mastery, bring solemn joy.
The arm that swings the forest-clearing axe,
Or hand that checks amid the gathering storm
The jerking helm upon a whitened sea,
Reins in the steed, or through the furrow drives
The ploughshare, thrill the mastering soul.
 Toil sweetens rest. Through the hot quivering day,
With legs astride, swinging the crooked scythe
The mower plies his task ; but evening comes,
And in his cottage porch where roses climb,
He sits at dusk, his youngest on his knee,
While, overhead, within its wicker cage
The thrush, eyeing the crimson west, pours forth
Its last and sweetest song of all the day.
There is a pleasure in cessation, in
The pause of absolute rest, that soft unlocks
The muscles tense, the strained and o'erwrought nerves,
Not less unwelcome than the glad rebound
With which the spirit plies a welcome task.
 Nor is man's life one dull unvarying tramp.
Pleasure is linked with change ; variety,
New sights, new sounds, awake new interests,

Expand, and with instruction store the mind;
And all insensibly. The eye that long
Has grown familiar with some well-known scene
Of quiet English beauty, hedgerows, fields
With daisied undulations, or of plains,
Meadows with bordering elms, or furzy heaths,
Seems like another sense, when now it looks
On alpine landscapes, towering mountain heights,
Snow-clad, ethereal against the sky,
Blue lakes, torrents that from the glacier steal
And with wild echoes every valley fill,
Pastures of dazzling green, and fringing pines,
Heights, depths, where death and desolation dwell.
  Sleep is the gift of God, the gift of love,
Sabbath of sickness, anodyne of pain.
How beautiful the mild forgetfulness,
Brief, temporary death, oblivion short,
That with its placid waters makes each day,
Howe'er perplexing and laborious,
An island rounded off with gentle peace,
With gentle peace enclosed in gentlest guise.
Were it not thus, the overburdened mind
Bearing its fast accumulating cares
Would sink beneath the load; the heart o'erwrought,
Eager to reach the goal of its desire,
Like the spent steed, would fall this side the mark.
The priceless opportunities of life
Are slowly measured to us, piece by piece,
That we more carefully may mark and gauge
The character and texture of our work,
Amend its errors, and adjust its aims.

The day is closing with its sanguine skies,
Like shining petals of the evening flower
Shutting in gloom: art thou dissatisfied
With this brief section of thy mortal life?
Few can reflect with pleasure unalloyed
E'en on so short a fragment as a day.
Amendment waits repentance; help is near.
Turn with regret sincere, in strength Divine
Frame thy resolves, determine yet again;
Beneath night's brooding shadow rest awhile;
Thy former ineffectual attempts
Forget, and aims imperfect, true, though foiled:
Wait thou in patience the blue hours' return,
And strive once more. The Observer of thy path
All-merciful, like some fond parent seems,
Who to the staggering child he dearly loves
Sets but a journey of a dozen steps,
Short stage, with many a cherupping word, sweet smile,
And fond encouragement: so for thy good
The little life of twelve short hours is given.
Use well thy chance, nor stain the spotless page
Of that brief register, with thy mistakes,
With murmuring, and petulance, and sin.

O'er the wide world, on good and bad alike,
Descends the mercifulness of gentle sleep.
Impartial night, that shrouds with low-browed gloom
The cloaked assassin, shrouds his victim too.
O shadowy land! where the unworthy rests
Unconscious of his guilt, the wicked soul
Is stripped of its poor rags of wickedness,
And in the innocence of sleep is dressed.

The king forgets the majesty of state
Wherewith his pride is robed, nor of his throne,
Ambition's pinnacle, nor sceptre dreams,
Nor sweeter sleeps upon his bed of down,
Within his palace, watched by sentinels,
Than the poor vagrant on the barn straw laid,
Who, all unconscious of his neediness,
Has slept a-hungry, and of banquets dreamed,
And dreamed himself a king. The judge puts off
His ermine, and unbends the heavy brow
That weighed a mortal's fate. The criminal
Condemned, who watched with anguished eye the light
Fade from the thick-barred windows of his cell,
Looking with apprehension to the dawn,
A temporary refuge finds in sleep,
The cleft of night's great rock, dreams of the past,
Of innocent boyhood dreams, mayhap, of hope,
Of self-respect, and liberty free-limbed.
The merchant from the tempest of his cares
Has harbour found, and sees before the gale
Ride prosperous his safe-returning fleet,
With sails gold-burnished in the evening sun,
Though the tusked rocks and churning foam have torn
And swallowed up entire his venture fair;
Unconscious one! Over the mighty crowds,
The sorrowing, toiling millions, master, man,
The tyrant and the slave, a sabbath rest
Falls with the night. The voice of harsh command
Ceases awhile; the taskmaster has dropped
His biting thong; the anvil rests silent,
Unsmitten, and the plough unyoked, nor flies

The busy shuttle through the clattering loom.
Even the sufferers are still; for sleep
With gentle hand has soothed the sick man's pain,
And in his dreams, in rude and sunburnt health
Of lusty youth, again he bounds along
The thymy hillside, hearing, as of yore,
The shining swallow twittering in the sun,
The brooklet's fall, the hum of bees. Their pains
Awhile forgot, the sufferers moveless lie,
As snowdrifts on the wide and wintry plain.
Now rests the wounded heart that through the day
Has dragged a numbed existence wearily,
And wished for death; the desolate soul bereaved,
O'erwhelmed with grief, its loss first realised,
Finds its beloved in the world of dreams,
Forgets for a brief space bereavement's pangs,
Forgets its hot salt tears; its pain is dulled;
The sympathetic touch of gentle sleep,
Like to a mother's kiss, has smoothed the face,
Unfolded every wrinkle, hushed each sob.
Even the maniac rests; the stormy brain
Distraught by terrible fancies, from its depths
Calls forth no more its images of dread:
The moonlit corridors are still; no shriek,
No sob, startles the ear or chills the soul.
  Ah! beautiful is sleep, sweet, kindly sleep,
Respite, brief death, the hollow of God's hand,
Balmy forgetfulness mild restful ease,
Dusky seclusion, reason's twilight dim,
Each day's Hesperia rich in golden fruit,
Around whose mystic shore old Nereus throws

His vexed waves with echoes all in vain,
Dim-veiled majestic night, thy handmaid, waits,
O sleep, thine almoner, to go with thee,
Soft-sandalled on thine embassy of love,
To wipe the bitter tear, to lull the breast,
Befriend the friendless, and the mourner cheer.
Sleep builds the waste, the battlements of life
Pulled down by busy care's destructive hand;
Sleep with its full and rocking tide flows in,
Obliterates the hoof-marks of despair,
Commits to vast oblivion's depths our shame,
And gives the morn the smooth and shining strand.
 Among the proud traditions of our race
The proudest runs that man was made like God.
Over his primal beauty there have passed
The blight of sin, the baleful shade of death,
Till man is but a ruin of himself;
Yet ruined, desolate, still yielding proof
Of high original. Here in the book
Of human nature the reflective mind,
With clearness, like to that which rests upon
The page revealed, can read what man has been,
What God would have him be; how He regards
The creature He has formed in His own image.
Wondrous unfathomable mystery!
The creature man, our own familiar selves:
Involving contradictions infinite;
Ambition vast, yet grovelling as the mole;
At once a god, and yet the slave of slaves;
The servitor of passion, reason's judge;
Truckling with Satan, yet with bended knee

Fealty declaring to the Will Supreme ;
Pawning for wretched sops his noblest pride,
Buying earth's tinsel, yet relinquishing
Without a sigh his brightest jewel hopes,
The heir of immortality, time's slave !
In virtue affluent, or, pitiful,
The pauper soul, that from its tyrant lusts
Begs for an alms, nor feels its own disgrace :
How capable of power, of happiness,
Invested with the faculty divine
Of reason, and the upward-seeking thoughts
Of purity with their severe constraints,
Yet welcome as the path to godlikeness ;
For though we oft complain of life's sore loads,
And the strait limits of our narrow path,
Wishing that we might choose our lot, might rise
And shake us free from these sore galling chains
Of present circumstance, yet Thou, O Lord,
Hast given, if not the choice of fortune, choice
Of character, what persons we would be ;
In highest form and effort of freewill,
How good, how godlike, merciful, and true ;
Nor limits hast Thou set to this grand range
Of goodness, truth, fidelity, and love :
Man's truest beauty as his truest wealth.
For commerce with a world of things external
Husk, frond, and scarf, outward betokening
Of inward life, not yet the essences,
The hidden life equipped to know, first steps
To ampler knowledge of sublimer sort
And intimate acquaintance with pure truth,

THE SONG OF SORROW.

Immediate blending, energy transfused,
Moulding the soul to issues ultimate :
Our life not in one single function spent,
But with resources of our being ample ;
Here placed in this dim tenement of clay
Wherein may stream, through media interposed,
The effluence and images of things
Remote, at best but indistinctly seen,
Yet potent to awake the slumbering powers,
And fashion to immortal destinies.
Here pass, as through the portals of the mind,
If wisdom and discrimination true
Keep sentinel, the riches of the world,
Best things of earth, and free to all earth's sons,
The tribute of this wide material scene
To Heaven's vicegerent paid, the gold of truth,
Fine gold, uncankered, incorruptible,
And the rich harvestings of beauty's fields,
Pearls from reflection's depths, gems from the mine
Of wisdom, by incessant labour won ;
Here traitors pass, if prurient fancy yield
The king's highway, a heart that loves too well
The night of ignorance, too readily gives
Ingress and welcome to suggestions, sights,
Forbidden to the purer spiritual eye ;
Foul traitors of the soul, temptations dark,
Though vested as the messengers of light.
Alas! that through the soul's high temple porch,
Lust's foul incentives, hateful forms of sin,
Or aught that might not swell the choiring powers,
Or kindle to diviner height the flame

Of true devotion's ecstasy, should pass,
To desecrate the temple of the soul.
   Yet man, this speck of insignificance,
This tiny emmet on the world's huge mass,
Itself, amid the universe of worlds,
A twinkling point, yet man down angel paths
Can gaze, and to the human eye is given
So glorious range, to see the endless maze
Of worlds unnumbered, yea, a universe.
To the tent door the voice of God still seems
To call the mind reflective, thence to gaze
Into the glorious starlit gulf of night,
And from earth's threshold insignificant
The greatness of infinity survey.
   Quick to distinguish form, graceful or rude,
Gigantic or minute, the difference
Of varying colours, how the ready eye
Reaps its swift harvest in the changing field
Of wondrous vision, now with distant worlds
Conversing, then with earth, compacted fair
Of wide extremes, built up of kindly love ;
The twinkling dewdrop's prism upon the bent,
Or glowworm with its sphere of gold green light
Amid the dewy grass, or giant pine,
Wrestling with merciless and ruffian blasts,
Or the red lightning in the quivering clouds ;
The ear that serves without being asked, and
      notes
The cricket's chirp, or thunder's cavalcade,
As movement of innumerable hosts,
Swift to obey, as messenger of thought,

These bring significant echoes from without,
And patient sit and wait at reason's door.
Reflection's magic faculty conjoins
With the perceptive power, enriching life.
The scene removes, its loveliness remains.
The wizard mind calls from the past abyss
Dead thoughts again to tread the silent stage,
React their parts, with voice inaudible
And shadowy action of the pithless limbs,
Tricked in brave colours of reality,
Then move in slow procession to the bourn
Of things forgotten, or detained before
The gaze contemplative ; the grossness gone,
Reality's keen edge and commonness
Removed, a tenderness is flung o'er all,
A grace th' original had not, or, perchance,
Not guessed, from superficial view concealed.
Thus gifted to review in stern assize
Past actions, of their quality to judge,
The motive gauge and its sincerity,
To see in juster light life's meaner acts,
Unworthinesses indistinctly seen
In heat of action, or perhaps despised,
To hold to inward reprobation stern,
Gather the slackened reins with firmer grasp,
And reattempt the goal with steadier eye,
Seems it not merciful to put the past
In fee to fallible mortals ? thus t' afford
A glimpse, ere the inexorable page
For ever close from view, that from regret
Resolve may come ? What sign more evident

Of thoughtfulness, than that which would prolong
The pleasures of the past in shadowy form,
That the reflective soul might chew the cud
Of meditation, and extract from thence
The lurking sweetness unperceived at first.
   Thus musing on the awful power that hides
Within the secret cells, recesses dark
Of our mysterious being, all the words,
The facts of life inextricably part
Of human character, by recklessness
Imported, or by culpable default,
Inwoven by the loom of things, the powers
Mechanical, agents that work around
Unconsciously, and unsuspected shape
To other ends, the doubt may gather form,
Whether a greater love would not have sought
To obliterate past inefficiency,
By dropping in th' abyss follies and sins
Unregistered. This, Lord, is known to Thee,
And all our future all unknown to us,
And Thou'st in wisdom otherwise decreed.
We are but shadows of our former selves;
We are but shadows of our future selves;
The thwarting hand of sin has fallen across
The spiritual mechanism, and has turned
The higher capabilities of man
From their original. Dimly we guess
What heights sublime man might unfallen have reached,
Had not the daring eager wings been clipped
Of his most godlike power, imprisoning him
To base and lower uses of the world.

The soul unspotted, undefaced by sin,
In memory would have found a treasure-house
Of all the choicest pleasures of the past.
Now, unillumined by celestial light,
That ray benignant from a farther shore,
The trembling consciousness too often shrinks,
Nor dares the portal of the catacombs
Of memory, the graveyard of the past.
    Like to some ruined temple, such as give
To Nile's green marge or Libya's yellow sands
Pathetic beauty; columns, architraves
Stupendous, capitals and pediments
All strewn as if an earthquake's hand had wrecked
Their symmetry; by their own ruins dark,
Or dimly seen, the narthex yet intact,
Or by the torch's lurid gleam, or ray
Of noonday sun made visible, where gleam
Paintings grotesque and quaint, in pigments fresh,
Of dread Anubis crowned with jackal's head
Leading dead souls to great Osiris' bar,
Defunct conventionalities, revealed
But meaningless, yet clothed with sanctity,
As having once expressed the deepest thoughts,
Strange and unspeakable, the hopes of men,
The faith, the fears of the forgotten dead
Now tombed in pyramid, or mountain-side,
Or desert sand, sleeping beneath the crook
Of stern Osiris, Thoth, or Horus fierce;
Ruined man lies. Is Lethe but a dream?
Or shall the soul through death's lustration rise
Purged of defilement in the memory?

THE MORNING SONG.

Yet, even now, in this disjointed state,
When like a wayward child the errant will
Gathers its useless weeds and wayside flowers,
And in forgetfulness the petals picks
And strews them to the wind, the virtuous glean
Rich golden ears in Nature's bounteous field,
To bear their patiently collected sheaf
When peaceful evening calls them to their home.
 For happiness, Thy creatures Thou hast formed,
O God, and when this great design they miss,
'Tis by traversing the conditions plain
That shape their lot. Still art Thou found on earth,
Not 'mid the verdant glades of Paradise,
But in this gloomy sin-disordered world,
Too oft Thy blest propinquity unknown.
For life is full of sweet divine arrests,
Love's gentle hands, 'gainst which we dare not strive.
Yet like the sighing of the autumnal wind
Through yellowing woods, so through the lettered world
Escapes the sigh of disappointment. Man
Knows not his proper good. Thou art our good;
The path of Thy commandments is the path
Where man may meet with Thee; and he who seeks
With resolution firm and filial care
Shall find, amid familiar common scenes
Of modern life, all too mechanical,
'Mid Nature's shifting ever-pleasant gleams,
Him who has made us and who loves us well!
For we are Thine, O Lord, and like the flowers
That offer up their beauty to the sun
That called them into being, these our lives

THE SONG OF SORROW.

Should we to Thy great honour dedicate.
The burden that majestically rolls
Down the long colonnade of bygone years,
The anthem of the generations past,
Experience of the wisest and the best,
The worthiest of our race, religion's theme,
And theme of Nature's psalm : " To every man
The Lord is loving; tender mercy rests
O'er all His works." Love everywhere has writ
Its mystic language ; this fair spacious world,
Blue canopied, and the all-glorious sun,
And sweeping wind, and fresh reviving air,
The leaping wave that sparkles in the light,
Night's solemn spectacle of fretted fire,
The imperial azure of infinity,
Each star that shines, each note of sweetness dropped,
Each flower that blooms, with simple eloquence
Tell their evangel, and to listening souls
Proclaim our God to be a God of love!

BOOK THE FOURTH

THE SONG OF HUMAN LIFE

THE ARGUMENT.

Whence came love's natural ties?—The pleasant land of childhood—Early associations with the dawn and springtime—Man changes but the natural scene remains—Boys' voices at play—The child spirit lives—Sweetness of life—Deliberate aim in life necessary—The mountain path—What has man to do upon the earth?—Emptiness of life without purpose—Our life is what we make it—The noblest style of life—Nature's neutrality—The noontide surge of trees—The ruined banqueting hall—Friendship—The spectre of evil example—The foam track of the ship at night—Married love—The wife's jewels—Love's paradise regained—Home touches the heart—The calm mountain lake—The Canadian emigrant—Home always beautiful—Round the hearth—Winter evening home scene—Sickness—The face of the dead—Grievousness of death—The pillars on which home happiness rests—Religious associations with home—A summer Sabbath remembered—Sweetness of the children's love—Angel faces through the dusk—Influence of children on their parents—The bereavements of time—Where are the children gone?—Love of country—English miserable homes—What may be done—Appeal to Christian statesmen—The golden dream—Time a second deluge—Good deeds engraven on most enduring material—Time saps man's strength—The cliff undermined—Great law of change—The closing scene.

BOOK THE FOURTH.

THE SONG OF HUMAN LIFE.

NOW will I sing of things all beautiful;
Of fair humanity and its bright hopes
And brighter promises; of human love,
The sweetest fruit of earthly paradise,
Prolific source of human happiness,
The proof and pledge of a sublimer love,
Which, all embracing in its tenderness,
Looks through each glance, speaks through each gentle
　　word
Of soft endearment, tells in each caress
Of a diviner tenderness and care.
O dear mysterious bonds, that link the soul
To kindred souls in blest captivity!
The attractions of this mortal life ye bring,
And compensation for woes manifold.
　　Whence came these natural ties? What chance produced
These tender charities? This loving care,
And yearning sympathy of human souls,

Clinging affection and confiding trust,
Sprang they from savage instincts dumbly led
To these high issues? Nay; from love love came,
Man's tenderness from tenderness divine;
For Thou, O Lord, wouldst win our lingering love
By the soft words, the smiles, and gentle tones
Of those we dearly love; Thy gospel this
That Thou wouldst have us read, Thy blest evangel.
For it is love alone that can unlock
The mysteries of love; the summer blows
For love, for love the world its brightness wears,
And all its varied prospects give delight,
Wakening our busy hopes. The frosty heart,
Dimly discerning through its own cold gloom,
Finds desolation, neither can perceive
The sanctity and glory of our life,
With its divine relations. Give, O Love
Supreme, the seeing eye, the accepting heart.

O pleasant land of childhood, fairy realm,
The Eden of the individual life,
How oft to thee fond recollection turns
In its far exile with but vain regrets!
The bounding pulse, the spirits glad and high,
The nimble fancy in its vivid play,
That from materials slight would build a world
All beautiful, these wrought their charm. Bright hope
O'erarched the path of life with rainbow hues.
Life was a holiday, and gentle peace
The welcome pillow smoothed for sweetest sleep;
Not yet had care wrinkled the brow, nor cast
O'er the fair morning sky a sullen gloom,

Nor pale disease so filled with boding fears
The present moment till that life but seemed
An endless vista darkening into night.
The hurry and the bustle and the tramp,
Anxieties, responsibilities,
The ceaseless exigence of barking cares
Not yet had trooped to exclude the larger thoughts,
Thoughts beyond earth, and yearnings indistinct
Earth cannot satisfy. Fair was the world
With its new pleasures opening up around.
Sights, sounds, familiar grown, now trivial,
Had then peculiar charm. The opening dawn,
In all its glorious golden mystery,
That through the curtained chamber windows crept;
The crow of early morning cock; the song
Of carolling lark mounting aloft to heaven;
Fresh smell of cowslips, or the primrose faint,
Or daisy with meek look of wonderment;
And all the pleasures sweet and new what time
The budding lilacs and the cawing rooks
Told that mild spring with lengthening days was near;
The mossy nest with its blue spotted eggs,
Seen in the hawthorn hedge; or crow's hoarse note,
Heard o'er the furrows of the fresh ploughed field;
Or corncrake in the crimson glimmering eve,
Heard in the mowing grass, or whirring wings
Of startled partridges among the corn;
A happy world it seemed and framed for joy.
Keenly alive, the quick intelligent mind
Was conscious of the beauty all around,

Not threadworn, faded, and familiar grown,
But the fair vesture of the daily life.
 Thus onward move our days ; thus moves the world,
In fluctuation fixed ; all unimpaired
The beauty of the natural scene remains.
Years pass ; the cock still by the hillside crows ;
Morn dawns, eve dies, the rustling autumn comes ;
The furze-bush crackles in the midday sun ;
The blackbird flutes upon the fitful breeze,
And the white-breasted swallow skims the fields ;
The sunlight from the dewy clover drinks,
And still the world is fresh, still bright and fair.
The past becomes the pathos of the present.
Now through the trees, boys' voices at their play
Are heard, recalling boyhood's days. Once more
The listener is a boy again. Once more
The arm swings the swift cricket bat, the feet
Scarce touch the dusty sunburnt grass ; the heart
Thumps like a hammer ; still the crown of sweat
Circles the scarlet brow, and the shrill joy
Of boyish victory makes the echoes ring.
Amid the crowd of customary things
Lives the child spirit ; while the fire of youth
Lingers and smoulders 'neath the ashes dead
Of years gone by, of passions long extinct.
Though by conventionalities engirt,
Familiar with the world, the willing mind
Still loves the clover and the violet,
The hedge-rose in the sighing days of June,
And pleasant ministry of natural things.
Sweet is the clean hillside blown of west winds,

Where the white road is edged with sparkling grass
Washed by the slanting shower; and sweet the thyme
That blossoms in the sun upon the hills,
Where hum the orange velvet bees their tune;
And the warm fragrance of the new-mown hay,
And sweet the fresh clean smell of rustling wheat
Crackling in th' August sun; the glorious air,
The purple hills, the winding river's light,
Our life, O God, is good, and sweet it is
To live in this Thy bright and pleasant world.
   As when one climbing some steep mountain side,
Where winds the track past yellow-lichened rocks,
Or through the blossoming broom and golden moss,
Wild mountain lake splashed with the stormy light,
Gray desolate slopes where ragged mists updrive
And the poised eagle screams to echoes wild,
Upward to voiceless heights where mounded clouds
Fleecy as wintry snow, surround the path,
Reaches at length the gateway of the cliffs,
And sees far spread below a prospect wide
Of shining stream, dark wood, pasture, and tilth,
Where lies his course, pauses to note with care
Whither his steps will tend; so, wisely, youth,
Pondering the future with deliberate choice,
Seeks the best path; refusing through the world
To go like paltry pedlar with his wares,
Selling his powers for earth's poor small returns,
But fired with quick ambition, or to know
Or do things worthy of his manliness;
Not with the surfaces of things content,
But mingling with their meanings, well assured

That Nature does not fool her progeny,
But to each life assigns its proper end,
Co-working with the mind intelligent
That blends its individual purposes
With her more general aim ; so Nature teaches,
Stirring the mind, resolving to refuse
To rustle in the straw of low content,
In misconception of the rational life,
But on broad wing to rise, and spend its strength
To worthiest ends ; like the well-feathered dart
That flies straight to its mark, the energy
Of youth must choose and keep its end ; not like
The drifting leisurely sail, that with the wind
Goes gadding o'er the crinkled deep, or stops,
Coquettish like, to dream upon the wave,
Over her mirrored beauty, helpless toy
At mercy of the elements. To man
Is given the power to reach the loftiest ends,
Ends unperceived but by the thoughtful mind,
That through the crowd of ordinary things
With settled purpose makes its steady way,
Despite necessity, whose towering cliffs
Oft seem to bar the access to the prow
Adventurous, till farther vistas ope.
For in the silence of reflection's hour
The clamorous voices of distracting cares
Die off, and duty's solemn voice is heard
Admonitory ; to the inward eye
Rise in their due proportion life's great claims,
Pleading discharge, or to the recreant will
Give stern rebuke, and prick our negligence.

For what hath man to do upon the earth ?
To sleep, to eat, to propagate his kind,
Dress and undress, to burrow like a mole
In learning, throwing rubbish heaps to mark
The life-track ; seek for poor and trivial joys,
Amusement, gold, feather and ribbon aims ;
Equipment seek for life, brass for the face,
And hinges for the knees, wallet for gain,
Destroy the simple wholesomeness of life,
And by dull repetition blunt the edge
Of fancied happiness grown wearisome ;
Get gold, and in the winning spend bright life,
Drudge like a mule and blows for labours take ;
Beneath a burden nigh intolerable
To groan and sweat, yet patiently endure ;
Bearing the slow procession of the days,
Then, like the autumn sunflower, rot on the stalk ?
Had not man's higher nature worthier ends
Life were a snare, a bitter mockery.

Be it for him to seek life's noblest style,
Nor grudge to walk the muddy common ways,
Bating all niceness, with the end in view ;
A life of purity and upward aim,
Silent, unconscious as the meekest flower
Of its own fragrance and its loveliness ;
A life not spent in selfish indolence,
Unnerved by soft indulgence, castled round
By wealth from all true knowledge of the woes,
The common sufferings of our race ; at hand
The key of luxury, temptation sore,
Perhaps the sorest, and to live for self,

That wretchedest of tasks, to yearn and pine,
And know not how to spend the golden hours;
To have a heart eaten with sinful pride,
Dissatisfied, that never knows its wants,
Pride nourished by distinctions brief at best,
Oft undeserved, that in its selfishness
Counts it a condescension but to know
Poor human nature, poor even at the best,
And sorely needing all the kindliness,
And all the sympathy that each can give.
To thine own self be hard ; duty exact,
And self-denial the concomitant
Of duty ; but to others lenience show.
Thus going forth in Christ-like charity,
True chivalry of soul, by thine own life
To better this rough world ; not to be served,
But serve ; and, humbly bending the proud neck,
Discharge the lowliest duties of thy life
With highest motives and a meek content,
Well pleased to serve though but in humblest guise
Master so great : this were t' enrich the world ;
Kind, generous, as the silent labouring tide
That, all unasked, sweeps on its breast all craft,
Navies steel-panoplied, or rich galleons,
Pleasure's light skiff, or the proud merchantman.
Give to the world a pattern ; there are minds
With high ambition smit, and fond desire
To lead a life of purpose, to infuse
Into the dull familiar daily round
The highest thoughts, who patterns seek, too oft
Swayed by the ineffective lives of such

THE SONG OF HUMAN LIFE.

As, grasping not the dignity of life,
Brave the ideal of an office high,
Complacent, and their narrow round who fill
With dull familiarity, nor feel
The observant gaze of yearning minds that crave
Loftier ideals ; nor in conscience stirred
Surpassing self to spend on loftier ends
Life's energies, that die to fructify.
We mould our life. For thus we are our own,
And this our life is to us as we make it,
Full of divinest meaning, or a tale
Vapid and dull, a spending of the years,
An unresisted drifting on the tide,
Swept onward to a destiny unknown.
For what makes life ? The sweet, the smart ; or pain
Or pleasure brief ; gain, loss ; neglect or care ;
Reverence, contempt ; hope, fear, or sore regret,
A tangled web, yet oft with golden threads,
That through our fingers shape their pattern fair.
Instant decision life's great purposes
Demand from early youth, immediate care ;
Not sowing memory with the seeds of sin,
Sure there to germinate, and harvest yield,
Or soon or late, of utter misery.
Nature revenges on the sluggish powers
That rise not to her mastery, and show
Their heavenly origin in their use of earth.
  Fair snow of daisies powders all the sward.
The wakening breeze wafts on its gentle wings
The smell of hawthorn 'neath the chestnut's bloom.
Soft surge of trees is swelling to a roar

That dies upon the wind again to rise;
The finch's twitter and the linnet's lay
Short broken on the silence of the noon,
An oasis of sound, break the still hour.
Now art thou one with nature, for the mind,
Recipient, lends itself full willingly
To all the enchantment of the passing hour;
Anon, the charm is gone, and loneliness,
Nature's neutrality, relentless, cold,
A drowsy sleepiness, give no response.
Nature appears a world far off, distinct,
Unsympathising with the sentient mind;
Ongoings unconcerned, on which man looks
A passing visitor and nothing more.
Walk on the sunlit grass, feel the warm beams,
And meet the cooling breeze, while treading down
The daisies under foot, and think how soon
Within death's darkness thou thyself must lie
Inactive, though successive Mays shall blush,
And breathe their fragrant odours o'er the land.
Virtue nor power can battlements upthrow
To exclude the invasion of all-conquering time.
Rank nettles crowd where ruddy hearthfires gleamed;
And through the ruined banquet-hall of kings
The chirping sparrow flies, or, straw in beak,
'Mid the groined Gothic builds its ragged nest;
The spider casts its web; in oriel high,
Refulgent once with the ensanguined pane,
The vine-stock sways in the wind; towers, palaces,
The glory of the realm, lie in the dust;
Given to the flickering bat and hooting owl.

Friendship to youth its choicest pleasures gives;
Nor friends are found like to the early friends,
Bosom companions, of most secret thoughts
Partakers with completest sympathy,
Trusted implicitly, though since the heart
Oft disappointed, slowly gives its troth;
Like as the early blossoms of the spring,
The snowdrop and the hiding violet,
Or shivering primrose on its southern bank,
That with too ready confidence appear
At the first glimpses of the sunbeams warm,
And find a bitter welcome in the wind,
The dry and chilling air. True friends are found,
And from this source, O Lord, hast Thou ordained
Some of the purest pleasures of our life
To spring. Pathos of love! the clinging fast
Of human souls in the abyss of being,
Blending of lives, the interlocking trust,
Sense of dependence, and the flow of heart
In sympathising with the need of those
Framed like ourselves! Nor thus alone to help,
But by most potent force of influence
To mould the character and destiny,
Kindly to care for all the retinue
By Nature chosen to surround our path,
And these to love; for none are locked in sin;
The sad crushed blossom of a wasted youth
May bloom again, and yield most precious fruit,
For in God's universe the amplest room
Exists for good intent, for upward aims,
All true ambitions of our native worth,

For truth, for tenderness, for simple faith,
For weakness, insignificance ; but none
For malice, selfishness, and avarice ;
For hatred, that from ignorance e'er springs,
None for deceit, and none for tyranny.
These are permitted by mysterious will
Of Providence, yet only for a time,
And in their train the miseries they bring
Stamp their true character and work their end.
  Not from the moonlit churchyard's solemn shade,
Nor midnight's thrilling hour of quaking gloom,
Nor aisle, nor catacomb, deserted vault,
Come the most dreaded spectres ; fear we more
The effects of ill example ; influence past,
The shadows of our former selves, old sins
Thought lightly of, yet in their hour endued
With perpetuity, with power to lure,
To entrap unwary souls, and lead the way
Down hell's dark path to everlasting woe.
O dreadful shades! mocking our bitter tears,
Haunting life's pathway with your purpose fell,
Have ye no form, no vulnerable parts ?
Come forth to light of day that we might see,
Might dread you more than gibbering ghost, blue haze
Of nightmarsh, skeleton form, or relics drear
Mattocked from out the earth ; come forth, and teach
How we may curb your fatal influence ;
May put a period to your vengeance dread.
For as a ship that ploughs the midnight sea
Will leave behind a track of foaming light,
So in good deeds we live a second life ;

Pure influence and works of high intent,
And tender charities and Godward thoughts
Will troop to encamp and fill the vacant place
From whence their author has departed, there
His memory to cherish, there embalmed
In lives redeemed, in souls from ruin snatched,
Dejection, or the sinful weariness
That wastes the precious energies of life,
To build for him most glorious sepulchre.

 Friendship's ideal and most perfect height
Is reached in love connubial, the type,
The emblem pure of a diviner love.
A woman's love comes forth to perfect man.
Clinging with fond tenacity, she guards
His name from shame, his inward soul from loss,
From secret unobserved declivities
To grossness, harsh and sordid views of life ;
Keeping his home in peace and sanctity :
And as the vine that clings around the elm
Shields the rough trunk, and the protecting boughs
Enriches with its clusters, while it decks
Their barrenness with beauty, so the love
Of woman perfects and enriches man,
Perfects itself, filling its nascent orb
Else dim, with a serene, all-golden light.
Such the ideal life ; oft reached, when reached,
A heaven on earth. A life of sympathy,
Of mutual confidence, respect, and care,
Mutual consideration, in the tide
Of life, not chafing 'gainst each other's faults,
But helpful ; of each other's weaknesses

Indulgent, to each other's faults most mild,
Each proves a guardian angel in disguise ;
Nourishing the generous thought, the noxious weed
In the fair garden of a trusting heart
Uprooting, and implanting in its stead
Heavenly desires, the seeds of purity,
With what is manly and true womanly.
Filling their days with truth and trustful love,
Life's changes sweetly verge towards the end
Of happiness. A life so privileged
Lies within reach. Hast thou, O man, declared,
In the glad nuptial hour, clasping the hand
Perchance now worn, upon whose finger thin
The wedding-ring moves loosely, thou wouldst love
And shield thy wife ? Thou art to her next God ;
She is but mortal, frail, and fallible,
And thou must be her best and truest friend,
Till thou present her faultless at God's throne.
Love is the key of every human heart :
Should it be so that time has stolen youth's charms,
Beneath a faded harsh exterior
Waits for affection's call a woman's heart.
Stand, as thy Lord, and knock. Renew the tones,
The gentle words, and deeds of earlier years,
And by thy side thy past ideal will come,
An angel as companion of thy life.
Kind silences and kindly tones disarm
Resentment, wooing timid confidence.
Thus shalt thou prove how hidden in mortal breast
Lie the unfathomed depths of holy love.
  Hast thou, O wife, thine earlier vows forgot,

And now familiar, grown unmindful too
Of him thou lovedst once ? Thy help he needs ;
He is but frail ; and in this hard rough world
Is tempted sore ; thou art his nearest friend,
And thou canst be to him God's minister.
Put on thee thine apparel Heaven bestowed,
And in the beauty incorruptible
Of gentle goodness clad, woman's true garb,
More beautiful than samite, cloth of gold,
The Tyrian purple, byssus, or the floss
Of finest silk, his heart will follow thee :
Put on thy jewels, meekness, quietness,
In God's sight precious, as in sight of man ;
Give him thy love gifts, tenderness in thought,
In word, and deed. His heart will answer thine.
Waken the rational soul to self-respect
With gentleness, that mightiest power with man ;
Conquer rude violence, the energy
Teach to develop in a nobler field.
For in the breast of each, how cumbered o'er
With necessary cares, by negligence
Forgot, and with its quick intelligent life
Crusted with covetousness, or vice, exists
The better soul with all its sympathies,
Glorious ambitions, tender shrinking hopes,
Sweet flower that waits to burst the encumbering clods,
And bless the kindliness that sets it free.

But as the mountain lake reflects heaven's blue
That arches it, now flecked with snowy clouds,
Drifting across the azure canopy,
Or, with the effulgence of the sun ablaze,

Rendering on earth, although in miniature,
The sky's vast amplitude; so is God's love
Nowhere more clearly seen than in the calm,
The blest retreat of home. Abode of love,
The refuge of the heart wearied with care,
Deceived, and disappointed with the world;
There find we peace when all without is storm;
There find we rest from labour's heaviest loads;
Home keeps its smile when all the world's a frown;
Home still confides when even friends distrust.
Blest pole star of the heart! constant to thee
Turn fondest thoughts and sad remembrances.
The lonely emigrant upon the deck
Leans o'er the moonlit bulwarks wistfully
Gazing upon the sea, the thought of home
Smites his stout heart, and melts him into tears.
Amid the silence of Canadian woods,
In his log-hut, axe, rifle, laid aside,
The exile rests. The Sabbath calm has brought
Thoughts of his home far o'er the eastern wave,
Thoughts of past days. Once more, as in a dream,
He hears the swallow twittering in the thatch,
The goldfinch singing in the orchard trees,
The hum of bees about the hollyhocks,
Or leisurely chiming of the old church clock;
And thinks he sees those he will see no more;
Feels gentle kisses from fond lips that ne'er
Will press again his lips in tenderest love.
Alas! for this fond, trusting heart of man,
That, loving, loses its most treasured joys.
The traveller, pausing on a distant shore,

Bethinks him of his home, and with bright face
And quickened step, resumes his onward course,
Glad to anticipate the joys that wait
To welcome his return.   All love their home ;
Peasant or peer, the monarch on the throne,
Or the tired labourer that at set of sun,
Shouldering his tools, trudges the homeward path,
Smiling as he bethinks him of the child
That, 'neath the honeysuckle porch at dusk,
Lifts for her father's kiss her sweet bright face.
   For home is always beautiful.   At dawn,
When the pale morning to the casement bears
Fragrance of flowers, grave musk and blushing rose,
Sweet pea of delicate and piquant smell,
As gentle voices, rousing slumbering sense,
Giving good morrow to the loiterer.
The birds are on the wing ; the clamorous crows,
The streams of cawing rooks flow to the hills,
Or jackdaws hiccuping across the fields.
The smiling sun peeps 'neath the eastern elms,
As if right glad to welcome yet again
The odorous fresh-cheeked flowers, his daughters fair,
Kissing their dewy lips.   The amorous wind
Toys with the tresses of the lady birch,
Whose bright leaves glisten in the golden sun.
Upon the dew-wet lawn, hoary, festooned
With gossamer threads, the birds with bold bright eye
Alight, throwing their shadows o'er the grass.
Or, in the hush of sultry summer noon,
When, through the lattice and the open door,
The languid breeze comes laden with perfume,

THE MORNING SONG.

From drooping flowers, scarlet parterres abloom,
Blown o'er a drowsy land of whispering woods;
Or, when the daylight fades with gentle hush,
Mantling the silent hills in deepening shades,
And evening's holy sky, placid, serene,
Broods as forgiving all that man has done,
What time the heron sweeps in gathering dusk,
Low on the darkened marge of woodland lake,
And the last gleam of light fades lingeringly
O'er the calm wave, in quiet glimmering peace;
Then in the home glad voices come and go,
And notes of song, and merry laugh are heard.
    But chiefly shines the pleasant light of home
When all without is drear, and the cold world
Forbidding, or when winter's frosty breath
Has dimmed the brightness of the landscape broad,
Shrouding the fields with snow, and the chill air
With foggy vapours filled, or blinding drift;
When night without is dark with storm and rain,
And roving winds that set the trees aroar,
Shaking each casement, then the blazing fire
Within the warm and closely-curtained room
Shines with its ruddiest lustre. By the hearth,
His youngest prattler climbing to his knee,
The father sits; and in the lamplight soft,
Comeliest amid her blooming daughters fair,
The mother, seated by the table, plies
Her busy needle, calm and well content;
Extended on the hearth-rug one bright child
Plays with the lively kitten, brisk as he;
The chessboard's mimic field engages some,

All silently, intent with glistening eye,
With busy thoughts discussing the next move,
The progress and the chances of the game ;
Meanwhile deft fingers from the ivory keys
Bring forth sweet music, and with pure clear voice
The singer sings of pleasant summer days,
Of hope, of love, pathos of human life ;
And all without is darkness, wind, and rain,
And all within warmth, harmony, and peace.

 Abode of calm! the haven of the soul,
Where troubles cease to vex, and fretting cares
Will vanish as the morning's rising mists ;
Affliction comes ; prosperity's bright hour
Is clouded, for a temporary shade
Eclipses the bright noon. A sufferer lies
In the hushed chamber ; quick affection's ear
Keeps listening through the hours of awful night
For moan or cry that from the loved one comes
In the dread struggle, moan, unconscious cry,
Betokening the outflowing of the tide
Of health, towards the ocean vast of death ;
Quick sympathy flows forth in gentle word
And tender act, better than oil and wine
For sorrow's wound. The ministry of love
Is sorrow's best medicament ; the hand,
The soft low voice, the loving thoughtfulness,
That hastens to assuage the sufferer's pains,
Brings God's sweet anodyne of sympathy.

 Ah me! by what sore bonds are human souls
Linked to each other ; in what fires severe
Are forged those links. The darkened room, chill fear,

That trembling finds its omens all around ;
Vigil of anguish, bitter lonely hours,
Prolonged suspense, the agony of hope,
When apprehension scarce will let hope live,
Watching and grief with mighty hands to mould
This poor humanity's unyielding clay :
Then comes death's awful fact, inexorable !
We stand upon the low dark marge of life,
And cry in desolate grief, "Come back, come back !"
Yet hear we no response from out death's night.
The face beloved changed with a mortal change,
The icy kiss laid on the marble brow,
The iron sleep, the rigid, moveless form,
And the strange stillness haunt the grieving mind ;
The empty room, the vacant chair, the voice
Once known so well, so loved, now heard no more.
The hour returns, but not the well-known step,
For which love's ear expectant listens still ;
The table's spread, the chair placed by the hearth,
The dear familiar face is seen no more !
Then live we in a dream, bruised, numbed, and sore,
With constant miserable sense of loss,
Of missing one, long loved, haunting the thoughts ;
Deadness to everything ; time's flight unmarked,
Or strangely magnified, that when an hour
Had passed since the dread cruel blow it seemed
An age, till time's revolving weeks recalled
The past in all its freshness ; from the life
Something has gone that ne'er can be replaced.
Again, and yet again, the pining mind
Goes o'er the story, picturing all afresh,

Feeding on grief, and jealous of the hours
That bear us from the irrevocable past,
Nor stay ourselves but on the hand of God.
We build our poor philosophy, and rest,
Yet at the sight of some familiar thing,
Garment once worn, handwriting known too well,
Chance utterance of the cherished name, start back
As wounded, and the dark o'erwhelming flood
Returns in all its bitterness once more.
Ah! Lord, how grievous is this dreadful death
That haunts our earth; how sorely it afflicts
Our sorrowing hearts; no single penalty
But manifold, for, in the death of those
We love, we taste afresh death's bitterness;
Yet from the depths of our great troubles come
The pearls of confidence, of hope, of love,
And all the tenderness that springs from grief,
And soft allowance for another's faults,
And ready sympathy with others' woes.

 Neither on riches nor on rank depends
The happiness of home. Its corner-stone
And its foundation firm is love; which wanting
All else were mockery and empty show,
How specious e'er, rich, cultured, or refined.
Like the best things of life, the joys of home
Lie near at hand. Good temper, thoughtfulness,
Mutual consideration and good sense,
Contentment, these combined, still more than these,
Religious principle, the fear of God,
And in its farthest and most secret shrine
The love of God. Fond memory will recall

Past days of calm serenity and peace,
When on the Sabbath air the Sabbath bells
Sang their sweet music through the resting land.
Still shines the sun in lingering memory's sky.
All breathes of peace, of restfulness, and calm.
The fields seem resting; 'neath the willow's shade,
The farmer's horse, respited from his toil,
Stands dreamily with long and bushy tail
Whisking his shining flanks. The balmy air,
The wind that blew across the daisied fields,
Reviving, fresh, as if it breathed the love
Of Him whose kindliness ordained for man
The holy day, how did it rest o'er all
Like to a benediction on the land.
Smooth waters round their wooded islands gleamed,
That gave 'mid drooping boughs glimpses of green
Goldened with buttercups; swans glided by,
Like mimic clouds upon the nether blue;
Onward the river flowed; the bells chimed on;
And, as beneath God's smile, the land had peace.
    As on a cloudy day when mists enfold
The city's wilderness of spires and towers,
Faintly distinguished in the common haze,
A casual ray will touch some lofty fane,
That with its gilded cross mounts far on high,
Revealing it all white, ethereal,
The sunbeam pointing to the house of God,
So in the mist and maze of life Heaven shows,
As with the finger of the sunbeam's light,
Religion, man's chief end, his duty chief.
    Most prominent amid the welcome thoughts

That make of home a fragrant memory
Are the remembrance of devotion's times,
The cloistered silence of the hour of prayer ;
Gathered for worship, then the father's voice,
Both priest and shepherd of his little flock,
Was heard in solemn, reverent tones to read
The sacred page, and on the mute bowed heads
Of those who knelt around t' implore God's grace,
To equip them for the day, or through the night
To guard them in the helplessness of sleep.

   Here, in the narrow precincts of the home,
Here, wouldst Thou have us learn, O Lord, the way
From earth to heaven ; here live the highest life,
The life of purpose and self-sacrifice ;
Silent fruition of unuttered thoughts,
And grateful non-occasions for discourse,
Wherein the mind recruits its flagging powers ;
The living in most near and intimate view
The life that by its silent teachings moulds
The life of others, shaping them to forms
Worthiest of man : nor only by the deed,
But by the thoughts that in the saying come
Edged with their virgin freshness, quick to form
The plastic mind, and to the opening powers
Alluring ; precious husbandry that sows
True thoughts, dropped in the mind of youth as seeds,
Whence spring the love of truth, of constancy,
Pureness, sincerity, unselfishness,
The fairest flowers that grace humanity ;
To watch them grow, to prune, to train, direct
The aspiring thought to ends commensurate

THE MORNING SONG.

With man's high origin and destiny,
Would seem a task worthy of Paradise.
   But who may tell the simple joys of home,
And all the sweetness of the children's love,
Clinging like tendrils round the parent's heart;
Clear ringing laughter, and the footsteps light
Of busy feet, that patter on the stairs,
Bright looks of sunshine, arch and merry eyes,
And fond parental names though feebly lisped,
Though feebly lisped, yet with deep fondness heard.
How, at returning eve, child faces watch,
Sweet angel faces through the dusk they seem,
All radiant with delight, and eyes of love
Search through the gathering gloom to welcome him.
Clinging around his neck twine little arms,
And soft warm kisses press upon his cheek,
Cold with the blowing of the outer wind,
While on his bosom rest bright golden curls;
The hearthfire burns for him a ruddier light,
And every flickering shadow in his home
Bids him a welcome from the cold, dark world.
   Like some young grove planted towards the north,
That, growing, shields the home from wintry blasts,
Children arise, and guard him with their love;
For him the lifted hands, the lisping tongues
Of innocence, oft plead in simple prayers;
Nor can I find that Heaven will disregard
The intercessions of a little child.
The gifts of love, that like fresh flowers best please
In their first freshness, these are likewise his:
Upon the learner's meek inquiring face

To look, and satisfy the mind with truth :
Warn of life's treacherous sea, where most we fear
When that prosperity's full gale blows fair ;
The timid heart dreading each moment next
Lest, plunging on some hidden rock, its hopes
Find utter wreck, the lurking peril show ;
By precept and example, pointing out
The better way, careful as well to teach
How that with velvet touch the wasp of sin
Will sting the soul, and of false teachings warn,
Of base philosophy that ever brings
On nations as on individual man
A devastation worse than floods or fire.

 But as the summer sky long time will show
A settled fairness, day succeeding day
In golden beauty, though no other change
Betokens the sure steady lapse of time,
Than deepening hues in wood and harvest-field,
Blue mists upcurling o'er the mellowing oaks,
And coral berries gleaming in the hedge,
Whirr of brown sparrows in the stubble fields,
And hazy landscapes, though in nooks retired,
Green nooks, the heart of woods, foxgloves still bloom,
With silvery ferns spangled with dew of light ;
Until by slow gradations autumn comes,
Closing at length earth's mighty portals dim,
The treasure-house of Nature's plenitude :
So fade the brightness and the joys of home :
The past becomes irrevocably past.

 Home has its plunderers. Not death alone,
But stealthy and slow-pacing time, bereaves,

In changes oft, each change howe'er unmarked,
A death without the bitterness of death,
Gentle bereavement welcome e'en to love.
For love well pleased will note the youthful frame
Develop into broader lineaments,
Stalwart, of manlier build, or sweet new grace
Of dawning womanhood; the golden curls,
Shorn from the ampler brow, not without sigh,
The lisping utterances of youth exchanged
For deeper tones; and oft the heart will cry,
Where are the children gone? Revisiting
Familiar scenes, the home of earlier years,
Insensibly the mind shrinks from each change
That seems to block our access to the past,
Where fancy wanders back beguiled. Still shines
The pleasant glint of sunshine on the brook
In wavy lines; still open lies the path
Along the fields where once the children played;
Soft hush of slumberous leaves is on the air;
Low piping wood-notes of the summer day;
Short heather songs in the blue quiet noon;
Echo, still listening, waits among the hills,
Still cries the heart, Where are the children gone?
   The love of country from the love of home
Develops. While a sanctity exists,
And reverence due to universal man,
That knows no bounds of climate, class, or time,
Yet must the link that to our native shore
Binds willing souls be reverenced; for the man
That thrills not at his country's name is cold;
That at the sound of the familiar speech,

Perchance o'erheard upon some foreign shore,
Lends not a willing ear, is sure a son
Unworthy of the land that gave him birth.
The Swiss in exile, for his native land
Pines secretly; glimpses of snow-clad heights,
The châlet on the glorious mountain's side,
Blue lakes, and fringing woods his vision haunt.
Old Scotia binds her sons with links of steel;
Calls willing thoughts from earth's most distant shores
To her gray-lichened rocks and heathery slopes;
And thou, our England, home of liberty,
Mother of many nations, art enthroned
Within our hearts; and should the call arise,
Thousands were ready to avouch that love
Even to death.   Linked with the mighty past,
As a rich heirloom, the historic fame
Of this rude island fixed 'mid stormy seas
Is theirs.   Yet England's greatness sprang, and still
Must spring from out her people's homes.   Here grow
The principles of strength and purity
That make a nation great : thence men come forth
God-fearing, armed with simple truth, with love
Of rectitude, justice, humanity.
Alas! too oft the sacredness of home,
And all its genial kindly influence,
For thousands of our people are but dreams,
Its happiness a figment most unreal.
  Are we content such things should be ?   Content ?
Nay!   This hath touched the sorrow of my soul,
For I have lived amid the teeming throngs,
Have known their wretchedness, and felt their woes :

Suffered the pangs of disappointed hopes,
Th' apparent failure of remedial schemes,
Or slight success, and sorrowfully yearned
O'er the great mass of human misery.
England, my country, Christian England called,
Rich art thou, populous, renowned, and great,
Yet are ten thousands of thy people steeped
In ignorance and vice! This must not be!
Greed builds our crowded cities : avarice,
The worst and meanest spirit from hell, throws up
These dismal streets, thronged with their noisome dens
Called homes of men, men stabled worse than kine,
Where, 'neath dense canopy of smoke, the crowds
Breathe the foul air, and herd like beasts, and die.
These are our brethren : these have natural rights
To breathe God's air, feel the warm sun, to see
The pleasant face of Nature, and to know
The kindliness that sweetens human life :
These have inherent right higher to rise,
But scarce have chance to live. To lie, to steal,
Blaspheme, corrupt each other, fight and work
And die ; these may they do, but are debarred
From much that elevates and honours man.
Yet God's creation these, yea, even as they
Of finer mould ; for 'neath the exterior rough
Of many a horny-handed son of toil
Are found the elements of truest man ;
Kindness, a spirit generous, unselfish,
And capable of true and gentle deeds,
Manhood sincere. By what accursed fate,
What social exigency fell, have these

THE SONG OF HUMAN LIFE.

Been thrown 'neath mammon's cruel chariot wheels?
At the slaves' cry the heart of England woke;
She broke their fetters, she proclaimed them free.
But these our slaves at home, our countrymen,
By thousands told, born thralls, condemned are they
To lifelong struggle, that they may but live.
Who pities them, who hears their weary sighs?
O dismal beating of the weary feet
Along the stony deserts of our streets!
O pale-faced workers, whose pathetic look
But says, " To-day we work, to-morrow die!"
These are the general mass that throngs the streets,
Ordinary, who feel the curse of labour's curse,
The overdriving that excludes the hopes
That help to dignify humanity,
Making this life more than mechanical,
And man than worms' meat; the incessant toil
That makes them barter for the passing hour
Of pleasure, things of highest worth;
Plucks from the cheek of modesty its rose,
And robs the spirit of its spur of fame;
Till, driven and worn, at length the wearied soul,
Losing its hope, drags life, like some spent horse,
Crook-legged and spavined, from whose withered flanks
The whip has scourged the last and lingering strain.
And what can life for these twice-banished do,
Who find not in religion's holy calm
Refuge, and sanctuary from the noisy world;
Rich mingling harmonies, uplifting thoughts;
Glimpses of angels, and the spotless hope;
Who scarce can hear amid the horrid din

The holy music of the good man's life.
Theirs hard and common drudgery unredeemed:
Even Nature's sanctuary to them denied,
Refuge to find from loud intrusive cares,
Refreshing silence in the open air,
Or the dim solemn gloom of ancient woods,
Or salt sea breeze like cool hand on the brow:
Nature's sweet ministry to wearied minds;
But toil instead, privation, squalor, noise.
Shame on complacency that tolerates
Existent evil, calm to allow such ills;
Suffering the rankling wounds to go unhealed;
Counting the present a necessity;
That thinks the poorer classes must exist
With all their miseries unremedied.
Exist they must; but not as some would deem,
Like a fermenting and corrupting heap
On which the flowers of pride and swollen pomp
May grow; the refuse heap on which the shards,
The cuttings, and the superfluity
Of selfishness be thrown as charity:
This were unmeet: but what in truth they are,
Society's smirched hands and toiling feet,
Foundations of the national edifice.
  O Christian statesmen! if the sacred name
Ye bear have a compulsive force;
If ye the great Redeemer would obey,
Rendering His gospel in your calling high,
Forget not the great brotherhood of man,
The charity sublime the Saviour taught:
How Christ the poor befriended, and their cause

Upheld, commiseration taught, pity,
A tenderness and mercifulness extreme,
Taught that the meanest and the worst of men
E'en at their worst estate, were sons of God,
Though fallen and lost; and that for this He came
To rescue them. For His sake be their friend.
Even if the instincts of humanity,
Though exigent, and to the inward ear
Clamorous, assail not in their earnestness.
A nobler work invites your energies
Than common statecraft, and a nobler fight
Than that for party victory. A name
Illustrious among the brightest names
Enriching our proud annals may be won
By him who would befriend the struggling crowd,
Against the unnatural conditions plead
Of social life, plead for the children's rights,
The friendless and obscure of human kind.
Our people are your care, your first, your chief;
Ye are the shepherds of the national flock;
See that it be not wasted, worried, torn,
By human covetousness, by ignorance.
Let your great power be interposed to check
Insatiate mammon, that, like dragon old
In legendary tale, its victims claims;
Poisons the air that all perforce must breathe;
Pollutes the water all perforce must drink;
Disfigures the fair face of mother earth,
Blasts vegetation, taints the running stream;
Corrupts man's food; the healing properties
Of natural drugs adulterates, and cheats

L

The dying of their hope, while it condemns
To pale faced servitude the struggling crowds.
With what intent ? That but a few, and they
Already rich, might heap up greater wealth.
Our people, not our money, makes us rich.
 Vice, like some blight, some baneful canker-worm
Frets the fair flower of national industry,
Gorging its fill. Upon the nation lies
The curse of drink, Britain's disgrace, the cause
Of unimagined woes, which, if unchecked,
Seem to forecast the national overthrow.
Nor should remedial measures rest untried
As costly, doubtful, or e'en dangerous ;
Danger oft proves danger's best remedy.
Knowledge outruns slow-paced morality ;
We boast us of our scientific lore,
What marvels electricity unfolds ;
But the new blaze of science only sheds
A ghastlier light on man, revealing painfully
His meagre increment of moral good,
Faint as the earth-shine of the crescent moon ;
Wiser, has man become more dutiful,
More generous, considerate, and true ?
What boots it to have harnessed all the powers
Of nature, distance to annihilate,
And net the throbbing globe with human thought ;
To fill the world with echoes of the fame
Of England's prowess, if our people fail,
If there remain a base residuum
Beneath the glitter of the national wealth,
The poor down-trodden, ground to dust, in vice

THE SONG OF HUMAN LIFE.

Nurtured yet banned : abuse unremedied,
Because antique ; and frightful evils borne
Under the pitiful plea of social use.
Who makes society ? Who gives it laws ?
Is it some dumb and blood-smeared fiend that claims
These victims, helpless innocence and youth,
The feeble, and the friendless ; that exacts,
And stints, and starves, and works, till life becomes
Dismal and wretched slavery, and the poor
Fly to strong drink for refuge from their woes ;
Or death ? From the appealing drownèd face
Wash off the dreadful river's muddy waves ;
From graves of shame ten thousand spectres rise
To impeach a deaf and avaricious age
Whose god is gold, whose end but wretched self ;
Of cruelty, of quickness to forget
The duty owing to our fellow-men.
Still goes the law, armed with her sword and rope,
To enforce her dumb and dreary negatives,
As men were brutes, restrained by dint of force ;
Still flows war's torrent red, the hand of man
Is stained and crimsoned with his brother's blood ;
While over all dense night of ignorance hangs.

  Is there no hope ? Must life be spent in dread
And we as criminals condemned, but wait
The passing hours, and snatch our furtive joys ?
Must we but sorrow o'er our brethren's woes,
Wanting a moral lever ? Hope remains ;
For in our Christian faith the potency
Of a most glorious future lies enshrined.

  Heartsore, appalled, I dreamed me a fair dream,

The golden future of humanity,
When God's great law of love shall rule the world;
When manliness shall godliness become,
Brute force not reverenced first and chief as now,
But lashed behind the wheels of reason's car;
When to the general man shall be applied
In the uplifting of the general life,
The laws that rule the Christian family,
The appeal to reason, gentleness, and trust;
When what is right, and just, and merciful
Shall be the canon of all human deeds.
Then rising in her might the Christian Church
Clad in pure charity, her fairest robes,
Shall the corruption in her alms cast forth,
The price of blood, condoning avarice,
Shall stretch abroad her ample loving hands
To lead the nations in God's path of love;
Then shall be exorcised that baleful shade,
Spectre unreal, that haunts the visible Church,
Rigidity of form, or unctuous phrase
And guise of earnestness with heart of dust,
Presenting her great evidence, good deeds,
That noblest ritual of the Christian Church,
Then shall she teach the sacredness of man,
The world his fatherland, and heaven his home.
 Still must abide faith in humanity:
An upward path for all. None is so poor,
So weakened and so hampered by the past,
Filled with remorse and shame, lying hard bound
In chains of habit, forged in long past years;
Life's daylight ebbing, and the spirit worn

With bitterness of disappointed schemes,
Yet still bright hope remains ; deliverance
Comes of repentance, happiness and peace
Too long delayed may yet be called his own.
The hand of God is strong ; His strength is ours.
  O time! that sparest not man's proudest works,
But spreadest in low ruin of the dust
The tower, the citadel, palace, or arch
Triumphal, or sky-piercing pyramid,
Thou sparest not their authors, for they pass
Like shadows on the wall, and leave no trace.
The greatest feel thy power, the strongest fail.
Little has earth to offer as the lure
Of our ambition, for oblivion comes,
A second deluge, with wild wasteful flood
E'er creeping higher on the heights of time,
Submerging 'neath its black and hungry waves
All, yea all, though counted strong or great,
O'erwhelming e'en the relics of the past.
Here wouldst thou build ; but canst thou not obtain
Material to endure ? The granite crumbles,
The solid marble yields like drifting smoke ;
For as the stealthy centuries hold their course,
The most substantial masonry gives way ;
Mouldering and envious time with venomous tooth
Gnaws the sepulchral brass, blackens, corrodes ;
Blurring the brightest, wrecking loftiest hopes.
Man is the noblest monument of man.
In wholesome influence, godlike charity,
In rescuing to self-respect, to hope,
And by example to a purer life

Leading the way, here in amended lives,
Thy virtue all insensibly will grave
Its record in undying characters;
The sun will fade, the solid earth will yield,
And from their spheres the stars be shaken forth,
Ere these decay, throughout eternity
With lustre shining that can never pale.

By slow degrees life's noon at length is passed,
And the oncoming shadows of the night
Darken around; the soul confronts the thought
That life's bright fire at length shall slowly fade,
Flicker, and in the total gloom expire.
Nor is the thought, though sorrowful, unwelcome;
Nor can I hold that life's best things come first,
And that the virtuous must, as years pass by,
Drop their choice treasures, youth, and strength, and friends,
And stripped of all to death's grim portal stoop
All desolate; nay, but the best comes last.
Goodness is beauty and perpetual youth.
The ripe results of age, experience,
And tenderness, wide-hearted charity,
And all the virtues won in blessed strife
Are but the first-fruits of a life to come,
The equipment and the promise of the skies.
Who to the sunrise look, upon whose face
The glory of the coming brightness shines
Can with complacency observe the flow,
The outward ebbing of the tide of life.
Happy who realise the night is near,
Who recognise their age, nor lag behind

With early weaknesses, frivolities,
And show of youth, but put on them the garb
Of silent gravity and self-command,
That, fitting, governs best the present hour ;
Content to accept the facts of life, oft dumb,
Inexorable ; and with theories scant
To meet the inevitable with constant hope
Justice supreme will life's mistakes construe
In mercy, and the intention own, despite
Of opportunity, or in default
Of knowledge acquired. For every age is good :
And sail we ever on a deeper sea,
And with more flowing wind to farther shores.

    Time saps the strength of man. Like some white cliff
That jutting seaward rears its glistening front,
Seen by the mariner out many a mile :
Flowers bloom around its brow, the clover blows,
The grass sinks its bright tresses in the wind ;
While far below, against its base, long years
The sea with sullen and resistless plunge
Has broken ceaselessly : days change and pass,
Days when through fog and driving mists it looms
Ghost-like, and o'er the black and weedy marge
Of the spent tide, the gusty storm-blasts lash
The creeping serpents of the hissing foam ;
Or, when through wintry and tempestuous nights
The fierce white surf tears up the hollow bays,
Thundering with spouting foam against the cliffs,
Thence sweeping to the wild and wasteful deep ;
Or, when the summer broods in utter calm,
And the white silent ships all motionless,

Deep laden merchantmen that point afar,
On distant voyage bent, are dimly seen
Upon the horizon's blurred and misty edge;
Or breathes the wind across the moving plain,
Crisped billows of the fresh and breezy sea:
The cliff erect, as ramparting the land,
Stands firm; emblem of strength and permanence!
At length change comes; through fissures unobserved
The trickling rain, or secret driven spray,
Finds lodgment, and the midnight frost congeals;
Then when the morning sun, with the new strength
Of the returning spring, smites with warm beams,
The icy wedges yield, and the huge mass
Falls prone with sound of thunder on the strand.
 Around us all are perishable things
With their monitions constantly renewed.
The hills remain unchanged; the streams flow on;
The forest trees outlive man's little span:
'Tis true. All other things run their swift course;
The favourite steed, the placid kine, the flocks
That browse the pastures round about the home.
The old man looks upon his dog grown old,
Long his companion, friend for every mood,
Than many a friend more faithful, frisking round
Through many a year in daily customed walk,
Now feeble grown, moping and deaf and blind;
Some morning shows him stretched upon the sward
Beneath the pine, his black and rusty hairs
Beaded with dews of night, and strangely still,
No more to answer to his master's call.
And with mute eloquence the moveless form

Tells with all simple unconsidered things
The common fate. In the dead quiet fall
The yellowing leaves. A subtle power goes forth,
Writes on the reddening woods and misty skies
" Behold !" Earth's beauty, like the expiring flame
That trembles in the socket, dies away
To utter loneliness of wintry death.
The world is full of waning, fading life,
Changes, departures, sorrowful farewells,
As Nature whispers in her gentler tones,
Speaking through dumb and inarticulate mouths
To instruct the patient and submissive mind,
That fights not with the simple facts of life,
But of them makes its constant lasting friends,
The seasonal changes of this transient world
Accepting, using them to highest ends,
Making dull time subservient to man,
The wasting and the wearing of the years,
As instruments of wisdom well designed
To further the great ends of rational life.

Give place, give place, and yet again, give place :
Such is the law of this our mortal life ;
And petty circumstance awaits the hour
How bright or brave ; custom aweary grows,
And lusty strength now lagging halts afoot ;
Life's glory tarnishes, its brightness fades.
Old faces change ; new faces crowd the scene ;
And other interests engage the mind,
And other masters rule the passing hour.
Time onward creeps ; invades our sanctities ;
On our seclusion deep the daylight brings.

So fares life's great debate; so flies the hour,
So goes the day; the longest day goes by,
Growing and fading in the changing sky,
Till all our days unnoticed glide away;
The evening comes, old age sits down to count,
And counting finds the number fully told.
Like one outwearied with a day of toil,
O'erwrought, exhausted, longs for utter rest,
To lapse in brown obscurity of night,
And for a while become one with the world
Of things inanimate in deep repose;
Grateful for having lived, and glad to drop
Into the welcoming arms of restful death,
So man draws to his end, so longs for rest.
Thus runs the circle brief of human life
With changes few, each change accompanied
By new developments of love, new bonds;
Daughters and sons have grown around him, formed
By his example, by his precepts led:
And as his spirit nears death's shadowy bourn
Their hands of love sustain like angel hands.
His loved ones gather for the last farewell
Around his bed: then comes life's solemn close.
Love's accents linger last upon the ear:
Love smooths the pillow, holds the cooling draught
To the parched lips, or fans the heated brow;
Clasps his now feeble hand, with tender words
Whispers of hope, and, smiling 'midst its tears,
Commends the loved one with a last fond kiss
To God's unfathomed love and blessedness.

BOOK THE FIFTH

THE SONG OF THE PAST

THE ARGUMENT.

The abysm of the past—Nature's scriveners—Theories of the earth's origin—The geological epochs—Primeval man—Cave dwellers—Other views—The golden age—How is the enigma to be solved?—Former races of men—Revelation's light—Paradise—Our first parents—Perfect humanity—The fall—The retinue of sin—Thence sprang need of revelation—Genius the gift of God—Architectural power—The sculptor's power—Beauty slumbering in marble—Divine philosophy—Poetic genius—The pastoral, lyric, tragic, epic muse—The dreams and deeds of art—The glowing canvas—Musical genius—The sphere of art—Great cities of the past—The chosen land—The pastoral scene—How the chosen race was educated—Morn at Sinai—The great revelation of human duty to love God.

BOOK THE FIFTH.

THE SONG OF THE PAST.

 MIGHTY past, thou fathomless abyss!
Within whose depths profound the
    mightiest deeds
Of mightiest men have vanished, on
    whose bourn
And dim horizon, fading fast away,
Linger the glittering pageantry of time
To blend, dissolving as the summer clouds,
Or unsubstantial spectres; all the fame
And the proud triumphs of the past lie hid
In thy embracing and Cimmerian gloom,
Beyond the flood of this most cheerful light
And pleasing consciousness of life. There lie
Millions unnumbered, powerful and great,
The good, the beautiful, master and slave,
All insignificant alike; the tramp
Of war resounds in history's great march;
Clamour of labour and loud trumpetings

Of fame that challenged the dull power of death,
With all past worthy deeds unchronicled,
Are, like mid-ocean's sounds, all hushed : the waves
That break upon the shore of the quick present
As the spent surge alone are heard. Life's deeds
Have registered themselves with diamond pen
In Nature's archives, deeds of excellence,
Or deeds of shame, in her dread muniments
By jealous hands engraved, by jealous eyes
Close-sentinelled for vindication clear.
Earth is an auditorium, where the winds,
The waves, light, heat, and air, God's scriveners,
Hear and inscribe life's busy doings, words,
E'en shadowy flickerings of the nimble thoughts,
Or bold presentment of unchallenged deeds.
Though trenched with graves, the field of ocean sown
With that which once was man, old earth becomes
A sepulchre ; yet unresponsive all
To man's fond questions, silent as the grave.
   How the great fabric of this earth was formed,
Launched by the Almighty fiat in th' abyss,
Or sprung from nucleus ethereal,
Which in the swirlings and the eddyings
Of forces vast, unknown, that ever stream,
Grew by agglomeration, until smit
By kindly solar heat, alternating
With pulse of day and night, the germs of life
Were cherished to their full development,
Dimly we guess. A mighty hand engraved
In jagged coast lines, serrate mountain tops
That climb and dent the empyrean blue,

And fundamental strata deeply laid,
Full evidence of weird primeval days,
When the great natural powers, now slumbering,
Slipped from the leash at the Almighty word,
Clashed in gigantic conflict, and from thence,
Confusion dire, rose this great edifice,
The home of man.   Imagination sees
Wild chaos as in scaldic lore, vast depths
Of gathering gloom, dark wastes of thick-ribbed ice,
Whirlwinds of mist, fogs, snowstorms dense, the breath
Of Niflheim, and sparks and flakes of fire,
Wind-driven, the volcano's lurid glare
With crimson hues lighting the enfolded gloom
Of primal night, as yet unvisited
By the beneficent and genial day,
The lash of oceans and convulsive throes
Of earthquakes with broad continents in grip ;
Or grinding ice-floes toppling in the waves,
Rending of mountains and upheavals vast,
As when with his stern crew Enceladus
Tore the Thessalian hill from its deep roots
To scale from Pelion's height the walls of heaven.

   Whole cycles pass, where there were none to mark
Nor hand to chronicle time's changeless flow.
Monsters uncouth shielded, with tusk and barb,
Or pterodactyl, dinotherium huge,
Or mastodons of vast unwieldy bulk
Wallowed in slime, or with contortions grim
And bellowings loud, struggled for mastery,
Basked on savannahs green, or hung their folds
Round the great conifers, whose rugged trunks

Slumber in stone, or carboniferous,
Splutter their gaseous jets of welcome flame
To light the happy faces round our hearths.
O'er these vast forests centuries as years,
And days as hours, went by, and all unmarked,
With silence undisturbed, but when the wind
Tore for itself a path, or slow decay
Brought from its towering height the giant pine,
Wakening the echoes in these solitudes.
And autumns came, sepulchral autumns wan,
Strewing the garniture of continents
Upon the ground, and autumn rains bedrenched
Earth's russet pall. Thus slowly, if we read
The story of our globe aright, the world
Assumed its aspect now familiar.
The stage was cleared for man, whose mighty deeds
Heroical should consecrate the rocks,
The mountain-pass, the streams, the very dust
On which the actors trod, mute witnesses
Of the high virtues that ennoble man.

 Here roams the wistful thought still bent to find
In heaven or earth, impatient of delay,
Fresh evidences, if forthcoming still,
Of a paternal love. When man appeared,
Our primal sire, how looked he, in what garb
Arrayed, how gazed abroad on this strange world,
His new-found realm, without competitor,
Earth's lord and king, science would fain discern.
Caverns low-browed, in whose remoter gloom
Hyenas shrank, whence savage eyes gleamed forth
In ages past, of wolf, unwieldy bear,

Or tigress lithe, crouching on velvet paw,
Were these the home of the primeval man?
Sheer down the face of cliffs precipitous,
Past where the choughs and yellow-footed kites
Wheel circling, past the gray, old, lichened rocks
That cap the beetling front, and over which
The streamlet tinkles, swinging in the wind,
Dashing its powdery spray to rainbow dust
That glistens in the sun, half-down, where sways
The bramble, while the browsing kine below
Seem small as sheep, fissures and crevices
Are found in which a page of history
Rude chronicled appears. The torch has gleamed
On floors of ancient caves, the mattock turned
Shingle of river beds, and from the soil
Relics of earlier times have been unearthed,
Hatchets, flint arrow-heads, and knives of stone,
Charred embers, fibulæ, and polished bones,
Upon whose surface smooth rude art has limned
The forms of animals; human remains,
Interred mayhap with ceremonial slight,
Or, dreadful thought! the relics of a feast,
The cannibal instincts of their rude compeers
Have left; these seem to show humanity
In undeveloped wild original.
Well might the thought appal that man has sprung
From savage loins, from fugitives, half clad,
With matted locks peering amid the trees,
Who in the forests dark in ambush lay,
Blew with a silent puff the poisoned dart
With murderous intent, then clubbed their foes,

And in the cave, cleaving their victims' bones,
Their horrid Thyestæan banquet held ;
Tradition's faint and fleeting voices speak
Of a degraded era in the past,
Ere man knew fire ; then digged he in the earth
For roots as food, sought what the forest gave,
Acorns, crude berries, unripe fruits, and made
His cheerless home by burrowing in the soil,
Till the great son of Japetus from heaven
Brought in his fennel rod the nimble flame,
Mother of arts, and life of industry.

 Yet in the picture dark are other lines.
Tradition with a consentaneous voice
Tells of another age, when Vingolf rose,
Or Gladsheim, turreted with shining gold,
Where the All-Father sat and reigned as king ;
The age of gold, when mild Astræa ruled ;
Saturnian days, ere chains were forged to bind
The lawless, when the balances were held
In equipoise. Earth then had rest, nor pain
Nor grief were known ; calm seas, and fertile fields
Goldened with harvests, smiled 'neath cloudless skies.

 How read we the enigma ? Is our race
Advancing from a dark, degraded past,
Emerging from brutality's thick night,
From savage instincts, bestial lusts, and vice,
And superstitions base, or have we here
The evidence of some catastrophe
That has befallen the onward march of man ?
Oblivion hides full soon the monuments
Of human greatness ; the all-conquering dust

Drifts o'er man's glory, and its brightness dies,
While mighty empires, proudest dynasties,
Pass from this terrene stage, nor leave behind
Posterity scarce other evidence
Than a few potsherds, or an obolus
Dropped from the greasy wallet of a slave.
    Primeval earth in ages long remote,
Under conditions similar to ours
Climatical, through centuries untold,
Shedding husked fruits, ripening its yellow grain,
O'er widespread fertile acres, might have been
The home of beings similar to man,
Not dowered so high, yet with compelling hand
Ruling the earth, and all unconsciously
Forerunners, yet the servants of our race.
Fighting with savage beasts, the forest dense
With flinty hatchet, or o'ermastering fire
Reducing to the sun, these might have cleared
The stage for man's more highly favoured race.
Apart from revelation all remains
Ambiguous. Misleading voices come,
The utterance and the echo intermixed,
From the deep cave where time conceals its spoils.
The doubtful mind still hanging in suspense
Judgment refuses, waiting ampler proof.
    As when the night, calm, merciful, but now
Divinely vengeful, threw o'er Egypt's plains
A pall of tangible gloom, horror, and dread,
Goshen had light ; so in the page revealed,
'Gainst the dark background of th' oblivious past,
The sunshine sleeps o'er Eden. God's chief work—

No monster, strange, disfigured, man appears
When first he treads earth's stage, grovelling with beasts,
In reason's twilight, but as perfect man,
Serene, majestic, consciously endowed
With likeness to his Maker, likest Him
In free determination of the will,
And gifted with all knowledge requisite
For gift so perilous; Nature's rich crown,
And ultimate purpose of creating love.

There blooms the garden fair. Masters of song,
Who with no trembling hand, inapt, have touched
The sacred lyre, but with strong confidence,
And glorious consciousness of facile power,
Have told the loveliness of Paradise,
Building their stately edifice of song;
Our own Mæonides, like his compeer,
Who, by the Ægean sunned life's dark abyss
With dreams ecstatic, mused in lonely gloom
The splendid vision. Matchless melody,
With proud triumphant majesty of song,
And long-sustained sublimity, his thoughts
Have mingled with the national renown.
He, musing on God's Paradise, has sung
Its peerless beauty, and its joys undreamed;
How love decked its gay bowers, and from the waste
Fenced off this choice, peculiar, scene of bliss.
All that could stimulate, or gratify,
All that could pleasure give, ravish the ear,
Delight each sense, was there. A spacious scene
Diversified of hill, and vale, and grove,
The glistening river, and the moveless lake

Where shadows brooding slept, the brooklet's fall,
Or covert fount ; glades where the eye might rove
Discursive, nearer glimpse of thickets, copse,
Or the dim grove, odorous with fragrant plants,
Or blossoming trees ; arrayed in loveliness.
All flowers were there, the children of the sun.
Not yet the curse, had earth's prolific power
Stunted, nor thorns, nor weeds, nor cankerworm,
Mildew nor blight, had nipped th' aspiring life.
Fruits of all kinds hung pendent from the boughs,
That drooped beneath their fragrant generous load,
Not green and immature, but blushing ripe
Amid the leaves, or on the verdant mead
Lay for acceptance.   Here, on every hand,
The arching boughs cloistered the fragrant shade.
Nature's exuberance of flowers and fruit,
All that could please the mind, delight, allure,
Told of the Unseen Donor, and the thoughts
Called forth in glad acknowledgment and praise.
Not in pleased sense, most rapturous embrace,
Nor quickening to the intensest height the frame
Material of sensibility
Is man's true good.   These are but channels, ducts,
To feed the lamp of reason.   Higher source
Has he of happiness, accordant more
With natures rational and immortal framed.
 Bowered 'midst Eden's unimagined bliss
Were our progenitors, the original pair
From whose prolific loins the mighty stream
Of human life has flown, covering the earth :
They in perfection stood, pure, beautiful,

THE MORNING SONG.

Modest, in virgin innocence arrayed,
Sin and its daughter shame alike unknown;
No image from the clear, unruffled soul
But the Divine reflected. Sin's foul breath,
Like to the canker on the flower that mars
Its blushing beauty, sapping vigorous life,
Not yet had blighted the ethereal grace
Of perfected and pure humanity.
Nor statelier swung aloft the towering palm,
In fruitful pillared life, than our great sire;
Nor early summer rose in blushing pride,
Hiding beneath its veil of glistening dew,
Was e'er so sweet as his fair consort, decked
In purity, in wisdom, grace divine.
Pleasures around them smiled on every hand;
No broken lights were there, pain's anguished sob,
Nor sigh, the utterance of the burdened soul,
Nor interrupted cadences of joy.
Death lurked without, and all his horrid brood,
Sorrow and disappointment, wretchedness
And bitter woe. Nor was life's chief delight
Awanting; thither came celestial guests,
Th' Ineffable Presence, too, not corporal,
Nor visible, but to the listening ear
Announced; awful propinquity! When eve
With evening's star, her faithful servitor,
Lighting its lamp above the dusky grove,
Gleamed in the thickening shades came the Supreme;
Man new-create, and in the image formed
Of Deity, divine companionship
Enjoyed, favour divine, and love, whose bliss

All unimagined by our feebler thought,
Eternity must show. O happy pair!
Guileless, all unsuspecting the dread change
Already imminent, with sore distress,
How have your children 'neath the sad entail
Of your offence groaned heavily; the offence
That from our race diverted the full stream,
And fructifying river of God's love;
How have they their sore banishment bewailed.
Turning with lingering gaze towards Paradise,
As the poor exile on the pathless deep,
When night falls on the sea, thinks of his home,
And fondly looks where yet the sunset's gold
Lights faintly the far-distant mountain-tops
Of the dear fatherland. Thorns strew our path,
Darkness envelops us, and doubt and fear;
Yet e'en the blank and vacant countenance
Of grief will smile as think we that our race
Was cradled in the tenderness of God.

    Man fell. So runs the oracle. God's will
In greater matters or indifferent,
Explicity declared, no parley waits,
Unworthy hesitation, but demands
Alacrity, instant obedience,
The absolute surrender of man's will
In things or great or small. Presumption grew
Too daring, and forgot the sole command
Of the Great Author of life's happiness.
If burdened with restrictions numberless,
Or hard the task, surpassing human power,
With tension long protracted of the will,

A plea in mitigation might be urged.
'Twas a light burden, 'twas an easy yoke
That the rebellious will of man disdained.
　Now o'er the original brightness of earth's sky
Gathered disastrous gloom, and boding change,
Fell consequence, when the deliberate hand
Plucked sin's dread fruit; yet was the worst unseen!
Slow gathering in the process of the years.
The night of God's displeasure dark closed round;
And as the light ebbs from th' ensanguined west,
The sun departing bearing all the grace
That beautified the land, the hues of flowers,
With play of light and shade, variety
Of colour or of form commingled hid
In brown obscurity and deepening gloom;
So were the manifold delights withdrawn
Of the lost Paradise; then hither trooped
A grisly horde, to claim these derelicts;
Grim, shadowy death his skeleton hand put forth
Demanding; coward fear, with joints unlocked,
Slunk to the citadel, there lay entrenched;
Enthroned within the bright and daylight hall
Of conscience, sat despair, the worst of sins;
And ignorant envy came with hellish leer,
Cunning, with eyes askance, and white-lipped rage,
And dark revenge, and feverish, panting lust,
And red-eyed grief, and pain with quivering mouth:
Thus passed sin's retinue. Dogging their heels,
Diseases came, a foul and fetid host,
Trembling, or with contortions dire convulsed,
Pale feeble dolorous crew, and 'mid them care,

That hungered on its food and barked for more ;
And weary age, decrepit, footing slow
The dusty path to death. These claimed their own.
  Alas poor exiles! whither must they flee
Whom God has banished, whither flee from Him
Whose presence fills all bounds of space and time ?
Or where escape His constant awful frown ?
The refuges of lies no shelter give,
Distance, nor darkness, nor the farthest star
That holds its outpost on the verge remote
Of dark infinity, nor murkiest hell
Can them conceal from dread Omnipotence.
  Why the hot thunderbolt of wrath divine
Suspended hung, nor with extinction smote ;
Or why to millions yet unborn, the sins
Of their progenitors by strict entail,
Descending with unmitigated force,
Disaster brought, remain mysterious,
Though generations numberless have passed
Since that sad day. The world's great history
Spanning ten thousand times ten thousand lives,
Slow moving centuries, all time may be
But a mere speck in vast infinity,
The eternity to come, where God will show
The riches of His grace. Then may be seen
In its true grandeur, ample symmetry,
Redemption's scheme ; what compensations rich
Balanced the perils of this mortal state ;
Then, in far-widening scenes will be displayed,
More visibly, the equity divine.
  Though lost, yet not irrevocably lost

Was the Creator's love; though forfeited
The high distinguishing regard that crowned
Existence, hope remained to cheer man's gloom.
Were it impossible to scale the heights
How miserable were man! Existence then
Would but a curse have been; the excluded soul,
Despairing 'neath eternal banishment
By absolute decree, might have reproached
The power that gave it life, and cursed the boon.
Thee must we bless for ever, O our God!
Thou didst not thus ordain. The sonship lost,
Lost too, the pricelesss co-relationship
With heaven's immaculate hosts, the beauty lost
That purity bestows on rational souls,
And inward self-respect, and consciousness
Of rectitude, guerdon of patient hearts
Affiant of the truth, but chiefly lost
God's sovereign love. Yet with the punishment
Came hope, and the dark thunder-cloud was edged
With silvery light. Henceforth must man's offence,
With its concomitants of death and pain,
Guilt and unrest, determine how the tide
Of Heaven's benevolence must earthward flow.
To leave the yearning heart all unappeased,
Unsatisfied, to ignore these deep-laid wants,
And the bewildered reason to desert,
Upon its perilous and darkened way,
Leaving the guilty conscience all unshriven,
This were no proof of love. To these deep wants
    Nor bowers, nor glistening streams, nor flowerets
        fair,

Extensive prospect ravishing every sense
Could minister, or happiness bestow.
  How far in the original scheme of things,
Man's reason might have read beneficence
Divine, vocal each breeze, full eloquent
The myriad tongues of new-created life
Emerging from the abyss, all jubilant,
Each crannied separate nook in this vast frame
Rich stored with latent proofs, suggestions deep
To stir prolific thought, we but surmise.
Henceforth, alas! the splendid page was blurred.
Nature's grand, faded palimpsest requires
Interpreting, to fill the void, and clear
Th' evangel of its ambiguity.
As on a stormy day the fringing light
Will shoot betwixt the clouds, and in the haze
And nebulous expanse the noonday sun
A faint and ineffective disc appears,
Scarce visible, and soon again obscured;
Thus o'er the heavens of God's unclouded love
Drifted the darkness, while base earth-born mists
Climbed high, and jealously assayed to quench
Th' ineffable brightness of the love supreme.
  From Thee, O Lord, and from Thy glorious love,
As from life's fount the splendid gifts have come,
Of human genius; all the loveliness,
The beauty, and the goodness, and the power,
That have adorned our frail humanity,
Its aim exalted and its commonness
Redeemed, taught it self-reverence, nobler hopes,
To reprobation all its vices held,

And witnessed for the beautiful and true :
Glances from Thy perfections, these, O Lord,
And lingering traces of the godlikeness
In which Thou madest Thy frail creature man.
 The fertile brain, and quick compelling hand,
That with unhesitating sweep obeys
The will's behests, the comprehensive glance
Of inward vision, with perfection's charms
Enraptured, sought the desert to reclaim,
Enriching life. From the constructive mind
Majestic temples rose, by slow degrees,
Towering to heaven in all their stateliness
Dome, cupola, or spire, or minaret,
Noble entablatures that met the gaze
Like a celestial vision, rose to view,
The snowy marble mounting to the sky,
Parts manifold in symmetry conjoined,
Embodied aspirations of the soul
That, dreading chaos, sought with earnest aim
The world's Great Architect to imitate.
 Genius from marble catacombs called forth
Visions of loveliness, embodied thoughts
Of purity, that modest shrank, as shamed
Beneath the awful blue of spotless heaven ;
Statues that glimmered 'mid the olives gray
Calm in perpetual serenity ;
Placid, in beauty's most alluring grace,
Stood womanhood, with modesty arrayed,
With modesty defended ; manhood grave,
Bearded and stern, with power in every line,
Excised all trace of weakness, meanness, lust,

And in his noblest frame expressed, quiet,
Bold, resolute, and kind. Seized by its art,
The movement and the mirth of days gone by,
The quick and thrilling life congealed to stone,
With flowing drapery and prancing steeds,
And laughter whose last echo has just died,
The conqueror's triumphs, arms, and spoils of war,
Processions bacchanalian, satyrs, fauns
That with the merry antics of the glade,
Under the thyrsus, crowned with vine leaves, played.
In the deep pathos of perpetual grief
Mourns Niobe, or locked in anguish fast
Wrestles Laocoon in endless strife.

Divine philosophy haunting the grove,
All powerful to mould life's energies,
In its seclusion sought the dignity
Of man to exalt, to wean from antique fable,
And childish faith that in its loneliness
Peopled the cloudy mountain-top, the woods,
With vanishing forms of loveliness and grace,
Nymphs whose bright hair spread o'er the golden wave,
Green ocean depths, the subterranean world,
Lurid with swarthy Vulcan's sounding forge,
Commerced with higher themes and worthier man,
More consonant with reason, native lode
Of truth, deep lying but approachable
By patient thought. Here reasoned Socrates,
With caustic speech, and nobler Plato dreamed,
And built him commonwealths of thought, and reigned,
Pacific sovereign, all of wisdom crowned;

Or, like some eagle, to the topmost heights
Of speculation soared, on tireless wing;
Of gods, of men, of nature, of the frame
And the substantial essence of the world;
Musings of death, that death itself might spare,
Wisdom profound, too rich to strew the wastes
Of dark oblivion. Or, his scholar great,
Keen-witted Stagyrite, whose lynx-like eyes
Tracked error to its cave, causes explored,
Surveyed the wide domain of human lore,
Its limitations, and its boundless stores.

  Not from the rocks sprang the poetic soul,
Ilissus, or Castalia's charmed wave,
Or the Lebethran fount, where dreams in death
Eurydice's lorn mate, while nightingales
Bewail him with their golden-throated songs;
The haunting presence of the pastoral muse
Scattering white violets o'er the shepherd's tomb,
Bewept the fate of Daphne, early lost,
And shrined his memory in melodious verse.
The grasshopper in Sicily's hot fields
That chirped at noon, the browsing goat that cropped
The vine's young tendrils, or the meadow flowers,
Waving their shining floss upon the wind,
Caught in the amber of poetic verse
Live in immortal beauty, with the love,
And fresh delight of centuries long past
That ne'er can die; this testified of power
Sprung not of man; for in the breezy pines
That rocked on Pindus came no other sounds
Than natural echoes. Dripping water grots,

And bosky dells, all interspersed with glades,
Blue glimpses 'mid the hills, and shivering reeds
Fringing the vagrant streams else desolate,
Or clear cold springs in valleys far remote,
Were but by fancy peopled, musing thought
That framed a world within the visible world,
Fair pleasant dreams, but dreams, and nothing more.
   The passionate rapture of the lyric soul,
Pindaric strains, Anacreon's golden string,
Wanting full oft the stop of reason's palm,
Yet towering to the height of ecstasy ;
The tragic muse treading the breathless stage
Strewn with Cilician saffron, while at hand
Panchæan odours smoked, oppressed with woe
Lamented in her sad majestic strains
Prometheus' endless pangs, dread brooding fate
Of Agamemnon's line ; or brighter yet,
Conspicuous, the prime singer of the dawn,
Whose martial soul exulting in the strife
And clash of arms, sang forth his pictured strains,
All thrilling with the conflict resolute ;
Sparks from the fire Promethean, rich gifts,
From a divine and all-enriching mind.
   But not to ancient days alone, the gift,
And impulse irresistible of song,
The solemn joy of the creative hour,
The masterful endeavour, and the glow
Of soul, conceptions clamouring to the birth,
The swift accomplishment, th' embodied thought
That asks not for permission to come forth,
But claims of right existence, and with power

Unchallenged, wide acceptance finds unsought.
The spirit of beauty, like the breath of spring
Passed o'er the human world ; the canvas glowed
With high imaginings, all radiant
With hues of Nature's choosings, landscapes wide,
Swimming in golden sunlight, cradled lakes
Among the hills, peaceful and blue, or woods,
Or sounding strands, ocean's white fringe of foam,
And rainbow spray blown on the damp sea breeze ;
Or the rapt musings of th' enthusiast soul,
Visions of heaven and heavenly faces sweet,
Radiant of peace, of confidence and love ;
Heroic deeds that breed heroic souls
All self-forgetful, and the canvas moves,
The speaking marble thrills with noblest life.

 The words of power that made the senate ring,
Persuasion's silvery accents, and the force
Compulsive multitudes to sway, and urge
To action swift in thrilling sympathy,
The deeds that glorified the battlefield,
That gave to Marathon, Thermopylæ,
Or Salamis, their grand undying fame,
Immortal fame of which the world is proud,
All that the patriot soul could dare or do,
These were, O Lord of victory, Thine own.

 And Thine the strains that float majestical
Out of the ancient caves of silence, called
By the creative mind in passing pomp
Of sound, deep-folded harmony all built
On undisturbed repose, from conflict sprung,
Resolved to blending concords which conduct

The soul to musing rest, on ample wing
Mounting the heaven of heavens, zenith of hope,
Then like the stricken eagle falling low
To depths despairing, wanderings forlorn ;
The soul-compelling volume on whose breast
Subordinate feelings play, as changing lights
Suffusing gild the high and towering clouds,
Awakening longings deep and undefined,
Thoughts half developed, and suggestions high
Too high for words, pleased melancholy rapt
In her own sweetness to a willing trance,
Enraptured in the twilight of its grief.
Delightful art! the language of the soul
In its pathetic tenderness. Now leads
The simple child-like strain, in willing bonds,
The captive thoughts, won by its innocence,
And from their cells tumultuous feelings rush,
And hidden tears, and longings of desire,
To hear the passing sweetness. Like the roar
Of chariot wheels unnumbered, battle driven,
Or shifting thunders rolling far to die,
Or ocean's mighty diapason, rise
The massive chords that tell of deep-built trust,
Of endless love, of absolute repose.

 These are Thy gifts, O Lord ; nor these alone.
All that redeems from savage rudeness, all
That can subdue to order, decency,
And self-possession, prize oft dearly won
In nations or the individual life,
By self-denial, and stern mastery
Of will, all that can add to life new grace,

Or loveliness, or zest, can elevate
Or deck the roughened path with smiling hope,
Are all Thy gifts; Thine too, fair liberty,
Of justice born, and resolution high,
Pride of strong nations, guerdon of the brave ;
Thine gentle peace that woos brown labour's toil,
And firm compacted bonds of brotherhood
That nations make, firmer than tensest steel,
Consideration mutual, patriot love,
Thine all that makes man strong or great or good.
 Thus, as the landscape with its varied lights,
Here cloudy, dark, there interspersed with gleams
And sullen shade, while in more favoured spots
Dart the slant beams of the effulgent sun,
So, o'er the landscape of the historic past,
Rested these transitory gleams of love,
Soon to expand to universal noon.
 Great cities with the hum of multitudes
Astir, in plenitude of power and wealth,
Sat by the Mediterranean waves, and flecked
Its crispèd waters with their snow-white sails.
Girding her loins, imperial Babylon
Reigned as a queen, proud Egypt's dusky realm
Beneath its palms; fertile and populous,
A hundred cities in their towered pomp
Of temples, palaces, and pyramids,
Grew to its splendour : o'er the desert far
Of tawny Libya, Ethiopia swart,
Or mystic Seba of the torrid south,
Her sceptre stretched. Not to Assyria,
Ancient of empires, or the Median realm,

Cathay, or distant tribes of golden Ind,
The benediction came of Heaven's high love.
But on one family, the seed elect,
Chosen and segregate for highest ends,
Whence was to spring the visible pledge of love,
Messiah, Prince of Peace, Incarnate Love,
Concentred the divine, all-kindling rays.

    The pastoral scene invites ; sweet-smelling fields
Extending far beneath the open sky ;
Rich ample pastures where from morn till night
The shepherd wanders with his browsing flocks,
That, thirsty, bleat at eve beneath the palms,
Shading the well ; the breezy tent door cool,
Where by his tufted spear the chieftain sits ;
'Mid scenes like these the choice of Heaven appears.
Nor came the Deity as abstract spirit,
Mysterious Presence unresolvable
By man's dim faculties, but in the guise,
The form accessible of man, addressed
With human speech ; to Enoch thus, Noah,
To Abraham, sublime old patriarch,
The friend of God. Called from his couch at night
By audible voice, to his tent door the sire
Went forth, and 'neath the starry canopy
Heard speak that awful Voice, whose are the stars,
And whose this varied all-containing earth,
In dread proximity, communion holding
With th' Unseen. 'Neath Mamre's oak at noon
The patriarch hailed the mystic Travellers,
And angels entertained. As friend with friend
Converses, Abraham conversed with God,

Revealing thus the quality of man
Whom God delights to honour, and on whom
Divine beneficence descends : fearless,
Manly, and generous, and in simple faith
Unstaggering, life's fee ungrudgingly
He paid to God, the tribute of his trust.
Thus was revealed th' Almighty Fatherhood,
Defending, caring for, not weighing down
With th' abundance of earth's luxuries,
And lavish store of this world's passing wealth,
Himself imparting, richest prize of all.

The chosen seed, now to a nation grown,
Are moulded by vicissitudes foretold ;
Their greatness straitened, their ambition checked
By harsh oppression. Here the captives learned
The might of love's deliverance ; not for them
To be a sentiment inoperative,
Gilding captivity, slowly deduced
From patient processes of reasoning,
But fact acknowledged in its potency.
Their chains were severed by th' Almighty hand ;
Yet in the fires of their affliction sore
Links binding to each other and to God
Were forged, closer than consanguinity,
Born of one sorrow to one common hope.
Wrenched from their dire captivity at length,
His outstretched arm wrought for their liberty.
For them no arduous and exhaustive strife,
Bought with expenditure of tears and blood,
And disappointment's oft-repeated stroke ;
The gates of night swung back their portals dim

Exit to give, and merciless death, abroad
Upon the shuddering wind, palsying their foes,
Shrank at the measured tramp of their great host.
No blow was struck but by Omnipotence,
Nor was their path engirt with serried hosts
Of Heaven's battalions summoned for their aid;
Forth to the desert marched their harnessed ranks,
While in their van blazed as a cresset fire,
Shekinah, with its unextinguished flame;
Not yet their danger passed; before them yawned
The Red Sea waves, more tyrannous than man,
While in their rear, locked fast within the hills,
Thundered the chariot wheels of Egypt's hosts,
Pursuing, with fell vengeance armed. The sea,
Obedient to command omnipotent,
Heard Amram's son, and 'neath his potent rod
Parting its billows, owned its God, and fled;
And through the echoing night betwixt the waves,
The hurrying stream of fugitives passed o'er,
Till on the farther strand triumphantly
They sang deliverance. Thus, in the fires
Of national trouble fused, welded by blows
Of fierce adversity, they stood prepared
To accept the mandates of their Heavenly King.

 Morn broke on Sinai's peopled wilderness,
Where in their tents the chosen people lay,
Expectant of the vengeance of their King.
Nor slight the offence; the first of God's behests,
Writ by the Almighty Hand, had been transgressed
With high affront. Called by a voice divine,
In the gray dawn, climbing the lonely mount,

Moses had gone, and all around him fell
The cloud, the presence-chamber of the King;
In awful solitude the Lord passed by,
With circumstance of majesty, as later
The rugged Tishbite in his mountain clift
Heard the strong wind that tore with giant grip
The solid rocks, or felt the earthquake's spasm,
Or saw the lambent tongue of lightning glance;
Then, 'neath the shadow of these terrors dread,
Was heard in human speech the still small voice,
As man to man addressed, proclaiming thence
The style and dignity of the Supreme:
"Jehovah, Lord, gracious and merciful,
Longsuffering, and in truth and goodness e'er
Abundant." Thus would He reveal Himself,
By kindly attributes, not by the blaze,
O'ermastering of unapproachèd light,
Of absolute perfection, Light of Light,
Within whose circle dread none dare intrude,
Whom none can see and live. Love speaks in love.
The gentleness of Nature now has voice,
And with the loftiest sanction comes to man
In audible speech; now is the groundwork laid
Whence duty may arise. Were God but power,
Mere power, nay, dreadful thought, malevolence,
Or wisdom pure, unmixed with tenderness,
Neglectful of the creatures of His hand,
This must determine the approach. But love
Demands our love, spring of life's worthiest deeds,
Perpetual sentinel within the breast,

Bright efflorescence, fairest flower of man,
Itself most fragrant, and like twilight dew
That calls forth fragrance from the grateful flowers,
Love covers with its sweetness meanest things,
Thus making them acceptable to love ;
Love is life's primal duty, Heaven's light yoke !
Bind it as wristlets on thy hands, O man !
Thus consecrating labour ; on thy brow
Wear it as crown, thy privilege, thy joy ;
As frontlets 'twixt thine eyes let it be placed
Ever to tell that thou art not thine own,
And this to be life's object ; in thy home
To be the gracious soul of all thy life,
Thy commerce intimate with those most dear.
Give life's chief duty the chief prominence
In all thy thoughts, and bear where'er thou goest
Our life's first law : " The Lord is God, one Lord,
And thou shalt love the Lord thy God with all
Thy heart, with all thy soul, with all thy might ;"
So runs the message, worthy to be writ
Upon the dome of heaven in living gold ;
So down the generations comes to us,
As through some minster aisle come anthem strains
Majestic, with the full-toned organ's voice.
O happy day ! when first was heard by man
Command so glorious, privilege so great,
The privilege of being, fairest crown
Of life, and of life's joys. How dark the heart,
Blind and insensate to its truest good,
That turns from such a rendering of life,
Turns from ideal so sublimely high,

Counts it impossible, or, graver charge,
Writes it as insignificant for man.
  Thus, through the revelation of God's love,
More necessary through man's fallen state,
The broken lines of nature, now no more
A paradise but garden run to waste,
And desolation, having lost their power
Directive, and their continuity,
Runs like a thread of gold the promise fair
Of restoration, paradise regained,
Embodied in the embodiment of love.
This cherished hope, chief heirloom of our race,
Was jealously transmitted, age by age,
Across the chasm, the vast abyss of time,
And grave of nations. Intimations new
At intervals were given, new types whose lines
Wore to distincter shape as years rolled by,
Oft misconstrued, the ethical meaning lost,
And the bright promise of the future merged
In present greatness. Centuries thus passed
Noiseless and unobserved. Then, in due course,
The promise was redeemed, Messiah came,
Emmanuel, God with man, and God was love.
The startled heavens resounded to the joy
Of angel harmonies, " Goodwill to man."

BOOK THE SIXTH

THE SONG OF INCARNATE LOVE

THE ARGUMENT.

The advent of Christ—The land of Galilee—Appearance of Emmanuel—
Why thus disguised?—The Mount of Beatitudes—Teachings of the
Fatherhood of God—The prodigal son—Christ's life of sublime charity
—His lightning-like glance—Christ unknown—Return from Perea—
Blessing little children—Gadara's crowds fed—Midnight storm—
Christ walks the waves—Fruitless toil of the fishers—Morning on
the Capernaum coast—The draught of fishes—Nain and its life—The
widow's friend—Death rebuked—Bethany and its hallowed associa-
tions—The grand revelation of life after death—Thus passed Christ's
ministry.

BOOK THE SIXTH.

THE SONG OF INCARNATE LOVE.

THEE, Bethlehem, amid thine olive groves,
And thy sweet fields where once the angels sang,
Cradle of Christ, my pilgrim thoughts would haunt;
Thee, Nazareth, with consecrated calm
Brooding around, upon whose sunlit hills,
When the doves murmured in the orange groves,
And spring with emerald tinctured all the fields,
The Youth Divine once strayed, thee would I seek.
My heart leaps forth to sing Emmanuel's praise,
Not coldly, or perforce, but with deep fervour,
By gratitude impelled, and love's constraint,
Pleased in the throbbing pulses of my song,
Though all unmeet, to assay so high a theme.
Again, O Holy One, Thine aid I seek,
Pure Spirit of truth, to whom belongs to take
The things of Christ, Himself the Truth, to man

Revealing wealth untold, unsearchable,
Possessed through faith's clear vision by the soul;
As mortal feebleness may bear, fibres
Thin spun of mortal strength, direct my song.
Heaven's ecstasy alone can reach the height
Fully to celebrate the King of Heaven.
Rank above rank 'neath th' empyrean dome
Cerulean, upward from the peopled floor,
The amethystine pavement, crystal sea,
The thousand thousands raise their endless song,
Exalting this great Saviour of the world,
Ambassador of Love, and Friend of man!
Mortals full well might dread with hasty thought,
Or daring vagrant fancy to invade
The precincts bright, supreme Intelligence
To affront, to reach with sinful hands to strike
The unpolluted lyre.   Distinctly limned,
Majestical, before the inward eye,
Give the forthtelling power, befitting speech,
Marshalled with melody of thought, pleased strains,
The music of the soul, anguished full oft,
Inadequate, yet lest my song should droop,
Uphold, exalt, O breath, infuse new life,
Fitly to celebrate so grand a theme.

 Not yet returned, in thine acknowledged might,
O Warrior King, thou com'st from victory,
Where with Thine arrows sharp, Thine enemies
Transfixed, have known Thy power; not yet in robes
Of majesty arrayed, Thy sacred head
Bedropped with oil of gladness, aloes, myrrh,
And cassia from Thy garments all diffused,

And by Thy side, redeemed from jealous death,
Fair purchase of Thy love, Thy royal Bride
Triumphant led ; but in Thy lowliness ;
Stranger 'midst earth's illusions unconfessed,
Acknowledged but by few.   No star bedecked
Thy regal brow, no halo lingered round
With visible brightness, afterglow of Heaven
Attendant, but as man with men to dwell,
Though chief of men, yet lowliest 'mid the crowd.
Not Thine the palace with its gilded roof,
Nor couch of silken ease, nor deference,
Obsequious pomp and homaged stateliness,
Deep reverence, and awe that relegates
From thought or act, from too familiar touch,
The consecrated King.   Unrecognised,
Obscure, amid the common throng Thy walk ;
Thy life the common life, mingling with all,
And undistinguishable 'mid the throng.
Sprung amid poverty with poverty
Familiar, Thy manhood slowly shaped
Itself, developed 'mid the lowliest things
To loftiest issues.   On the mountain-side,
Beneath the imperial azure of the night,
Thou prayedst, or on a stony pillow slept.
Though unacknowledged, King of kings, uncrowned,
Unsceptred, till the hour of anguish came,
And daring hands Thy world-wide purpose mocked
Derisively.   Unroll, thou curtain dark ;
Rend, O thou veil, that hidest from our view
The sanctuary of Christ's most holy life ;
Show what the centuries have wrought, thrones wrecked,

The up-piled loftiness of human pride
Levelled to dust, empires decayed, the lust,
The tyranny, strugglings unchronicled,
And agony, appealing loud to Heaven,
Or mutely borne; unclose, O ravening dark!
And to the eye of faith once more present,
Amid His compeers on the Syrian strand,
The Sinless One, God manifest in flesh!
 Fair smiles the light on pleasant Galilee,
On hills, and ripening plains, blue lake's expanse,
With ever-whispering waves and smiling shores
Rolling in fertile uplands from the sun,
Where white-towered cities dream beside the wave,
Or flanked by Gadara's precipitous cliffs.
Like summer's glistening swaths before the scythe,
Successive generations here have lived,
Here flourished, and to dark oblivion passed.
Warriors have fought, and to their stripling sons
Retold their tales of former bravery;
Women have plied their necessary cares
Domestic, children played, and weary age
Waited death's summons 'neath the trellised vine.
A scattered feeble folk possession hold
Of this renownèd stage. The centuries
Have told their musing tale, the contents brief
Of history's varied page, harsh din of war,
The trumpet's challenge, victory's brazen shout,
Or lullaby of drowsy peace. Unchanged
The land remains, from Lebanon, snow-crowned,
To the fierce blasted wilderness, El Ghor;
Esdraelon's plain, where oft embattled hosts

Have glittered in the sun, now with spring flowers
Bedecked, or golden breadth of tawny grain :
From Carmel's mount, where the great prophet dwelt,
Or Tabor's shadowing oaks, to Jordan's stream
Escaping from the oleander groves
That fringe Gennesareth, the tamarisks,
Or palms, unrolling through the sweltering gorge
To blood-stained Masada, the leaden depths
Of th' asphaltic lake, Jordan, whose wave
Baptismal crowned the Son of God.   Stands yet
Upon its rocky heights, Jerusalem,
Though smitten with the mace of war full oft,
Whose ramparts long the foeman's battering ram
Resisted, down whose echoing streets the tramp
Of armèd men resounded, whence the shriek
Of agony uprose, or victory's cry,
When volleying through the cedar roofs the smoke,
Red-spotted, licked the beauty of God's house.
Zion forlorn remains ; still at its feet
The wintry Kidron murmurs of the past,
Tells of Gethsemane and all its love,
The anguish of its dark mysterious pains.

The scene remains : the human element
Has changed.   Yet here once dwelt, once breathed,
  once walked
Earth's paragon, noblest and chief of men,
Once spake serenest words of wisdom, clear,
Yet deep, surpassing all that man e'er spake,
Here harvested more precious truths than all
That diligent hands caring the spacious field
Of knowledge through past centuries have gleaned.

Here stood the Son of God, but how disguised!
Sublime concealment! not pre-eminent
Was He in form, with power terrific armed,
Nor as transfigured on the midnight mount,
Or when to John, in Patmos' lonely isle,
Revealed. A man in the integrity
Of perfect manhood, dignified, and grave,
Gentle, and unobtrusive as the dawn,
Yet in the stillness of His nature firm,
Deliberate, unyielding as the rock,
Spotless in purity as Lebanon's snow,
And armed with all the awful force of truth.
In Him a noble all-commanding grace
That won the confidence and ruled the soul.
Keen was His glance, and lightning-like His scorn,
Hypocrisy rebuking, awful, stern
In wrath, yet to the sad, the sorrowful,
His voice was full of brooding tenderness,
Soft as the mother dove's in summer shade.
Eyes of divinest tenderness, a heart
Had He to sorrow in the sorrow of our race :
No blanched recluse, no timid fugitive
From the dark wrestlings of life's bitter field,
But resolute, a victor in the fray ;
Before His generation stood He forth,
With gaze unblenched, a witness for the truth ;
Clad in the peasant garb of Galilee,
His hands disdaining not the peasant's task,
He daily wrought. Entering a human home,
He consecrated the thrice-blessed ties
That bind and elevate humanity.

Kissed by a mother's tenderness, the hands
Of fond affection stretched His infancy
To guard, He grew : the filial tie He owned,
Loved and was loved, discharged with gentleness
From day to day the duties of a child,
And to a fair and gracious manhood rose.
Tasting of youth's delights, and with a heart
All unrebuked, of bounding sympathy,
Thus from the arid ground of poverty,
Swept by the bitter wind, nipped by the frost,
Yet blooming in perpetual loveliness,
The mystic root its noble blossom threw,
Manhood's serene, unfading, perfect flower.
 Why thus disguised ? Why level thus with man ?
Or doubtful or ambiguous to the gaze
All-wondering : with no accoutrement
Of extreme power, or, if, invisible,
Subordinate, at intervals displayed,
Perceived by reason only, and the eye
Reflective, that but moral greatness notes ;
With no caparisoned pomp, no retinue
Of earthly greatness to arrest the glance
Inconstant, or convince the common mind.
Thus might the unreflective crowd pass on
Unnoticing, and to forgetfulness
Consign Him with life's trivialities.
Sublimely negligent of blatant fame,
Christ dropped the passing opportunity,
Silenced the outgoing echoes of the deed
That clamoured for renown, and onward walked
In His majestic silence unobserved.

God several ends by single means effects;
Christ's life was typical; He sinless lived,
Condemning sin, and teaching man to live.
Not for the rich, the wise exclusively,
Or great He lived, but gave for general man
The splendid lesson of a sinless life.
He came to seek and through His love to save
Man lost, that through His interposing love,
Self-sacrifice, the mediatorial end
Might be secured. The stamp of poverty
Was thus impressed upon His life; He stooped,
And disarrayed Himself of heaven's bright robes,
The russet garments of man's lowliness,
Man's lowliness in its most lowly guise,
To wear. Heaven's Messenger, the Royal Son,
Ambassador of Love, Christ's mission threw
Its greatness round life's commonness, redeemed
Life's poor externals, and to loftiest height
Exalted human hopes, as round on man
It cast a new and consecrating light.
To promulgate Heaven's latest law He came,
The law of love, Himself the evidence
Convincing, and irrefragable proof.
There stood He forth before the eyes of men
The embodiment of Love. Love spake through Him,
Love taught, the Love of God went to and fro
To seek its lost, Love wrought its tenderness
In tenderest deed, Love bowed the thorn-crowned head,
For man Love died, and passing through the tomb,
Sits crowned, divine, and everlasting Love.

Approach, O doubtful yet inquiring heart!
Still yearning for a higher sympathy,
If sympathy there be higher than man's,
Yet shrinking apprehensive, lest it find
That passionless fate compels our destiny,
Commands the lives of men, or casual drift
Fortuitous, determines man's well-being,
As forming part of this machinery
Of nature, with our lot assigned, an end
Discharged in action, till this conscious self
Be blown to nothingness and vacancy,
Extinct. List to th' Ambassador of Heaven.

While the stars glimmered on Gennesareth's wave,
All through the night, upon the mountain-top
The Saviour knelt in prayer, no sound to break
The silence of His oratory lone,
But flitting night-bird's cry, or jackal's howl;
All night He knelt upon the dew-wet grass;
The night wind as it swept heard pleadings loud,
Mayhap voices mysterious, not of earth,
As Christ communed with His eternal Sire,
Afresh commissioned, fortified by prayer,
Forth from the dark pavilion of the night
The Master came, when morning like a smile
Broke o'er the world: Himself the Light of Light,
Great Sun of Righteousness and Life of men,
Now dawning on the world with His first beams.
Gathering around Him multitudes drew nigh
Who from the white-towered cities of the lake,
The nestling villages, the olive groves
Of northern Galilee, or coasts remote

Of Tyre and Sidon, Hebron, Salem came,
Judea's ancient cities; seated round
Upon the grassy slopes, not for themselves
Alone they heard, but that the world might hear.
Then opened Christ His mouth. Blest utterance!
Translation of the mystic characters
Graven on the natural world, oft dimly guessed,
Which to the wavering and uncertain thought
Gives rest. The all-embracing Soul of things,
The Spirit animating this wide scene,
That life infuses and supports this frame,
Upholds and guides, Christ solemnly proclaims
To be the FATHER of the souls of men;
Exalted far beyond all mortal thought
In unimagined glory, yet towards man
Loving and tender, merciful and kind:
His the all-glittering sun that shines alike
Upon the evil and the good, and His
The shower that nourishes the milky stalk.
Though far removed from earth's distractions loud
Misleading shadows, disappointing hopes,
Yet e'er beholding from the secrecy
Of His divine existence, this vast stage
Of human life, noting the part well played,
The purpose owning, and the upright deed,
Befriending virtue howsoe'er obscure,
Reading the motive and the varying phase
Of inner life, hearing the secret prayer,
Though gently whispered; His the sustenance
Of these His creatures in their every want,
The observance of each life His constant care.

Wild birds that wheeling in the sunshine play,
Diving and balancing and with pleased song
Spending their little lives, are fed by Him,
Though sowing not nor garnering their food.
Fair regal lilies in their silken robes,
Perfumed, and canopied, as king ne'er was,
Spread o'er the landscape with a lavish hand,
Are all arrayed by Him. The Father's care
That decks this house, our earth, with flowers, that feeds
Its poorest servitors, will not deny
His children food, will not from them withhold
Secret support, most blessed intercourse,
Friendship, and hidden sympathy, and love.
 So ran the echoes : and like music since,
Sweeter than e'er discoursed from pipe or string,
Or human voice intelligent, descend
These glorious truths to this remoter age,
Oft faintly apprehended by the soul,
But in the stress, the agonising wrench
Of some great trouble, then, beyond all price.
Like to a child awakened by sweet strains,
That, wandering through the secret avenues,
Arouse the slumbering thoughts, so gently touched
That the pleased sleeper smiles and sleeps again,
Again to wake, as pleased, yet knows not why,
Opening fair innocent eyes as if afraid
To break the spell that bound it, thus the soul,
Pleased beyond words to find the page revealed,
Presents so dear a truth as God's great love,
Clearly expressed, still hesitates to grasp
And for itself to hold the truth as true.

Yet in immortal words the Saviour told
The path to God accessible; to none
Denied, but who themselves by negligence
Exclude, or dark despair, or unbelief,
That worst of sacrilege and first of sins.

 Forth from his childhood's home a younger son
Set out.—So taught the Saviour of mankind,
With luminous simplicity.—The world
Was full of smiles, false promises, and hopes
Delusive; to its brighter skies turned then
The prodigal, forgetful of the love
That sheltered him; untrue to home, to love
Untrue; reckless, extravagant, his all
Spent he on sin, and, 'neath a different name,
Bought wretchedness. At length his sin came home
To him in self-rejection, bitterness.
An exile, penniless, in misery
Degraded, clad in rags of beggary,
He fed the swine of aliens; with swine's food
Allayed his hunger; penitent at length
And hunger-bitten to his boyhood's home
He turned his wistful eyes, yet scarce dared hope
That his unnatural ingratitude
Would pardon find: yet trusts the father's love,
And in his sorrow homeward turns his face.

 The path of his return is watched. An eye,
The father's eye, still looks along the road,
The father's heart yearns o'er his missing child,
Till now, far off, his long-lost son he sees,
With instant recognition. Forth he runs,
He falls upon his neck, and kisses him,

Scarce listening to his sobbing utterance,
Rejoicing that the wanderer has come.
No stinted joy, no cold and stern rebuke;
The home flings wide its doors to welcome him,
Ringing with echoing glee. The son is found!
The son is more than all. Love finds her own,
And love with its belovèd must rejoice.
Robed, honoured, feasted, all the bitter past
Forgotten, this triumphant welcome home
Tells of the warmer welcome of the soul
That turns in penitence and faith to God;
The joy of angels, and the Father's kiss.

    Yet more. As God in Christ incarnated,
The Saviour lived the lesson He had taught
In a divine all tender charity,
A gentleness divine, allowance making
Ample and swift for the poor erring will,
Yielding encouragement to effort weak,
If but sincere, and preaching by His deeds
The creed sublime of pure humanity.
Nor would He have His people show their faith
By empty shibboleth, or lifeless rites,
But by a care for all their fellow-men,
Reverence for forms of reverence, nor by thought
Or unconsidered word t' affront the faith
Of the devout; the purer faith display
In widest charity, in sympathy,
And the sweet lesson of a blameless life.

    As perfect man He meekly bowed Himself
To grief's sore tyranny; with sweat His brow
Was oft bedewed; the tear-drop in His eye

Glistened and fell; refreshed was He by sleep;
Fatigued by labour, and to all restraints
Of this our burdened weak humanity
Submissive. To and fro the Saviour went
'Mongst men, mingling in all the scenes of life,
Pleasant, or painful to His higher sense.
He came unto His own, yet by His own
Was He rejected, and at birth and death
Disowned; the cratch His cradle, and His grave
A borrowed tomb; His throne usurped; His claims
Fiercely derided and His purpose mocked.
  The grand old patriarchal faith which found
The heavenly world contiguous, and maintained
Angelic intercourse, or, nobler yet,
Enjoyed divine companionship, had died.
Now Salem's temple desecrated stood;
God's priests but minions of Rome become,
Firebrands or fanatics, who sought alone
The nurture of revenge, blind, headlong zeal,
That served the altar with its blood-stained hands.
To this degenerate, disloyal age
Lowly, and all disguised, came the Divine.
Like Edom's shepherd, when the blazing thorn
Spoke from its tongue of flames, felt they not near
The Lord of heaven and earth, nor recognised
Beneath this frail exterior a power
Omnipotent? Though curbed with self-restraint,
Flashed forth His indignation like the bolt
Of summer lightning from the angry sky.
For sin to Him was loathsome, vile, and rank,
And not as it appeared to blunted sense

Of dull familiarity. Who turned,
With eyes of lightning glance, keenly to note
The Asian churches, searched He not His age,
The chosen people with their hopes and fears,
Pretensions, subterfuges, prejudice,
Their mercenary spirit, bigotry,
Rankness unpruned, intolerance, or pride,
And foul corruption, bred of long neglect?
The darkest plots, though tenfold dark and deep,
Shrouded in hatred's black obscurity,
Were known to Him; and pityingly He gazed
On the blind bond-slaves of iniquity.
His eye noted the thronging worshippers,
That swept with flowing text-embroidered robes
The marble steps, He searched their secret hearts,
Ready to recognise the right and good
Wherever found, yet swift to reprehend
With stern rebuke loud-tongued hypocrisy.

O Son of God, Most High, the King of kings,
Balanced upon whose will lie heaven and earth
With all their agencies, the universe,
Wider than widest thought of mortal man,
Who curb'st the forces of the human world,
Uprooting dynasties, and to the throne
The beggar elevating from the dust,
How little wert Thou known! Nature confessed
Her Lord; and at His glance terrific shrank,
The hoary sea, the deafening waves grew still,
Obedient to His word; while at His touch
Disease and death of all their terrors stripped,
Acknowledged Him; hell's opposition fled,

Though buttressed in its pride; Divinely armed,
Thus stood He in omnipotence complete.
How the Divine incarnated below,
As man with men, demeaned Himself on earth,
What deeds proceeded from those gracious Hands,
What words, and with what spirit accompanied;
How the eternal goings forth of Love
Enshrined themselves in noble act or word,
The loving, grateful heart still pines to know.

 From the Perean wilds the Saviour turned
In stress of spirit to Jerusalem,
To accomplish the great function of His life;
Around Him multitudes had thronged to bid
Their last farewell, where He had healed their sick.
Fond mothers come, bringing their babes to Him
That He might bless them; lingering, though rebuked,
Till interposed, the Master's voice forbids
The prohibition harsh, sweetly invites
The little ones, taking them in His arms
And blessing them. O glorious spectacle!
Incarnate God the shield of infancy,
The lover and protector of the weak!
Angels had sung above the darkened plains
Of startled Bethlehem, "Good will to man."
Good will to man shone in Christ's every act,
Accompanied His daily steps, and marked
His daily speech. He saw the human soul
Groping in darkness, burdened sore, and faint,
And seeing pitied, binding up its wounds.

 A shade had passed across the calm divine
Of Christ's serenity, the shade of death,

And, troubled to His being's inward depths,
From man He turned. The fearless speaker, John,
Witness for Christ, as for the purity
Of God, had been by Herod foully slain.
Capernaum was thronged. The Saviour calls
His tired disciples, wearied with the toil
Of their great mission late returned, embarks
And passes to the silence of the lake,
Far out of ear-shot of the busy hum
Whose turmoil sacrilegious might invade
The stillness of His grief. All silent now
The din contentious, tramp of restless crowds,
Passion's unholy clash, or forwardness
Of empty simulation, or the tongue
Of thoughtlessness, that, with incautious words,
Pricks the dull sorrow to the quick, with names
Too fondly cherished. From the peaceful cells
Of Nature's quiet their tired spirits drink
Needed repose: the large free air of day,
The fresh cool wind, the crispèd waves that bear
With soothing undulation their frail ship,
Wait with their gentle ministration round.
The grassy uplands on the farther shore,
That by gradations from the blue lake's strand
Receding rise, offer desired retreat.
Yet, ere arrived, the eye, the gathering crowds
Discerns, that break the wished-for solitude :
From the surrounding hills and open fields
The tiny sail by thousands had been watched
Of those who having heard Christ's precious words
Desired His further presence, and on foot

Had coasted round upon the farther shore
To give untimely welcome. Nor didst Thou,
Compassionate Redeemer, this refuse,
Nor access e'er deny to suppliants,
Though inconsiderate their earnestness,
Their plea inopportune. Far otherwise ;
Our breasts to individual griefs respond,
Thou to the crowd ; the multitude awaked
Thy sympathy. Like to a flock they seemed
Unshepherded and scattered on the hills,
Defenceless, and Thou yearnedst over them ;
Nor did compassion rest in sentiment,
But its expression sought, to ameliorate
Their sufferings and to minister support.
Thus wore the day towards eve, the hours being spent
In high discourse, or act of curative power.
The westering sun stooping from mid-day's throne,
Shrank behind Carmel, and with reddening ray
That burned across the lake, long shadows threw
Over the sward, while the crisp evening air
As parting day gathered its flowing skirts,
New vigour brought, with soft refreshing dews.
Upon the crowd Thy glance, O Lord, was turned ;
As far from home, night near, hungry, footsore,
And travel-wearied, still they lingered by.
Christ would not empty send the hungering throngs
Away. They, labouring first at His command,
To acquire the imperishable bread had left
The perishing : not loath, thus honours He
The precedence, and satisfies their wants.
No adequate supply had they to feed

A hungering crowd. Faith ever has enough,
Though the last handful, to obey its Lord,
And to obedience comes a full supply.
Five barley loaves, two fishes, these the store
The apostolic larder yields, scant fare
For those for whom provided, but for these,
A famished multitude, but mockery.
The hand of Christ was plenty's copious horn.
Forth at His word the blushing seasons pour
Their lavish treasures rich, recurrent gifts,
The plenitude of nature, wealth untold,
Exuberant, of flower, or fruit, or grain.
Who called the quails upon the desert wind,
The manna rained from heaven upon the sands,
Or bade the flinty-hearted cliff yield streams,
Could have commanded on the hillside green
Sumptuous repast, by hands angelical
Though all unseen administered. The stones
That idly lined Gennesareth's chiding shore,
Might have become, at His all-powerful word
Bread for the multitude. Thy blessing makes,
O Saviour, our abundance, while Thy frown
Is life's most barren dearth. Scarce had the words
Of holy benediction passed His lips
Than power went forth ; the scanty food increased,
And grew within the hand that carried it,
By distribution multiplied. His will,
His word, sunshine, and dew, and rain obey,
In operation instantaneous,
And all their kindly influences blend.
There sat the needy multitude as grew

The evening dusk, and 'midst them rose the form
Sublime of Him who every want supplies,
Of every heart, Himself the Living Bread.
   Constraining His disciples to embark,
The Master tarried to dismiss the crowds ;
Hastening ere yet the oncoming storm should break
Upon them shelterless. Then solemn night
Darkened the sea. The Master was alone,
And on the mountain-top again in prayer
Refreshment sought, though all the world was dark,
Lonely, and drear. Soon burst the gathering storm,
And vacant winds swept o'er the gloomy hills
With drenching rains. The lightning's sudden blaze
Cleaving the night, showed where the Watcher knelt
In all His awful earnestness of prayer.
Yet through night's darkness, trebly dark with storm,
Christ saw far off His timid trembling few,
Storm-tossed, and drenched, saw where the labouring
    bark
Out on the lake staggered amid the waves.
   Lonely had been the night since evening's dusk
Had hidden from their view the Master's form.
In long fierce conflict with the elements
The hours had passed ; nor came He when the storm
Swooped like a vulture on their foamy track.
But when thick midnight lay upon the waves,
And grim despair was piloting to death,
Regretfully their thoughts flew to the night,
Not long before, when on the selfsame lake
The storm from out its mountain eyry flew ;
When greedy for their death, tumultuous waves

Clambering the bulwark sought for easy prey;
Then was the Master with them; stretched in sleep,
He lay, till wakened by their urgent cries,
He from His slumbers rose, and with a word
Rebuked the storm. Were He but present now,
How glad were they, how safe! Useless regret!
Yet though death threatened them on every side,
Yawned in each wave, menaced in every blast,
Hurled his bright lightning shaft before their eyes,
Deliverance came, though in the darkest hour;
The fourth watch came, and with extremity
Help unexpected; for across the foam
A luminous form appeared, unearthly, weird,
And indistinct, yet was it their great Lord.
Misunderstood! to their untutored minds,
An apparition seemed He from the tomb,
A ghost which walked upon the restless waves,
The spirit of the storm: till from the din
Came the clear words, "'Tis I, be not afraid!"
Now indistinct, till nearer seen, their Lord
Came treading down the echoing halls of night,
As on a marble floor, diffusing wide
His radiance far o'er the tumultuous waves,
Nor arrowy rain, nor tumbling mountain waves,
Nor javelin-thrust of hasty lightning's gleam,
Nay, nor ten thousand deaths though ravenous
As famished wolves, shall keep the Saviour back
From His imperilled ones. Hither He comes,
From crest to crest of the proud billows borne,
With high imperiousness and firm resolve,
Not with vain show of superhuman might,

But for the succour of His own, the joy
Of His immediate presence. When reduced
By hunger in the wilderness saw they
How that the Master from the unseen stores
Of His creative might, brought sustenance;
Henceforth His people know that from the brink
And edge of death, how that His hand can snatch
From direst peril the confiding soul,
Now learn they that amid the storm's wild stress,
'Mid sorrow's blackest night He walks abroad,
Walks through the turmoil of the tempest fierce,
Unhindered, walks to rescue those He loves.
Christ makes the calm, Christ's presence makes our
    heaven.

    Nor did benignity alone appear;
A gracious friendliness thus intertwine
With the great purpose to disclose and give
To mortal thought, far as may be disclosed,
Subjects divine, those dear and cherished hopes
Which, reason as we may, must e'er remain
Man's truest comfort, as his truest wealth.
Christ's life exemplified in overt act,
Divine procedure brought to nearer view;
Silvering the clouds of gloomy providence.

    Hoisting their sails, eastward the fishers turned
Their prows. The night was darkening on the wave,
And evening's golden dusk lay on the hills
Of Galilee, deepening to purple gloom.
To these rough, humble, Jewish fishermen,
Bred to the lake, the landscape was well known,
The sloping shores, the distant mountains gray,

White towns that glimmered o'er the shining wave,
Towered and still, with lights like fireflies;
Familiar the ever-varying lake,
Lovely alike in storm, or calm, all times,
Or when the morning flushing Hermon's snow,
Whitened the silent wave with flooding glow,
Or midnight's moon threw o'er its wrinkled floor
A path of light, or noontide's quivering blaze.
Capernaum was their home. God-fearing men,
Serious and earnest, as the night fell fast
Upon the lonely lake, might they have sung
Some grand old psalm of peaceful confidence,
Or raised the prayer that Israel's God, who sleeps
Nor slumbers not, would them in safety keep.

Accustomed to their task, the night wore by,
As hopefully they plied their fisher craft;
The ruddy torch that shed around their skiff
Its useless glare, abandoned, now their lines
And nets they cast, yet at each venture met
By disappointment, labouring but in vain.
The hours with conversation were beguiled,
Nor topics wanted they, far nobler themes
Than tackling, boats, and sails, and fish, the change
Of wind or moon, or market's variation.
Not long returned from Jordan's sacred fords,
Disciples of the Baptist, we may deem
Their talk ran in its 'customed groove, of him
The stern recluse, son of the wilderness,
How to his desert eyes their life appeared,
How as the lightning flash opens the night
Conviction had disclosed their inmost hearts

And conscience, like the hammer of the Lord,
Accused. Like flowers towards the sun, their thoughts
Turned to the Coming One, greater than John.
The glistening wave of Jordan had becrowned
In baptism, the head of One whom John
Declared the Son of God. To two of these,
As Jesus walked, the Baptist had exclaimed,
Pointing to Christ, " Behold the Lamb of God!"
The whispering wave of midnight well might hear,
With labouring of the oar, or casting out
The net, converse on topics such as these.
    Night passed, and Gadara's mountain-crests stood black
Against the pale fair primrose sky of dawn,
The eastern stars, floating in crystal haze,
Grew dim, as weariedly the fishermen
Turned homewards, disappointed in their toil.
Now grew the light of morning overhead;
The birds, winging their way with chirp and song,
Welcomed the dawn; and the broad sun arose,
Flooding the hills of Bashan orange gold,
Gilding the wave-tops of the glittering lake,
Capernaum's towers, and white Tiberias,
The Tarichæan stronghold, Magdala,
With fields, the woods, the roads, and pleasant homes
Of busy Galilee; drawing near shore,
The eye discerned the early labourers
Forth to the cornfield bound, or bleating flocks,
Led by the shepherds from their nightly fold
Pasture to find, or where the olive groves,
Or fig, or pomegranate, or statelier palm

Moved in the morning breeze. Life was astir:
The fisher folk upon the shining strand
Hauled up their boats, mended or washed their nets;
Women with water-pitchers on their heads
Came from the well; hard-handed country-folk
Entered the town; and from Tiberias' walls
Might come the glance of burnished helm or spear
From Roman sentinel upon his rounds.
Now to the synagogue the worshippers
Wended their early way with reverent thought
To rest awhile beneath God's vine of peace.

  With grating keel upon the pebbly beach,
The weary fishermen make fast their boats,
And standing in the cool translucent wave,
Washing their nets, prepare for future toil.
All the night long, all the long night in vain,
So runs the story of unnumbered lives,
Effort prolonged, endeavour stoutly plied,
Yet all in vain, for disappointment still
Confronts the aim, and ill requites life's toil.
O human heart, alive with noble hopes,
Weighted with weakness and infirmity,
How oft has grim necessity compelled
Submission, yielded all unwillingly!
Fishers of men, Christ's ministers have oft
Wrought through a night lifelong in sorrow, pain,
And fruitlessness. Darkness, and buffeting storm
Have waited on their pains, and few results
Or none, till rendering up their solemn charge
Into Christ's hand in deep humility,
Have solemnly confessed, "The work, O Lord,

Is Thine, and Thine the ultimate result,
Success, or what to mortal vision seems
Failure, Thine, too, the ample recompense."
 The fishermen knee-deep in water stood,
Washing their nets, when now a crowd drew nigh
And with them One who stood conspicuous,
As shines the moon amid the stars of night.
To avoid the throng Christ enters Peter's boat,
And bids him thrust a little from the land,
Then sat Him down to teach. Upon the shore
The crowd expectant stood, or on the bank
Up-sloping from the lake reclined, then leaned
To hear the voice of Him who spake as man
Ne'er spake; and in the morning calm, broken
By plash of passing oar, rustle of leaf,
Or chirp of bird upon its hasty flight,
Christ's voice was heard. Now glancing on the crowd,
The sun-browned faces of the fishermen,
Who all attent sat by with folded arms,
And listening countenance, the Master spoke:
No tedious prettiness, nor rabbi's tales
Explaining nothing, disquisitions deep
On points minute, what Rabbi Shammai loosed,
Hillel, or Eleazar bound; Christ's texts
Were found near home, glistening upon the thorn,
Or fluttering in the wind, the upturned soil,
The cornfield birds, the sower's measured stride,
White villages far seen upon the hills,
The callow raven brood, children at play,
The net upon the shore, these gave Him all
He sought, the key to unlock the minds of men;

THE SONG OF INCARNATE LOVE.

And soon with firm and kindly hand He grasped
Their souls. Gracious was He; and from His eyes
Gleamed the pure fire of human sympathy;
His words, all luminous, were mirrored clear
Within the mind of every auditor,
Like midnight's stars upon the placid lake.
 The sermon ended; then the Saviour rose,
And by display of power miraculous
Would clench the truth proclaimed. Thick fogs and
  clouds
Of prejudice obscured His hearers' minds;
These by far-darting beams of energy
The newly-risen Sun of Righteousness,
The brightness of the eternal glory, pierced.
Turning to Simon, "Launch into the deep,"
Said He, "and for a draught let down your nets."
So spake great nature's Lord, whose piercing eye
Surveys old ocean's caverns vast and dark,
Though thousand fathoms deep, shrouded and dim,
Where gliding monsters twine, where scattered lie
Pearls 'mid the slime, as in derision spread;
So spake whose voice commands the underworld.
The net rope rattled o'er the vessel's side,
Its hidden meshes to the surface threw
Their tiny air-bells, and full soon the power
Of Christ was evidenced, for now the lake
Gave forth its glistening treasures in the sun.
So soon canst Thou our disappointment turn,
O Lord, to brimming and complete success.
 A gentleness of soul, a kindliness,
And pure compassion tenderer far than man's,

Christ manifested, and in tenderest form.
The tale of Nain's sore-stricken widow lives,
And all her grief; the love that glorified
Her sorrow, and its halo threw around
Her darkened home, form now a treasured theme.
Not far from wooded Tabor's outline dim,
Quivering in heat above Esdraelon's plain,
Stood Nain among the hills, rural, obscure,
Now consecrated by the love of Christ.
Its flat-roofed houses and white walls peered forth,
Seen by the traveller miles across the plain.
One day, one hour in the vast years gone by,
Has made its name immortal. Through the gate
Passed and repassed townsfolk and villagers;
The gossiping women to the well-side bound,
Or bridal parties with their noisy joy;
With their attendant retinues, rich Jews,
Turbaned and jewelled; from the neighbouring tombs
Out on the steep hillside, the mourners came;
Peasants to labour went, or from their walk
Across the hot and dusty plain beneath
Came wayfarers. Inside the walls went on
The business of ordinary life.
The trader sat, cross-legged, and watched his scales,
The keen-eyed merchant knowing well the world,
Measuring his textures from the costly bales,
Gossip and quarrel, chaffering or the shouts
Of children at their play, or from the school,
Conning their task in sing-song monotone,
The moan of sorrow mingling with the din
Of active life. Trouble and grief were there,

Too frequent denizens of human homes.
Now down the rocky street comes mournfully
A funeral procession; common sight!
Yet this was with a deeper pathos robed,
This hushed the noisiest, touched the coldest heart,
A widow following her only son
To his last resting-place, a son whose death
Had robbed her of her last, fond, cherished hope.
Emerging from the gate now comes to view
The funeral train, with solemn steps and slow,
Presenting death in saddest mystery,
Grief without palliation. From the plain
Approaching, Christ and His disciples come.
The Saviour looked upon the widow's grief,
Quick, suffering to detect, howe'er concealed,
Deeply compassionate, and drawing near
Stopped the procession, as He touched the bier;
Then stanched He with a word the mourner's tears.
Christ is unsought by her, she makes no prayer,
And no request by word or look prefers.
Her sorrow and her desolation plead,
In silent intercession with her tears;
Nor ineffectual their plea. We stand
Helpless before irrevocable loss,
Helpless to minister to those bereaved,
Muttering our scraps of poor philosophy,
Though feeling as we speak their worthlessness,
Thou dost not mock, O Christ, with empty words,
Nor vainly counsel to conceal the grief
That gnaws the heart. Thine was the word of power,
That in full flood subdues and banishes

Sorrow's imperious fears.   He touched the bier ;
The bearers stood.   Rigid beneath the pall
Lay the uncoffined face, no index now
Of busy thought or feeling's changeful play,
But with death's impress fixed, solemn and still.
Christ to the dead man speaks : " Young man, arise."
A flush of life thrilled the pale ashy face,
A tremor quivered through the ice-cold clay,
And, swathed and shrouded for the grave, the youth
Sat up and spoke.   Descending from the bier,
The dead rejoined the living, and once more
The mother clasped to heart her dear lost son.

    Thee, Bethany, and thy seclusion dear,
Sacred to friendship and to grief divine,
My willing thought would seek ; there linger near
What time the glimmering eve brought home the flocks,
And o'er the olives shone eve's dewy star
Full peacefully, when down the rocky slope
Came One whose wearied feet hallowed each path
They trod.   There, in the favoured home, to sit
With those meek souls, amid the deepening gloom,
In awful, though most blest propinquity
To Him who was the origin of life,
To listen to the Voice that made the world,
Attuned to friendship, sweet humanity,
Not pregnant with destructive power,
But linked with gentle wisdom's offices,
Instruction, and the moulding of the soul.
But chiefly on that memorable day,
By the sad grave of buried Lazarus
To hear the dead believer called to life.

Summoned from far by love's imperious cry
Of wistful earnestness, the Saviour came.
While hope remained the sisters' longing eyes
Down the steep slope that led to Jericho
Had turned, yet turned in vain. Jesus delayed,
Not casually or by constraint, but moved
By end deliberate ; now would He show
Before men's eyes a lesson for all time.
In solemn words had the Redeemer taught
The power of faith, how that believers live
Though they be dead, and on the grave's mouth lie
The jealous stone. O glorious living truth,
That who believe in Christ shall never die!
Come up, O Saviour, from the Perean wilds,
Assure our hearts ; this mountain hamlet make
The pulpit for so world-renowned a theme ;
Show death Thy vassal, show Thy power to save,
Touch the rock portals where Thy loved one lies ;
Put through the hole of death's all gloomy door
Thy hand of love, the jealous latchet lift,
That hides man from eternity's wide day.

Now goes the Saviour forth, stands near the tomb
Whose are the keys of Hades and of death,
About to unfold those iron leaves. Within
His servant lies, moveless, and on his brow
Gathers corruption's dew. Can the dead live ?
The dead in Christ, are they in safety kept,
Urned in deep silence and chill vacancy,
Though reft from love, and light, and this warm life ?
The echoless night of death gives no reply.
Go not, O Master, O Thou pitiful One,

Touch not the veil that hides what death has done
The sisters plead.   The stone is rolled away ;
Before the grave's mouth stands the Lord of life,
Stands at the portals of the realms of Death.
From far and near, O all ye sons of men,
Through the far centuries, hither turn your gaze,
Behold Christ's attestation of the truth,
Sanction sublime of our high gospel hopes!
"Lazarus, come forth!" and as the mighty word
Pierces the cavernous gloom, the dead man hears ;
Stirs in His sleep ; before their frighted eyes
The sheeted form, with face cloth bound, recumbent
Rises, and from the tomb comes forth.   Life's fire
Burns in the vacant eye, the pallid cheek
Is mantled o'er with the warm flush of health,
And strength revisiting the pithless limbs,
Once more he mingles with the living world.

  Thus passed Christ's ministry ; thus were His days
Filled with wise words and all with gentle deeds
Of pure beneficence and kindliness,
From Cana's wedding to the last sad feast
In Salem's upper room, a golden chain
Of deeds of mercy and of loving words,
Not casually but constantly displayed,
And pictured revelations in kind deeds
Of the great truths that shape our destiny.
Yearning for human souls, the lost He sought,
As seeks the shepherd on the hills his sheep,
Nor yet desisting till the strayed be found :
Came to the wayside where the beggar sat,
And broke th' immuring silence of the deaf.

His life was spent not in the cloister's shade,
In bookish leisure rapt in pensive thought;
The highways and the hedges were His haunts,
The open fields His minster, and the heavens
His clerestory, His pulpit was the street,
The country roadside, or the green hill-slope,
While in the home of sorrow did He stand
To give the bread of joy, the wine of love.
    For wouldst thou know the gist of that Christ came
To teach to man? Then listen to His words.
Come as the Pharisee who stole by night
To the lamp-lighted room to question Him.
Imagination hears the golden speech
Of Him who was the Truth: God's love set forth
In plainest words of most delightful power:
God's love declared to be revealed to man,
Not in the splendours of the natural world,
Large gifts to burdened sense, or wide display
Of generosity of this world's goods,
But all concentred in one priceless gift,
GOD'S SON,—to live, to love, to die for man.
Hence, paralysing doubt! No room exists
For busy questioning, for lagging will;
Now from Christ's lips the golden gospel comes;
Love is the law of life, life's origin
Is love, love is the atmosphere it breathes,
Love its directing force, and love its end.
    O wondrous breath! O wonder-working arm!
Majestic spectacle of Heavenly Love
Clothed with omnipotence, seeking man's good,
And pouring in humanity's deep wounds

A better balm than Gilead ever wept;
The hand of kindness to the blinded soul
Held forth to guide it to eternal rest.
O fairest dream of all the ages past!
Sweetest of stories, love incarnated!

BOOK THE SEVENTH

THE SONG OF LOVE'S TRIUMPH

THE ARGUMENT.

The perfect death—Marshalling of the powers of evil—The path to the Garden—The assault of evil—The picture of sin's results—Treachery—The arrest—Dawn of that most memorable of days—In the Prætorium—The coronation song—Ave Imperator!—The curse removed—Sentenced to die—The Via Dolorosa—The crisis of time—The deed of death—Noon darkness—Why this deed of violence and shame—The final hour—Death's victory—The procession to the tomb—The garden—Where the dead lie—The tyranny of death—The silent realm—The catacombs of dust—The treasures in the dust—The adventure of Alcides—Love's adventure—Triumph in Hades—Sabbath with the dead—The Sabbath night—Morning—The Lord of Love and Life arises—The women—The resurrection song of triumph.

BOOK THE SEVENTH.

THE SONG OF LOVE'S TRIUMPH.

RAY olives silvered by the Paschal moon,
Black pools of shade, and caverns dark of
   night,
Ye gloomy colonnades where sorrow
   dwells
And silence fills with ineffectual sighs,
Here let me hide; here rest in welcome gloom,
Who sing the dying sorrow of my Lord,
Darkling, yet hopeful by assistant grace,
'Mid heavenly sunshine, 'neath serener skies,
Before the Beatific Presence high
To fall and pour the heart's full gratitude.
   Who through the weary stage of thirty years
Had onward travelled o'er the sharded roads
Of life's humiliations, and had taught
By holy precept, by example fair,
The perfect life, the perfect death essays:
Not death illumined by the light of love,

Its ruggedness austere softened, subdued
By sorrowing affection, fond caress,
Lingering farewell, but with all circumstance
To aggravate the natural pang, and throw
Its jutting horrors into bold relief.
By persecution, by injustice fell
That cried for swift revenge, hounded to death,
Thy followers have stood at judgment seats,
On crimson sands of amphitheatres,
'Mid blazing piles, and looked to Thee, and learned
To die. Lesson sublime ! For Thou didst teach
How that man's nobler spirit may surmount
Earth's last and worst indignity, and rising,
Snatch the red triumph of the martyr fires,
The keen-edged sword, the lion's fangs defy,
Upborne amid the jealous ocean waves
May find Thy love can make e'en death itself
A trysting hour. Die though Thou wouldst, O Christ
Thou didst not choose the euthanasia
Of weary age, its burdens slowly loosed,
With gradual bereavement of decay ;
Nor wert Thou, like Beth-Peor's hoary chief,
Invisibly convoyed by angel guards,
From the dim precincts of this changeful life.
Around the hour of Thy untimely death
Were grouped in dread array, all that could daunt.
For in Thy death was more than nature's debt ;
The accumulated debt of sin Thou paidst,
Concentring its grim horrors on Thyself ;
The woes not of one life, but myriad lives,
Each with converging weight of anguish drear ;

Load self-imposed, a very world of woe!
In the abysses of Thy sorrow vast
Much may remain that mortals cannot know.
Pardon, O merciful One, what love misreads
Unwillingly, or with feigned personage,
Or circumstances feigned, presents; the pomp
Of Thy redeeming woe, love's tragedy
Must yet remain eternally unsung.

   The hour, the power of darkness, now had come,
When by inscrutable decree, the world
Was yielded to the dominance of sin.
The Prince of this world came; not to the eye
Were visible night's vast embattled hosts,
In serried phalanx, gonfalon, and spear;
No shade darkened the Paschal moon; no sound,
Rustling of dragon wings, nor hissings loud
Were heard of the roused serpent brood of hell,
To excess of malice wrought in their attempt
Supreme. Invisible, inaudible
Th' approach. From the warm lighted room where sat
In holy calm the Saviour with His band,
Went forth the traitor; th' occasion sought,
Now found, nor needed his malignance more.
Forth went he from companionship with Christ,
From holy fellowship with Christ's redeemed,
To endless shame, to execration dire,
And miserable scorn, the traitor's doom.
Scarce had the echoes of his footsteps died
Along the street, when from the upper room,
Rose in commingling strains of grateful praise
The eucharistic hymn, though with hushed voice,

And tender thoughts of Him, their Master, loved,
Though now o'erwhelmed with grief, and wounded sore
By treachery, keen barbed ingratitude.
The little group, descending to the street,
Stand in the moonlight. Through the city gate,
Adown the rough declivity they pass
To where, when swollen with the wintry rains
That lashed the olive groves, Kedron's hoarse stream
Its turbid waters swept; wonted retreat,
Seclusion of Gethsemane's deep shades,
Secret pavilion, where, unseen by man,
Heaven's pursuivants, cherub and seraph, came,
Attendant oft, before their veilèd King
Rendering meet service, or deriving thence
Authority for enterprise more vast,
Exploit more dangerous, or mission high,
To their proud loyalty most welcome task:
And midnight brooded o'er the city's towers.
Silent the dusky world: the temple courts,
Silent the crowds who during busy day
Chaffered and wrangled in the noisy streets,
Or thronged the temple steps; the fanatic
And lawless herd, armed legionaries, scribes,
Or furious zealots with their eyes of fire;
All silent in the holy truce of night.
And, 'neath the olive groves whose mounded shade
Covered the farther slope of Olivet,
The Saviour prayed, wrestling in anguish drear,
The sacred sorrow of Gethsemane.
 But who may tell the dark forbidding path
That Thou, O Christ, didst tread, our souls to win;

Here let me stand, within this nook obscure,
Listening to catch some echoes faint, far off,
Sweet strains that tell the sorrow of Thy love.
Yet who may fitly sing the theme sublime,
The sorrow and the triumph of that love,
The mighty stress and conflict infinite;
Who show hell's phalanx marshalled to confront
And Thy chivalric enterprise to daunt?
 Perchance, unseen by mortal eye, came fiends
Of horrid shape, uncouth, with flaming eyes,
Tongues edged with blasphemy, menaces dire,
And fearful sounds that smote the spiritual ear
With terror, agencies unseen but dread,
Of evil summoned to the great assault;
Monsters, mayhap misshapen, grim, that writhe
Upon the floor of hell, behemoths huge
That wallow in the fiery nether depths,
And, from the lurid pool of Phlegethon,
Serpents of monstrous bulk all intertwined
With scaly folds, malignant, from whose orbs
Shot baleful rays, and with them dragon forms
To assault the Great Invader of these realms
Of ancient gloom, or e'er the portals grim
Our Champion reach, relinquishment to effect
Of His great purpose. Shrouded in the night,
Wrestled the Saviour with His unseen foes;
Kneeling He prayed, or prone, now with loud cries
Of agony extreme, and now with tears.
O wondrous agony that bought the soul!
Sorrow divine, unfathomable depths
Of grief, medicament and sovereign balm

Of human woe! With anguish was the soul
Immaculate of the Redeemer pierced;
Affliction such as ne'er had overwhelmed
The greatest sufferer of man's suffering race.
   Perchance there rose, in that lone dreadful hour,
Before Christ's view, the hideousness of sin
Unveiled. Before His sympathetic gaze,
His tenderness divine, passed in review,
All scenes of human wretchedness and woe.
To Him uplifted hands made mute appeal,
Faces convulsed of myriad sufferers,
Pleading their wretchedness; unfriended hope,
And anguished innocence, dumb helplessness,
And beauty fretted by the cruel worm;
And lusty youth, dragging disabled powers;
And many a death-bed with its nameless dread,
Mortal distress that wildly stares, and rocks,
And beats the air with cold and bony palms,
Chiding the tardiness of pitiful death;
Distracting pain that in each fearful spasm,
Ground the clenched teeth, cursed life, and wooed despair;
And madness, with bright tearless eyes that burned
In their dry sockets, laughed with hideous laugh
Mocking its misery; dumb sorrow bent,
Drowned in its grief. To Christ's all-sentient mind
Were present both the future and the past
With all their dismal uniformity:
The slaughter dire of bloody battlefields,
Collisions of inflamed and angry souls;
Civil contention and domestic strife;
And all were His. For in that awful hour

He bore the heavy load of human grief,
And all the guilt of man, sin's bitter pangs,
Rebukes of conscience, stern remorse, whose fang
Gnaws out the heart of life ; the wrestlings, doubts,
And haunting fears that dog the sinner's steps,
And on the threshold of eternity
Hold him in grip ; and all sin's dire account
Stood to the Saviour's charge, charge self-imposed ;
O love unparalleled! Nor these alone :
The dreadful future of unpardoned sin,
Assailed His pitiful most loving soul,
Flames punitive, weeping and wailing dire,
That echoed from the prison of the lost ;
With these o'erpowered, o'erwrought, the God-Man sank
Upon the ground, staggering beneath His load!
Now to His blessed lips the chalice of death,
Essential bitterness and dregs of woe,
Was pressed. With meek uplifted eye Christ prayed
That, if 'twere possible, the cup might pass ;
Yet all submissive, sorrowful to death.
Now o'er His righteous soul immaculate,
Flowed sin's dark torrent worse than Stygian pool,
Or drear Cocytus. Terrors thronged Him round,
And evil in most formidable shape.
The blood piacular from every pore,
As by ten thousand agonies drawn forth,
Rushed as anticipating the rude nails,
And vengeful spear ; and the Redeemer rose
Clothed in the vesture of His sacred blood.
Alone the wine-press of God's wrath He trod,
Disputing to the utterance with these,

Our bitter foes. Yet would I sing, O Christ,
Thy love triumphant over every pang;
Most glorious theme to chant the praises high
Of the victorious love that trod on death.
Fierce the assault and vengeful the attack,
Yet firmly didst Thou stand, the shock repulse.
The dark abysses of Thy grief, O Christ,
We may not know; Thy love we know; blest theme
For everlasting gratitude and joy.

Treachery hath done its worst, and the false kiss
Delivered Thee to death. New echoes fill
These midnight groves now bright with torch-light red;
Tramp of armed men, voices, and din confused
Tell that a crowd draws near. There in the midst,
Bound as a robber, as a robber led,
Art Thou, O Holy One! Pale moonlight ne'er
Hath gleamed on sight more pitiful than this,
Nor crime more vile been cloaked by gentle night.
With glint of spear-point, helm, and burnished shield,
They pass; the traitor in their midst: and near,
God's priests, Messiah's witnesses, ordained
To stand, to announce when first Messiah's star
Should crown the brow of time to usher in
Eternal jubilee, yet, now, alas!
Apparitors of hell are marshalling
The Prince of Peace along the road of death.

Veil your meek eyes, ye midnight stars, with clouds,
Bury, O midnight streets, the soldiers' tramp,
Rabble of voices in oblivion deep,
In tenfold silence of unbroken night;
Nor let the dismal secret hence go forth,

From world to world in God's wide universe!
The Lord of Life through Salem's streets was haled
As if a malefactor, by the crowd
That cursed Him as He went, and for His blood
Thirsted like wolves. Forsaken by Thine own,
O Christ! false love or timid, that on stress
Of circumstance could yield Thee unto death,
Onward, alone, Thou wentest to Thy doom,
Nor meaner blood nor meaner agonies
Might mingle with Thy sacrifice sublime ;
Alone the onslaught fierce, alone the brunt
Malevolent of earth and hell conjoined,
Thou didst sustain, and welcome to Thy breast
Man's utmost violence, as thence to win
The souls of Thy redeemed to endless love.

   Now in the hall of Caiaphas, ere morn
Of that most sorrowful of days had dawned,
Stood the Redeemer, whilst the conclave sought
His innocent life, in form of justice sought,
Injustice absolute, endless disgrace,
That with foul blot and ineffaceable
Should human annals smirch with endless stain.
Meekly, all silently He bore Himself,
Though from the perjured lips of witnesses,
Suborned, faltered the lie, like poisoned dart
Aimed at His life. In conscious innocence
Serene, the calm and pitiful Observer
Of these malevolent designs, replied not ;
No word in self-defence, no protest deigned,
Nor confutation uttered. O'er the sea
Of passion driven, rudderless they swept.

At length, by adjuration bound, Christ's lips
Were opened to declare Himself Messiah.
Rending his priestly robes, with flashing eye
And angry brow, strode Caiaphas, and hurled
The accusation dark of blasphemy
Against the Spotless One, who stood arraigned
Before the elders of the chosen race.
 Over the eastern hills broke the fair dawn,
The innocent morn of that most dark of days,
Most guilty, yet most glorious of time's chain,
The day that brought salvation, wrought with woe;
There, in the courtyard, stood, as Jesus passed,
His recreant apostle; on his face
Perplexed, irresolute, the firelight gleamed.
Already from his craven lips had passed
Denial of his Lord, already burned
Remorse with its slow fires, a memory
To be lifelong of faithlessness. Christ turned,
With pitiful gaze upon the apostate looked,
Yet with reproach, a look that broke his heart.
 On through the streets, stirring with waking life,
To the Prætorium, from Caiaphas,
Close-guarded, the Illustrious Prisoner
Is sent to stand at Pilate's judgment bar,
Sent to His doom. Gleamed in the morning sun,
New risen o'er Olivet, the temple front,
A cloud of marble fretted o'er with gold.
The fountains glistened with their spangled plumes
Swayed in the wind, and restless flocks of doves
Tossed their white wings, or on the greensward played;
Amid the marble colonnades the glint

Of spear, where paced the sentinel was seen.
Bound as a criminal the Victim passed
The marble steps, beneath the cedar roof,
Where robed in purple with insignia
Begirt of his high office, as beseemed
Rome's majesty, Cæsar's vicegerent sat.
Worn and disfigured by the bloody trace
Of the dark conflict of Gethsemane,
The Saviour stood, helpless, yet with a might
Omnipotent endued; for at His beck,
To avenge His quarrel, legions stood attent,
All conquering, who the bright glaive would bare,
And with a righteous indignation fired,
Would burst the visible bourn, to aid their Lord.
Silent the Prisoner stood though clamorous shouts
And adjurations loud from envious priests
Came from the colonnade, with gestures fierce,
Accusing Him. Not now, "Art Thou the Christ?"
Asks the proud Roman, but, "Art Thou a King?"
With wondering scorn at His poor retinue.

   Waiting the issue of the desperate throw,
Supreme adventure of iniquity,
Now roused, now militant upon the stage
Of things mundane, and to its dreaded hand
Large possibilities brought near, Christ gazed
On all the pitiful turmoil seething round,
Wrapped in majestic silence, yet intent
Through personal insult or yet deeper pangs,
Or unimagined labours, to unlock
The gates of sin. Yet deeper depths await,
And a severer stress of that resolve

Magnanimous.   A robber was preferred,
As worthier life than He who was life's Lord.
Now through the judgment hall strange sounds are
   heard.
Alas! the furrowing scourge now seams and tears
His sacred back.   O shameful spectacle!
From which the startled thoughts unbidden turn,
And pale reflection summons up the blush
For our disgraced and fallen humanity.

  The coronation of my Lord, I sing,
Dolorous yet blessed theme!   From Pilate sent,
The Saviour stands, at Herod's judgment bar,
His back all bleeding, and His sacred face
Disfigured by the spitting and the grief,
And cruel blows of mercenary vice.
Before the haughty Asmonean prince,
With blood familiar and bred in sin,
Though questioned oft, the Spotless One spoke not,
With word nor work of power.   Again returned ;
The guilty hand of Pilate moves the veil
That hides the past, and to our view reveals
The sorrowful picture.   There, with purple robed,
Is seen the Saviour, crowned in mockery,
Bitter and pitiless, crowned with sharp thorns.
Rude violence upon His sovereign brow
Serene, planted this diadem of pain.
Unconscious all, in this their daring guilt,
That on their mockery and cruel spite,
The eyes of millions would henceforth be turned,
With reprehension grave.   Not helplessly
Relinquished to their will was Christ, nor thrown,

By force of circumstance within their power;
Love moved His heart; victim indeed was He,
Yet not with earthly weapons He contends;
Swords, staves, the dagger, battle-axe, and spear,
These were but coarse, rude implements to break
The stubborn will. Unarmed, yet fully armed,
And all caparisoned our Champion was,
In His celestial mail; salvation's helm,
With shield impervious of omnipotence,
And sword two-edged of an all-conquering love;
Triumphant Victim, Conqueror though conquered.
Not with coarse violence, reason's despite,
Would He, as they were wont, dishonour men;
Nor count them jungle beasts to be subdued
By force, the errant will to be regained
By the disabling of its fleshly shrine.
Passion He meets with reason's placid force,
Error with truth, and brute ferocity
With gentleness that shames the modesty
Of rational intelligence. Nor curse,
Nor malediction dire, nor thunderbolts
Are His artillery 'gainst His cruel foes,
Deluded ignorant men, but sighs, and tears
Compassionate, and friendly words, and prayers.
From point to point the daring sinners fly,
Yet love pursues, and where iniquity,
Wrought to the height of passion's turbulence,
Threatened with menace loud, o'erpassing love
Checked its advances with a mightier force;
Like as the surges of the wasteful flood,
Threatening with gaping billows to engulf

Th' imperilled shore, yet calmly break to rest
Upon the sunny beach of yielding sand.
  O pitiless jest! unconscious irony
That mocking mocked itself, mocked man e'en set
In highest state. Enthroned in merriment,
Arrayed in sport, was He, with laughter hailed,
And served with mock alacrity, deemed king
Of some faint shadowy realm of frenzied thought;
Yet King of Kings, in very truth, by right
Unchallenged, save by puny rebel man;
The King upon whose brow might justly rest
The crown of heaven, and whose all-mastering hand
Might grasp the sceptre of the universe;
Yet, as a Galilean bandit haled,
Red-handed in his crime, poor fanatic,
Or maniac from the tombs, mocked, set at naught,
To be the plaything of the hour, the butt,
And target of their ignorance and crime;
As vilest slave of commonest rights denied.
Supreme dishonour of heaven's majesty,
And ineffaceable; insult whose sting
Might justly rankle in the eternal breast!
  Yet calmer reason holds the mockery
Ill-placed, the subject wrong. The thorn-crowned
    King,
Exalted, wears sublimity undreamed,
And rising from the visionary realms,
The cloudy grandeurs of the past, still reigns;
Allegiance from the living present claims,
And happy loyalty. Not majesty
Divine they mock, but earthly majesty.

Misplaced derision! for on earthly state
They pour the vials of their bitter scorn.
For what is earthly pomp but as the gleam
And restless ripple of the summer fields,
Or glitter on the ever-moving waves?
And what its grandeur but the baseless dream
The short-lived fancies of the fickle hour;
All unsubstantial as the summer clouds
That ride the noonday sky in silent pomp,
And melt before the gazer's eye, nor leave
Nor speck nor stain to tell they once had been?
Death mocks the mightiest king; from out his hand,
Pithless, the sceptre falls, though sown with pearls,
Crusted with rubies, or with diamonds lit.
The crown of earth's most famous monarchy,
Is but a crown of thorns set thickly round
With harassing fears, ambitions, doubts, or cares
That gall and vex, not for a few brief hours,
As on the morning of that tragic day,
But for a lifetime. Mightiest of names
Linger in human chronicles awhile;
Their greatness dropped, then comes oblivion's hush,
And tired fame gives o'er her weary charge.
Soon fades the conqueror's palm; the laurel wreath
Droops ere the day of victory is done;
Chaplets of flowers though dripping all with dew,
Die in their smiles, and on the fainting wind
Soon languishes the loud Hosanna. Earth
Provides not for immortal victory.
Like dying echoes of a distant surge,
All former greatness breaks upon our shores

Passing away, and all the pageantry,
The pride and pomp of man glide from the view.
  Across the wreck of nineteen centuries,
The loyal subjects of the thorn-crowned King
See regal chairs o'erset, proud dynasties
Once potent as divinity, brought low;
Yet hail Christ monarch still. Pilate departs,
Though by centurions hedged and conquering spears.
Eagles and fasces, lictor, prætor all,
All disappear, and the imperial Cæsar,
Buttressed in all solidity of power
And portliness of fame, himself has gone!
No more Rome's galleys lash with servile oars
The Mediterranean foam, nor merchant fleets
Laden with orient wealth, crowd on the wind.
The imperial realm in all its stateliness
Has vanished like a thin and airy dream,
While this, our thorn-crowned King, though crowned
    in scorn,
Reigns still: His sceptre of weak reed has proved
Earth's mightiest sceptre; His derided power
An ever-widening sway, beneficent.
Millions to Him their glad allegiance own,
And hail Him, as they throng the road to death,
Ready to die for Christ their Conqueror!
  Yet find we in this sad pathetic scene
A meaning new. Crowned with His diadem
Of cruel thorns, bedewed with sweat of blood,
Our second Adam bears th' original curse
Of Paradise; His diadem of woe
Tells of vicarious pangs. Amid the thorns

No jewel gleamed, but the red drops of blood,
More precious than the costliest gems that hide
In dusky India's breast, or deck the brows
Of royalty, or beauty in its pride,
Were the rich jewels of our monarch's crown!
His pains are ours. There stood the accepted King,
Accepted in rejection, set at naught,
Yet welcomed King supreme of human grief.

   Now on Thy pilgrimage of love, O Christ,
Steadfast Thou sett'st Thyself; nor can the crowds,
With their fierce cries demanding instant death,
Nor treachery, nor cruelty, nor hate,
Fiendish and causeless, daunt Thy firm resolve.
Steep was the path to death, death in its last
Most terrible aspect, intensified
By pain extreme, embittered by the woes
From which men shrink, unreasoning violence,
Exposure, ignominy, bitterest sense
That stings the soul, injustice armed with hate ;
Nor may we know what pangs awaited Thee
Within the gates of death ; hatred tenfold
From spiritual foes unseen by human eye,
Malice unclogged, and by consentient flesh
Inert, unhampered, wrought by hopelessness
To desperation, and the fierce revenge
That finds the only respite from its woe
In plunging others in the depths of pain.

   The sentence is gone forth ; now art Thou doomed,
O Christ, to die! and wicked men would lay
By their free act upon Thy righteous soul
Death as a punishment, binding round Thee

The self-same chains, galling humanity,
Thou cam'st to break. Hell moves to marshal Thee,
And urge Thee on the road to bitter death.
   Wash thou thy hands, O Roman governor,
Protest with thy white lips and faltering tongue,
Then do the ill thou dread'st! Mock king art thou,
The bruisèd reed befits thy palsied hand
As sceptre ; for thine abject weakness gives
This life most precious to the dogs of death.
Blind victim, thou, who the All-Just could yield,
And with Him sacrifice thy manliness,
Honour, and truth, for tenure of high place,
Present convenience, miserable self-ease.
   Through narrow crowded streets to Calvary
Sets the procession forth. Brief time had passed,
A short four days, since welcoming crowds had met,
And hailed with loud hosannas their new King,
Whom now they lead to death. With stalwart tread
The Roman soldiers hedge their victim round,
Clearing the path, that the condemned may pass.
Last ignominy! for the Holy One
A murderer was preferred, and now with Him,
The soul of purity, of truth, of love,
Are linked two malefactors doomed to death.
Around His path the perjured, and the false,
The cruel scribe, and leering Pharisee,
Exulted in their cheap revenge of death.
There too were women, tearful in their love
And faithful tenderness, timid disciples,
Who by the sweetness, wisdom, gravity
Of the rejected Teacher had been drawn,

As by attraction irresistible,
To indulge in loftier hopes. Bearing His cross,
The Saviour staggering bends. Slow, dreadful hours
Of agony, the scourging and the blows,
Bitter contention, sleeplessness, had sapped
His physical strength. Another bears the cross.
Out through the gate they pass to Calvary,
Name of sad import, but hence consecrate
'Mid earth's most sacred places by the blood
That bought the soul. The hour at length has come,
The crisis of the world's great history,
Climax and topmost peak of centuried time,
Which, like the gilded cross that gleams aloft,
Capping the spire of some cathedral old,
High in the windy air 'mid drifting clouds,
O'er battlement and pinnacle and tower,
And kneeling worshippers and white-robed priests,
Echoes of prayer and blended song of praise,
Pre-eminent stands. Sprung of the past, the fruit
And outcome of precedent years, yet quick
To influence approaching centuries,
Keystone of time's great arch, stands Calvary's hour,
The Saviour's crowning hour of sacrifice.

Be dumb, ye echoes, tell it not abroad,
What sounds then smote the ear, as cruel hands
The hammer swung; thou universal light,
Reveal not to the gaze the tragic scene
When the Lord's tabernacle of the flesh
Was by the gusts of human passion rent
And fiendish hate, and prostrate laid in death.
Now lift your cross, ye cruel-handed men,

THE MORNING SONG.

Expose your pitiful deed, ere the swift night,
Haste anguish-stricken from her ebon cave
To shroud the form convulsed, the awful face,
Of our dear Lord.   O cross of agony!
Symbol of infinite compassion, love
Untold, how dost thou rise above the waves,
Stormy and dark of life's tempestuous sea,
The beacon of the soul, safety to show!
    Now is the stress, the tension dread of pain,
Now is the crucial hour, when on the soul
Of Christ is laid man's sin; and now He speaks,
Pathetical, not from sunlighted ease,
And peaceful circumstance, direction, choice,
And satisfaction deep, but when, if e'er
His thoughts might justly be engrossed with self,
Without rebuke, when outraged and betrayed,
With insults bitter the indignant soul
Might refuge find in silence, or invoke
A just revenge; life's tide was at its full;
Torn was His back; fresh from the cincturing thorns
His bleeding brows, and all His bodily powers
Not in dim twilight lulled of dreaming death,
But quick with resolute force, armed to resist
The mortal foe.   The crimson stream leaped forth
From envious wounds, new-trenched, river of life,
Purgation of the soul.   Sublimely calm,
With absolute forgetfulness of self,
Christ looked upon the faces of His foes.
Thoughts had He then for others, none for self;
No flaming eye, denunciation fierce,
Nor passionate outburst, sorrowful lament,

But pity's lingering glance, and gentle words
For these misguided creatures who would make
Iniquity their friend, evil their good.
O passing glimpse of tenderness divine!
Discovered by the violence of man,
As the spring storm that tears the russet sheath
Shows the hid flower. The love of Christ shines forth
Fair as the moon among the rifted clouds
Of midnight storm, calm in the tumult, fixed
Amidst the hurrying and unquiet rack.
Behold the Intercessor, Spokesman, Friend
Even of the worst! But a few hours before
With His disciples in the upper room
He stood, taught His great sacrament, and prayed
For those His friends. Though racked with agony,
His interceding voice the silence breaks,
Talking in darkness, as th' advantage swift
He seized to pray for these His cruel foes.
With unrelenting hate as hounds of death,
Had they pursued, had seized their innocent prey,
And in the darkness of death's threshold stood
With purpose fell to cast Him forth, and shut
Upon that life of pure benevolence
The iron gates. Lives there henceforth a heart
That can despair of mercy? Sin had reached
Its tide's full height, and all its savage waves
Engulfing this fair promise of the world,
Bright hope, and high ennoblement of man,
Rose in their wrath to culminating height,
And clapped their hands as by fierce tempest driven,
Dashing with hellish fury round the cross,

As if they would submerge this miracle
Of heavenly love, until man's quickening hopes
Into the pulseless and original gloom
Relapse of dark despair. Who dared to touch
With sacrilegious hand the ark that shrined
Glory ineffable ; who held supine
The sacred form, or who the hammer swung,
Or pierced with cruel nails the sacred palms
Of those most blessed hands, or who the cross
Uplifted with its throbbing load, we know not :
Yet this we know, Christ had forgiven them all,
And for their pardon prayed with dying breath.
O love divine, that like the setting sun
That breaks the cloud-bank of departing storm,
To tell a glad to-morrow, thy bright beams
Irradiated these most tragic scenes !

Thy thoughts, O Christ, fled from the noisy hour
Shouts, maledictions, gibes, and looks of hate,
And agonising spasm, and burning thirst,
And weary weight of woe, to Paradise,
Garden of God, whose cool and peaceful shades,
Fragrant retreats, allured th' escaping soul
To fly for sanctuary ; yet Thou wouldst not stay ;
Back to Thy cruel cross Thou camest, to him
Thy fellow-sufferer, hanging by Thy side,
Respite to bring to the rejected man,
All broken in his misery, who looked
With last imploring glance to Thee for help ;
Nor looked in vain : for soon Thy gentle voice,
Assurance gave that Thou wert strong to save,
And, e'en in dying, that Thou couldst unlock

The gates of Paradise, ingress to give
To this Thy late returning penitent.
   The day wore on till noon ; such noon had ne'er
Possessed the mid-day throne, since Egypt shook
In terror 'neath her sable pall, nor will,
Till in the peopled heavens the sign appear
To tell the Judge has come.   Night veiled the land,
Shrouding Siloam's glen, Hinnom's dread gorge,
Sepulchral Tophet, and the wooded slopes
Of Olivet, where stood, watching afar,
A group of Christ's disciples; the wide scene,
Temple and palace, pinnacle and tower,
The rocky bastions and the shadowy hills,
Faded and sank, till Calvary's cross lay hid,
Buried in gloom.   Hushed now the ribald cries,
The execrations deep ; awe-struck the crowd ;
And for a while the mocking tongues forgot
The moveless Sufferer, as deep darkness fell
Of premature night, starless and blank ; night reigned
Unbroken, save perchance when lightnings gleamed
With momentary shudder through the gloom.
For three long hours of mortal agony
Thus Nature cloaked the anguish of her Lord.
Silent He hung.   Here would I stay, my Lord,
Here by Thy cross in woeful sorrow stand,
And here lament Thy pangs unspeakable ;
Or, in the stillness, listening to the sigh,
The agonised moan, or feeble groan that told
The conflict sore within ; and here protest
With all the energy of this poor heart,

Craving, if e'er, for power of utterance,
Against earth's deep dishonour of her Lord.
   Here would I fill the echoes with my plaint,
And bid them through the changing years arraign
Those felon hands that wrought Him this despite.
No exigence of state called for His blood ;
Nor criminal and forfeited life was His.
The fair presentment of that holy life
Their malice had misread ; through coming time
Astonishment shall grow at this foul deed.
Holy Christ's life had been, beneficent,
And full of the divinest tenderness.
Eyes was He to the blind, feet to the lame,
Protector of the helpless, and of all
The friendless, friend. Not in the tawdry robes
Of earthly fame, the meretricious dress
Of thin veiled selfishness was He arrayed ;
In purity austere, unsullied worth.
Wisely and modestly through life's rough path
He bore Himself, gentle and affable,
Yet with majestic loyalty to truth.
Whom had He wronged, defrauded, or oppressed,
Or whom unjustly treated? When He spoke
His words were as a spring, a living stream
Pure as the mountain brook, wisdom unmixed,
Truth's winnowed grain, not mingled with the dust,
But for the furrow fit, the quickening cause
Of all that dignifies humanity,
Of happiness prolific, hope and love.
The truth He taught, not hesitatingly
As human teachers, but with certainty,

Unfaltering assurance, gravity,
And sweetness, as ne'er dropped from human lips.
　Bring forth, ye cruel scribes, ye craven priests,
And hireling guards, bring forth His deep affront.
Why smote ye Him, so noble and so true ?
The shadow of an accusation bring,
Smallest offence that in the well-poised scale
Of absolute justice calls for punishment.
Yet Him most perfect, gentle, tender, wise,
The innocent, the noble, and the good,
Unparalleled Son of earth and excellence,
Fair flower of man, of teeming millions chief,
Him truculent hands assail, Him they degrade,
For Him prefer a robber, through a path
Of coarsest violence and shame pursue :
Him with the mocking finger they deride,
Spit in His face and strike upon the mouth,
Blindfold and buffet Him in hellish sport,
Pluck from His beard the hair, and with the scourge
Furrow His sacred back ; with thorns they tear
His brow, they bind His hands, and, as the worst,
The vilest of our race, doom Him to death.
　There hung in pain, the Sufferer sublime,
Hung silent as the tomb. What thoughts possessed
His dying hour, what agonies extreme
When steadfastly confronting man's last foe,
Mortals know not. Mayhap around His head,
Thorn-crowned, swept in obscure and midnight gloom
Legions of hell, permitted thus to vex
His parting moments with their vengeful spleen.
No angel forms, as in Gethsemane,

Upheld His weary head, or to His lips,
Parched with death's fever, gave the cooling draught.
Left with His foes to wrestle till the last,
Who sought to drive Him from His purpose fixed;
For with His slight volition all were changed,
And all resistance would before Him melt,
And this dread scene, with all its horror clothed,
Into the rapturous glories of the skies
Would straight dissolve. Christ's love, all-conquering love,
That laughed at death, upbore Him as He trod
The billows dark and reached the farther shore.
  Six hours the Sufferer hung, in darkness three;
Beneath the pall that o'er the city lay
Cowered the multitude; some to their homes
Repaired, and to the temple some, as now
Drew near the hour of evening sacrifice,
And in the sacred fane the golden lamps
Shed their soft lustre on the frighted throng.
Now from that noblest altar, Calvary,
With darkness curtaining the crosses three,
By glancing lightnings shown, came the strange cry,
God had forsaken His expiring Son.
Mysterious utterance! Our sins had wrought
Their worst, had brought their utter bitterness,
And sense of God's estrangement had produced
In the God-Man, unlocking those close links
Of intimate complacency divine.
And now from depth to awful depth He sank
Of pains vicarious in death's dread abyss.
The worst was passed. To His parched lips that cried,

Moved with compassion, or mayhap awe-struck
By preternatural gloom, one to His lips
The sponge of wine upheld. And now returned
The natural light, as o'er His awful face
Drifted th' eclipse of death. He with last breath
Commends His spirit to His Father's hands,
Exclaims, "'Tis finished;" bows His head, and dies.
   'Twas at the hour, when, in the temple courts,
The low faint bleat of dying lamb was heard
That Christ, extended on the cross, expired ;
And, as His all-atoning life went forth,
From its rent tabernacle, wondering eyes
Awe-struck, beheld the temple veil down rent
By hand unseen, displaying to all eyes
The holiest with its golden mercy-seat,
Fit emblem of the yet auguster fact
That th' expiring Christ had passed within
The veil, the Holiest of the universe,
Making our earth the vestibule of heaven ;
And through triumphant love a living way
Opening from this poor anxious sorrowing life
To everlasting blessedness. Stone cold
Upon the tree of death the Saviour hangs,
Yet the great sacrifice completed stands,
And the dead Christ bears off the key of life.
   Now is thy hour of victory, O death!
Now reignest thou! Awhile upon the cross
The sacred form, pallid in death, now hangs,
The trophy of the victory of sin,
Till friendly hands remove. Hot tears of love
Beweep the sad descent. Full reverently,

As well becomes the corporal shrine where dwelt
God manifest in flesh, now humbled low,
Forth from His blessed hands the nails they draw,
And feet once busy on love's embassage.
His five poor bleeding wounds they wrap from view,
And veil His awful face from common eyes.
Bear Him full tenderly, ye loving ones!
Him whom we love; who loved us all to death;
For us bedew His form with tears, and kiss
His wounded feet. O Head, crowned in disdain,
O marble brow, with crimson lines deep-seamed.
Thorn-rent and scarred, sublime, severe in death,
Thou gazest through the past, O face divine,
With pitiful reproach that breaks the heart,
And in the breast of all thy faithful stirs
Deep reprehension, tender sympathy,
Sense of humiliation that Heaven's Lord
Should suffer such untold indignities.

   The stormy evening light withdrawing smote
Athwart the three dread crosses as in wrath,
Hasting to curtain o'er earth's darkest deed,
And close its darkest day with deepest night.
With scant procession to the grave they bore
Our Master; but with obsequies unmeet.
With what funereal honours, sable pomp
Shalt Thou, O Christ, be borne unto Thy grave?
If angels made the midnight sky resound
With their glad songs t' escort Thee to our earth,
Round Thy poor manger bed to stand attent
At Thy first sleep, shall not the darkening eve
Usher through eastern portals, draped in gloom,

White bands of angels issuing thence, to troop
Beneath night's cresset fires, in shadowy pomp,
Following their Lord in sorrow to His tomb?
Earth but a meagre ceremonial yields,
Scant retinue. Yet centuries unfold,
And as each passing year renews the tale,
Nay, each revolving hour, the sorrowful path
That from the cross conducted to Christ's grave,
Wants not for mourners, but is thronged in thought
With His redeemed, who tenderly bewail
The deep dishonour of their Master's death.
　Now in Thy grave at length to rest, O Christ,
Thou'rt borne. The haven of repose is reached.
Without Thy rocky bulwarks malice, hate,
Wrought like tempestuous waves. In death's deep calm,
Far from the tumult Thou art now removed.
Tears for man's woes Thou hadst, O merciful!
For Thine own sorrows none. Led as a lamb
Unmurmuringly, Thou gavest Thy murderers
Thy life that they might live. Before the storm
Like some tall mountain pine before the gale,
Meekly Thou bowed'st. Thy sword omnipotent
Slept undisturbed, though provocation oft
Tempted revenge. O soul of tenderness!
And love compassionate, Thou kindly wise,
Full were Thy hands of gifts, Thy heart of love;
Beneficent Thy life; Thy cruel death
A mystery was of mercy fathomless!
Shame on man's shameful recompense of love,
Ingratitude abhorred, rebellion foul,
Unnatural, sprung from hell's nether depths,

And by Satanic enmity inflamed.
Anear Thy tomb the grateful heart would mourn,
And tenderly recall Thy excellence.
One loving hand in life broke o'er Thy head
The precious unguent mingled with sad tears,
Of gratitude unspeakable the pledge;
So, as Thou liest within Thy rocky tomb,
Hushed in the silence of the last dread sleep,
The generations of Thy people haste
Fondly to watch around their slumbering Lord.
  Christ's tomb was in a garden. Pleasing thought
It was of antique piety to strip
Death of its aspect terrible, and place
In scenes most fair and grateful to the sense,
Th' expectant grave. Some in the mountain gorge,
Laid their loved dead, 'mid cloudy solitudes,
Or cliff deep scarped, with niches honeycombed,
Or, sepulchred in flame, gave to the winds
In airy vapours, while the scanty dust,
Immortal, was inurned by sorrowing love;
Millions of dead, forgotten, slumber yet
In unctuous churchyard clay, o'ergorged and rank,
Fretted with nettles, desolate, o'ergrown,
Round which the swirling tides of anxious life
Beat ceaselessly; in ocean's solitude;
Or quivering waste of burning desert sand;
These in seclusion sweet. Where slept at noon
Umbrageous cedars sweeping low around
Dependent boughs that drooped with resinous shade,
Or where the citron shook fragrant perfumes
With songs of birds and soft melodious lapse,

Or surly hush of streams in bosoming woods
Where roses clustered, camphire, spikenard sweet,
Or fragrant reeds and spices, born of the sun,
In bark, or dropping gum, or quivering leaves,
From whose invisible censers wandered forth
Wafts of refreshing fragrance on the air,
Upon the languid breeze in alleys dim ;
Or where flecked sunlight slept on golden grass ;
Through interlocking boughs the grave was found ;
The shadow in the sunshine, death in life.
   No sky is there so blue but clouds deface,
No calm so absolute but storms will rise,
No scene so fair but change will drape with gloom ;
Noon wears to night, and through the rifted clouds
The silver-handed morn night's curtains ope,
Fair day will dawn ; adversity is ne'er
So near at hand as when the heart unmoved
Rests in contentment with its purpose gained.
Amid the garden's pleasures lay the grave ;
Was it to sweeten death, or balance life
With needed seriousness ? Or, since man fell
In Eden's garden, lingered there a hope,
But half concealed, that through the tomb's dark gate
The soul again might pass, recover yet,
When death's dread sentence had been undergone,
Favour divine, and through the open gate
Unchallenged entrance find to Paradise ?
   O tyranny of death ! Enigma dread
Plaguing our mortal brain, ambition's leash,
Blank night of thought that walls the eager mind,
Love's sorest penalty, of bright-eyed youth

The dreaded nightmare haunting every hour,
Thou spectre grim that hold'st persistently
Joy's precincts, and the steps of good intent
Persistent dogg'st; armed like the cherubim,
Barring the access to the tree of life,
Thy merciless sword stretching athwart our plans,
How cunningly devised, how well concealed,
Quick to derange; breathing with icy breath
O'er the piled blossoms of our blushing hopes,
'Tis as the nipping frost, bitter, severe,
That leaves but desolation in its track.
We eye askance death's iron sceptre, armed
Of dark necessity, and yield perforce.
  Like him who tills, with labour infinite,
Some desert patch, reclaimed, and, now abloom
With the fair promises of future good,
Where creep the secret irrigating streams,
Where droop rich clustering vines and later suns
Embrown the whispering corn; in one dread hour
The robber horde makes desolate; the sword
Garners the precious fruits of toil and makes
A dreary wilderness. Dumb as a cliff
That inaccessible towers to the heavens,
Death utters no reply, though oft invoked
With passionate adjuration; dread abyss!
And voiceless, peopled but with echoes faint
Of human earnestness. No glimmering light
Arrests the wistful gaze that longing peers
Into the blank expanse. Necessity
Mysterious, man's inexorable doom!
Wert thou but life's long night, whose sleep profound

THE SONG OF LOVE'S TRIUMPH.

The firm-gripped muscle would relax, would smooth
Deep-furrowed brows by long endurance set,
Pour into troubled souls, grieving, perplexed,
The balm of ease, composing wearied limbs.
Fain would we welcome thee, O fearful death,
And thy repose; at evening wait thy call,
And, drowsy with life's day, yet hope to find
Within thine ebon cave soft-breathing peace,
The unbroken stillness of eternity;
Peaceful retirement in thy dreamless sleep,
Though in that long last sleep should never come
Revisitings from this brief fevered life,
Th' embrace of love, the kiss of children's lips,
And all the beauty of this changing world,
With free command of these dear powers of life.
Ah! menace of corruption's fingers dark,
Pollution foul, humiliation dread!
Dismemberment and dissipation e'en
Of man's original componental parts,
And doom of irreversible decay;
These meet our gaze, with apprehension fill
The questioning mind, fearing the total check,
Arraigned by conscience, grim apparitor,
To meet the future with life's great account
Unready, and uncertain what awaits;
The merciful construction of the life,
At best imperfect, or th' exaction hard;
Justice unjust! the uttermost farthing wrenched
From beggared nature by an austere judge.
Perplexed and apprehensive, doubtful, sad,
Man broods upon the mystery of death.

Sore burdened, wishing that he ne'er had borne
Life's heavy load, trudging the weary years;
That never had his conscious being emerged
From the deep primal quiet of the past,
To limp thus painfully life's sharded road.
Bereaved affection gazing o'er the sea
Where her most cherished treasures lie engulfed,
Pathetically cries, "Give back my dead;
Restore, devouring ocean, those once loved
Too tenderly, lent for too brief a time."
Nought but the inarticulate surge replies,
That ceaseless breaks upon th' eternal shore.

    O shadowy realm of dread all-powerful death,
Covering our earth, yea e'en to distant worlds
Extending far, thy vastness checks our thought,
Thy far-extending puissance appals
The sentient mind. The world is one vast grave.
The pyramids amid the desert sands;
Barrows beneath the thyme; rock chambers scooped
Near ruined cities, up whose marble steps
Lions now slink; or, silent catacombs
'Neath thronging cities' crowds; or, forests dark,
Where twisted boughs in dewy solitudes
Embrace mossed capitals, or, mouldering stones
That once proclaimed the sleeper's final bed,
His name, his title, his renown perchance
All perished, swallowed in oblivion's maw;
Or, 'neath the surging elms and cawing rooks
Of quiet village churchyards, thorn-bound graves,
With flowers bedecked, and words of sweetest trust;
Or, in the ocean's vast sarcophagus,

Where passionate winds and sad complaining waves
Chant requiems o'er forgotten myriads,
The dead lie sepulchred, and sleep their sleep,
No sound to break, no trouble to disturb,
The grand and holy silence of the dead.
  Vast are the catacombs of dust, the world
Whence Nature brings her elements resolved
And purified by death. Sleep's portals twain
Of weariness and strength, find counterpart
In this domain immense. Through mists, thick rains,
And sallow shattered leaves, stripped from their boughs,
We to thy postern stoop, low-browed, so low
That hope scarce dares to pass. The gate of life
Beyond uprises stately, fair. Low dawns,
And tender skies, and twittering birds, and flowers
Bid welcome to the early travellers.
Who can compute life's cyclings numberless,
Comminglings, periods of rest, who tell
The mazy dance of atoms, or what time
Th' informing spark of life begins to burn,
Or the essential spirit gathers round
Its cunningly-devised environment,
Organic tissues of this solid frame?
In the vast storehouse of the dust e'er lie
Unnumbered particles, inert, that wait
The imperious word of all-consuming life.
Urned in deep silence, yet the scanty dust
Condition of responsibility
Becomes to man, and burden sore of ills,
Under whose weary load he groans and sweats.
Freighted with life, like Charon's boat, the dust

s

Ferries man over to eternity
With its momentous dooms : too weakly deemed
As insignificant that builds up life,
Masters man's arrogance, how towering e'er,
And lying nearest to the hand of God.
   Material forms change ceaselessly, and yield
To love and hope scarce foothold, though despair
With her twin sister sorrow firmly tread.
In death's grand exodus spirits return
To God the giver, central Fount of life,
And final resting-place ; matter remains,
Sweeps its low arc, its declination finds
Its nadir in humility of dust,
Ambition's grave, mockery of human pride,
And solemn hiding of God's power. Frail man!
Discrowned, dishonoured, dust! Whether beneath
The clouds and free winds of our English hills,
Or smoky torchlight by swart Arabs flashed
In dark Egyptian pyramids, or where
Lamps perfumed throw their golden light around
Over the Escurial's marble glories dim :
To dust returned ! O bed of weariness,
Sleep's consummation, labour's ultimate sum ;
The strength of metals and the shock of war,
Fierce harvest sun, and stubborn glebe, and pith
Of corrugated oak, tire but the clay ;
And this, released from the commanding will,
Durance, and servitude of tireless life,
Inactive rests. How choice the treasures love
Has in the dust irrevocably lost!
Sweet faces vanished in the dusk of death,
The golden locks of children, bright-eyed grace,

Fair shapes of comeliness, vermilion cheeks,
Soft tinctured with the ruddy hues of health ;
Strength, manhood's pride, and beauty, woman's charm,
Familiar presentments fondly clasped,
All vanished, as the clouds of crimson dawn.
Leagued with the slower fires of sun, wind, rain,
Jealous, omnivorous time, have thither passed
The spoils of art and architectural pomp ;
Marble façades, and snowy minarets,
Spires, cupolas, and pinnacles that fret
The emulating clouds, and battlements,
Bastion, and fortress, by stern hand of war
Up-piled, and palaces magnificent,
Slowly have passed. The mouldering capital,
Pillar, with architrave, or pediment,
Of all the splendour of the past remain.
For nature's dissipating powers have seized
And scattered far upon the empty winds,
And restless waves, the pomp of centuries.
Sternest equality bids pride of blood
Its ancestry deduce, not from the page
Heraldic, cobwebbed vaults, cathedral crypts ;
These later links, but archives more remote,
The winds and waves of pre-diluvial times.

 The great Alcides by Mount Tænarus
Found access to the regions of the dead ;
With unassisted force dragged the cursed hound,
Reluctant Cerberus. Nor force alone,
But love, though fabulous, has dared t' invade
The silence and the mystery of death.
Orpheus bereft sought his Eurydice.

Sorrow awakening to its sweetest strains
His wistful lyre, till lurid Phlegethon
Checked its drear waves, and rugged Pluto wept ;
While from her trembling hands, Proserpina
Let fall her yet unfinished cypress wreath,
Narcissus, maiden hair, woven for her lord ;
The plaintive song of pining human love,
Subduing iron breasts, made death relent.
    The generations not unwillingly
Their graceful fables kept ; and unsubdued
Saw in the awful pyre the golden gates
Of immortality ; yet nobler hopes
Of nobler deeds begotten, claim the thoughts ;
Not visionary, sprung of sick desire,
Faint images projected on the sky,
By hope engendered, but more firmly based
On fact historical, record divine ;
No vague and shadowy myth of ancient days
Dim antique fable of the morning mists,
And golden dawn of man's generic life.
Thy name, O Christ, name above every name,
We celebrate.   Led by all-conquering love
Thou didst invade the tomb ; the Breaker, Thou,
Of death's dark battlements, a living way
And portal to the temple of the skies,
Thou gav'st to man ; Thyself the Conqueror,
Thyself the way ! To win Thine own from death,
Thy Church beloved, stooping Thou didst disrobe,
And in mortality's poor gear Thyself
Array ; bowing Thy sovereign head to die,
Thou in th' invisible didst claim Thine own.

Though faint and fainter in Thy dying pains
Upon the cross, Thy voice at length was lost
To mortal ears. Yet when the Sabbath dawned
Above the silence of the garden tomb,
First Sabbath of the dead, Hades had heard
Those silvery accents sweet, wondering to hear!
What hopes were wakened in the chastened breasts
Once disobedient, stands not revealed.
Nothing in vain Thou dost; too good to mock
The irrevocably damned with mercy feigned,
To hold a shadowy chalice to the lips
Of those beyond the reach of pitying love.

 High converse with the blest in Paradise,
On that most glorious Sabbath, when Thou dwell'dst
'Mid their exultant company, Thou hadst;
The prophets that with rapt seraphic fire
Told of Thine advent, hailing Thy glad day;
The long array of priests whose spotless robes,
Sprinkled with blood, told Thy redemptive work,
In holy function, sacrificial act;
The countless multitude of faithful souls,
Who meekly resting in the promises
Of grace assistant, strength, and peace, and rest,
Had dove-like nestled in the Saviour's breast.
Rapturous the welcome of Salvation's King,
Bearing the pledge of resurrection life,
To these His loved ones. By His side there stood
Th' ignoble one, last loved, on Calvary,
Just found, the dying thief compassionated,
Plucked from the burning by Christ's power in death,
Last trophy of the might of conquering love.

Now is He welcomed, His blest presence hailed,
By dearest names invoked, new risen sun,
Adding new splendour to the balmy light
Of Paradise, and to the ravished hearts
Of His redeemed, seeming as heaven begun.
    Meanwhile, upon earth's distant noisy shore,
And meretricious stage of pompous show,
Masked piety, anointed violence,
And empty ceremonial, yet of sin,
Alas, too real, disastrous in effect,
The guilty actors had withdrawn, and now
Stand dressed in other garb. Blood on their heads,
In the rash moment of their mad revenge,
Had they invoked, guilt ineffaceable,
Blood of the holiest that unpurged would draw
Vengeance in weltering floods upon their race.
The sated mob, slunk to obscurity,
'Shamed of their deadly work. The priests of God,
Of God in name, but ministers of hell,
Victims and dupes of Satan's power led on
To heinous deeds of sin, though cloaked with good,
Now robed in priestly dress approach the shrine,
The altar of the outraged Deity.
Dread mockery, profanity untold!
To approach the fount of justice absolute,
With fat of lambs, and unctuous smoke that climbed,
Blotting the heavens, and innocent victims' blood,
With due formality of priestly act,
Yet guilty of the darkest, foulest crime.
How must the sacred blood on Calvary's height,
Yet crimsoning the earth, have louder cried

Than Abel's, each accusing drop full-voiced
In protestations from th' ensanguined ground.
The winds that sighing swept, the rocks that rent,
The empty graves yielding their sheeted dead,
With this most solid universal earth,
Would find a tongue in their dumb mouths to arraign
The wickedness of man. The sacred corse,
Plain evidence, too plain, of sin's fell work,
Lying extended in the dewy gloom,
Mutely invoked stern justice to impeach
Before God's bar, the murderers of truth,
Of gentle pity, spotless innocence,
True manliness, and all too tender love.
Blood on the priestly vestments, blood that cried,
Blood on the priestly hands, not purgative,
But damnatory; on the shield of Rome
The blood, a blot whose tarnish would remain
Unhidden by her glories yet to be,
Splendour of victory, or laurels proud
Of the world-empire in its conquering might.
    Nature resumed her sway full peacefully,
Her troubles passed. As paralysed with dread
To see her agonised and dying Lord,
With darkness had she shrouded Him. The night,
Jealous, from nether caves had sprung to hide
And shroud from common view, from mocking eyes,
The awful tragedy, shrank to its realm;
Nor blot remained, nor lingering brooding shade,
Nor quivering spasm in rocky flank of earth.
Back flowed the light, and in its wonted course
The stream of things created onward flowed.

Now second evening came, and duskily
Shrouded the guilty city. Broad and calm
O'er Olivet, once more the Paschal moon
Silvering the olive groves, shone bright and full,
Edging with light, hill-tops and parapets,
And swelling domes, high battlements and towers,
The silent temple, or the querulous stream
Of glistening Kedron, mourning as it flowed
Past sad Gethsemane. A deeper hush
O'er the secluded garden now prevailed,
That brooded with its world of mystery,
Eternal burden of unuttered woe.
Before His tomb, His royal bed of death,
Where from redemptive labour Christ reposed,
Second creation, making of a world,
And second Sabbath kept, by jealousy
And fear fast sealed, firm locked, paced to and fro
The Roman sentinel, holding his watch ;
And as the hours of midnight now drew on,
Till the third dawn the Prisoner had named
When living, as His resurrection time,
Strictly their guard they kept. All through the night,
With deepening silence, as the vast concave
Wheeling with stars innumerable swept round,
As if heaven's host their funeral torches held
Round night's great catafalque, honouring their Lord.
All night ; nor rustling leaf, nor stir of bird
Nocturnal 'mid the dewy trees, footfall,
Nor early cock-crow on the morning air,
Unnoticed passed. Ears had they for such sounds
But none for th' angelic footfalls light,

Of the celestial guards who drew anear
The visible bourn, attendant on their Lord,
And all unseen by mortal eye approached,
Since now He rested from redemption's task,
Watching the Sleeper, if mayhap to note
The first faint tremor of returning life
Thrill through the shrouded form, the covered face;
To hail the first far-darting beams of life
Shooting athwart the darkness of the tomb,
To celebrate His power who came to snatch
From envious death, and claim the mournful gage,
The trophy of an all-enduring love,
And sad memorial of His passion; pledge
Of everlasting union with man,
His wounded clay! by mediatorial power
A second incarnation to assume.

O great High Priest, whose loins were girt with love,
Whose flaming eyes outshone the lightning's gleam,
And burning feet seemed as the fiery brass;
None saw the lifted veil, none heard Thy voice,
As sound of many waters, when Thou gav'st
Thy salutation to our sin-struck earth,
When from the Holiest Thou cam'st to bless
And seek Thine own. In Bethlehem's crowded inn,
Thy first faint cry of human feebleness
Was heard, and in Thy virgin mother's arms
Thine infant form was laid, for thy first sleep.

No mortal eye saw now the cerements burst,
Secret, as when at th' Almighty word,
The pulse of life within the slumbering earth
Begins to stir, and in ten thousand spires,

Of emerald velvet of the budding woods,
Or blossoms blushing as the cheek of youth,
Nature arising from her wintry tomb
Renews her beauty.   Thus, all secretly,
The Saviour rose, thus silently assumed
His outraged clay.   In mockery of man,
Who as with vaporous clouds had sought to quench
The sun, and with the dewy-beaded cobwebs
To bind the lusty morn, rising, Christ passed
The rocky barrier of the tomb.   To Him
As ineffectual shadows were the stone,
The seal, the guard with intercepting spears.
The stony portals and the rampart dense
Of living rock faded as vapours touched
By the new-risen sun.   The dusk of dawn
Was on His face.   The earthquake was His herald;
With tremulous pangs as apprehending wrath,
Shivered the coward earth to know Him nigh.
The stone was roll'd away; the sentinels
Lay as if dead, while through the open gate,
And blackness of the tomb, a radiance gleamed,
While snowy angels hovered round the scene.

  In the gray morn the faithful women come,
First visitants, disciples these, with one
Whom gratitude had brought in loving haste,
To anoint Him, dead, whom living she had loved,
Forgiven much ; nor terrified by death,
The quaking dawn, deserted garden paths,
Nor ghostly silence of that garden tomb,
The hour unmeet, unguarded company,
Love bore its light and in that light they walked.

Upon the mournful crucifixion eve,
Sitting apart, these noted where the Lord
Was laid, and watched the place, despite the guard.
Bearing their fragrant spices to anoint
Their buried Master, down the dewy paths
They went confidingly, with loving speech;
Anear the sepulchre troubled they stand,
Perplexed, not knowing to remove the stone
That blocked the tomb. O feebleness of faith!
Thrice had the Saviour plainly prophesied
His resurrection; e'en the time was named,
The third eventful day. How had their grief,
Tempestuous wrought, submerged the argosy
Of this so glorious hope; yet, desolate,
From memory's ocean depths how plucked they not
The pearl of so great promise to redeem
Bitter bereavement? Offerings for the dead
Crowded their hands, unguents and sweet perfumes;
No glimmering hope, offspring of faith remained.
Him dead, irrevocably dead they deemed,
Bewept, immured; to the voracious past
Resigned, the shadowy bourn, th' abyss dreaded
Of pitiful love. Had they but hoped to greet
Their risen King, according to His word,
Joy scarce had tarried till the laggard dawn,
Should bring its incense from the glowing east,
Ere swift of foot to meet Him had they fled;
There in the star-lit vestibule of night
Impatiently to tarry with their gifts,
Eager to welcome their returning Lord.
   So fared the women. Having reached their goal,

Astonishment befell them. From the tomb
Was rolled away the stone, and on it sat
An angel clad in garments white like snow;
His face as lightning shone. From angel lips
The glad intelligence at first was given
To man of the Redeemer's birth : and now
From angel lips the glad assurance comes,
The Saviour lives! and from death's caverns deep,
Loosening the grave-clothes, through the open gates
Comes to revisit earth. O glorious news!
Floating like some proud banner on the air,
Perpetual message, pledge of victory,
As rose, for generations yet unborn,
The full-orbed gospel of redeeming love.

  Now dawned immortal day; now as each year
Slowly revolves in festival of spring,
Emerging from her wintry tomb, fresh-clad
In beauty Nature comes to hail her Lord
Triumphantly returning from the dead;
All strewn with flowers His path, a tenderer blue
The sky assumes; and on the fragrant air
Ten thousand blossoms pour their innocent lives.
The sun fresh brightness wears, his virgin lamp
New trimmed, as summoned by the midnight cry
To meet the Bridegroom, come to claim His Bride.
Life stirs, throbbing and pulsing through the maze
Of things created; nature's tide 's aflow,
Ocean of wealth and beauty, with glad waves
Lifting their voices multitudinous.
O glorious festival! O spring-time fair!
For ever consecrated to the hope,

Thrice-blessed hope of immortality.
Nature and grace combine to bring the world
This new evangel of Christ's victory
O'er death, man's sullen and relentless foe.
Now through the temple of the universe,
These outer courts, dim, distant, smitten with sin,
Welcomes resound hailing the King returned,
Once dead, but now alive for evermore.
   Break into singing, O ye blossoming fields,
That glistening in your dews with freshness shine,
Filling the balmy hours with odorous joy ;
Lift up your voices, O ye woods and groves,
Ye meadows green and echoing woodlands dim,
And carolling birds, and gently whispering winds,
And glistening streams with your melodious flow ;
Thou vault of blue to the crisped ocean give
Echoes redoubled, let the messenger wind
Glad burden carry to earth's distant shores ;
O feeble heart, fly forth, though feeble winged,
Sing thy surprise, sing of thy risen Lord,
Rise to the greatness of the lofty theme,
Joining the world's great anthem of delight.
Heaven's music blesses earth ; now through the aisle
Of centuries long drawn, receding fast,
Christ's Holy Church, His chosen Bride, exults,
Robed in the righteousness immaculate
Of her dear Lord, lifts the immortal song,
Full-cadenced, sweet, as ocean's deep-voiced waves,
Pure adoration, gratitude, and love :
   " Thee we adore, O Christ, Redeemer Thou,
Incarnate Love, twice-born on earth, yet now

Immortal in the energy divine
Of mediatorial power, acknowledged Head
Of the whole family in heaven and earth!
To slender faith, unbalanced yet to mount
Th' empyrean of celestial love,
Cowering 'mid visible things with broken wing,
Thee, in Thy mystery of humility,
Too slow are we to hail, bemused, perplexed,
Beclouded, blinded with excessive light;
True man, of very manhood perfected
By suffering, till the veiled divinity
Blended in truest sympathy with man.
This was Thy gospel confident, and this
Thy pledge, when pointing to Thy tomb Thou bad'st
Man watch the bursting of the bands of death.
Thy tomb of living rock close sentinelled
Withdrew its jealous bolts at Thy command,
And to the vast pretensions of Thy life,
Crowned with the grand pretensions of Thy death,
Gave absolute assurance. From Thy tomb
Forth stepp'st Thou, Conqueror, upon this earth,
Sin-ruined, and Thy victory achieved,
Betokened by no desolations wide,
And miserable circumstance of war,
Cities in smoking ruins, homes of men
Blackened and roofless in the pitiless wind,
Fields wasted, vines uptorn and trampled corn.
The battlefield's dread agonies, the cry
Of brave men in their anguish, the appeal
Of sobbing orphans, or of widowed love,
Not these the adjuncts of Thy victory.

With man's dread foes Thy might omnipotent
Was measured, sin, all-prevalent death, Satan
Th' usurper old ; these felt the might, these bowed
Before the sceptre of our conquering King!
Ride on in power, O Mighty One, ride on,
Take to Thyself the kingdom Thou hast won
All worthily! Forth issuing from the grave,
Forth from the dreaded grave by man abhorred,
As through the gate of immortality,
Come Thy redeemed ; no lingering taint of death,
Nor trace of ashy paleness on the face,
Nor apprehensive fear, paralysis
Of will, but sunshine there, and light of love
Immortal. Mighty host, ten thousand times
Ten thousand told, and thousands numberless,
Washed in Thy blood, O Lamb of God, and clad
In robes of everlasting righteousness
Purchased by Thee, these follow in Thy train,
And to heaven's golden gates turn joyful steps.

" But chiefly Thee we praise ; and glad accept
Salvation's pledge, Thy grand and perfect work.
With faint and dying lips Thou didst declare
Thy task was finished. Finish'd the array,
The preparation slow and full detail
Of truth revealed ; faint shadows acted oft
Unconsciously, dumb picturings of truth,
Yet making known with sweet simplicity
The great transaction of vicarious love ;
Complete Thy work, complete Thy sacrifice ;
Then, in humility sublime, Thou bowed'st
Thy sacred Head, hanging in pallid death.

Three days of silence passed, no voice proclaimed
Thy sacrifice accepted; now Thou com'st
Through the rent veil, Jesus, our great High Priest!
Thyself the Apostle of new life and love.
Our grisly foe, Thy minion death, withdraws
The sable curtains of the tomb and shows
The world its great Redeemer, now no more
To die. Thy coming forth in trumpet tones
Proclaims the sanction of almighty love.
Unhindered, now we claim the priceless boon
Accruing from Thy blood; now unabashed,
Gaze on heaven's sunlit battlements, nor deem
The upward path as inaccessible.
Ours the deliverance, Thine the bitter pain;
The spotlessness oft craved brought nigh by Thee,
And priceless benefits of grace divine.
  "Salvation's King! our blest Redeemer hail!
Forth from the secret silent tomb Thou com'st,
The firstfruits of the dead, the promise fair
Of harvest yet to be, when from the dust
Thy quickening word will call the sleepers forth.
Our life is bound in Thine, in Thee we died,
And rising, rise with Thee, Great Federal Head.
Death brandishes in vain o'er Thy redeemed
His pointless spear; his terrors are no more,
His menace vain, for Thou, O Conqueror,
Hast captive led captivity, and robbed
The spoiler of his spoils, making our foe
Our bondman, and Thy tributary slave!"

BOOK THE EIGHTH

THE SONG OF THE MILITANT HOST

THE ARGUMENT.

The Alps — March of the nations — Rome's zenith — The catacombs and their inhabitants — Life of the persecuted — The pangs of martyrdom — English village church — Peaceful Sabbath described — Thoughts of trials of early confessors and martyrs — The Coliseum — The Christian martyrs — Night on the arena — Address to martyrs — Their glorious testimony — Persecution in vain — Inroads of heresy — The pacific march of Christ's Church — Influence of Christianity on art, laws, manners — The Bible — Rise of crusading enterprise — Motive pure — The going forth of the host — Failure of the enterprise — Knightly orders — Chivalry — Missionary effort — The Master's command — Rise of the new philosophy — Each country has its heroes — Modern effort — Ultimate triumph.

BOOK THE EIGHTH.

THE SONG OF THE MILITANT HOST.

GLITTERING Alpine peaks that climb
   the heavens,
Piercing the azure with your snowy cliffs,
Titanic battlements of living rock ;
Or, somewhile seen, as apparitions faint,
Startling and shadowy, as that once ye died
And passed into your state of endless rest ;
Saintly, removed, ye seem, and on the point
To vanish as I gaze ; the purple hills
Crouch round your throne sublime ; the misty vales,
Where wandering echoes of the avalanche,
Or diapason of the thunder's roar
Prolonged, is heard, recede in silent gloom ;
The notched and fringing pines with sweeping boughs
'Gainst the pure ermine of perpetual snow,
Or mounded clouds, or the cerulean sky,
Stand forth distinct : a peace sabbatical
Breathes in the air and broods upon the lake,

That slumbers, like a nether sky, below,
And fills your ancient solitudes, removed
Far from the turmoil of man's busy world.
Ye have a sanctity, ye sunlit peaks,
A majesty and power to elevate
The soul, to stir within us noblest thoughts,
Whispering ambitions worthy of our race.
Withdrawn in your proud loneliness, your voice,
Silent withal, yet penetrates the soul.
Crowned are ye with your icy diadems,
And caped with snow; round your imperial thrones
The bloom of distance like a purple robe
Is flung, across whose amplitude, the storm
Retreating, weaves its jewelled rainbow hues.
The glorious pine-woods with their myriad spires,
Sky-pointing, clothe your nether slopes, sheer cliffs,
Gray-lined, precipitous, and jagged rocks,
With emerald patches where the sunlight sleeps;
Yours the majestic movements of the clouds,
That in the mid air form before the eyes,
And drifting upwards trail their rustling skirts,
Or in procession march and countermarch
Till the breeze casts them as a filmy veil
Over the landscape; with consentient voice
Of God ye speak, of that primeval day
Of sounding darkness, when the Almighty Hand,
Moving with plastic energy divine,
Framed this great world with all its ordered parts;
When the vast natural powers, now slumbering leashed,
Slipping their bands, tore continents in twain,
Upheaved those mighty bastions, and the depths

Of these low vales delved with the glacier's plough ;
Of God, who built your fastnesses, ye speak,
Who, still upholding earth's majestic frame,
Pillars its strength, and binds its myriad links,
Breathes in its life, and in its beauty smiles,
Rears your vast forms, beneath the awful sky
Your frozen solitudes outspreads, snow-wastes,
Hushed in deep silence, where the eagle's scream
Disturbs the loneliness, regions of clouds,
Of brooding mists, and ever-restless winds,
And desolation of the dreadful prime.
Of God ye speak, with voices eloquent,
Whose echoes find their echoes in our breast,
Prompting the homage due to One so great,
Reverence, and deep humility, and trust,
That in the shadow of His greatness rests,
With absolute submission and content :
Him ye proclaim as chief, who, justly chief,
Holds the pre-eminence, and your high theme
Fills the live echoes with the truth sublime.

   Yet have ye too a voice full eloquent
Of man, amid his mutability,
Immovable ; of confidence ye speak,
And duty, aspirations sprung of truth ;
Of the yet loftier path, that mounts above
Your towering peaks, a path the eagle knows not,
Nor the vulture scans, which wisdom treads.
To us, O lofty and aspiring heights,
To us the informing spark, kinship divine,
August, and daily made more intimate
With Him who made you, and whose sovereign love

Called us in being, and for us, this frame
Of universal things existence gave,
With its fair garniture. His love enshrined
In our mortality, frail walls of dust,
Is the sublimest fact in man, the life
Of life, of love the love, guerdon and crown,
Firing th' ambition that with gaze unblenched
Mounts to the zenith on its pinions bold,
Seeking the favour of th' Omnipotent.

Yet once more, O ye snow-clad witnesses!
I bid ye testify, as well ye may,
Of that exalted, conquering, spirit in man
That dwarfs your vastness, and our pettiness
Redeems. Frail as the moth that flickers o'er
Your pasture flowers, or, for a moment brief,
Lights on the rock to spread its painted wings,
Then flutters on,—man seems. Before your thrones,
Have passed the generations in their pomp,
Like the slow march of evening's golden clouds.
And ye have seen the outcome ultimate
Of slowly-working principles in life
That baffle nearer scrutiny. Man's pomp,
His majesty, and far-resounding fame
Passed like an echo on the passing wind.
Perchance have come t' invade your Sabbath calm,
Cries manifold of human agony,
Ambition foiled, and disappointment sore,
And tyranny that drives to bitterest ends
Its victims, war's alarms, and vengeful cries
Blown on the wind, the litany of woe,
Or when in fateful moments stalked abroad

The demon persecution, as from hell
Sent on dread mission, when your grassy slopes
Were dabbled with the blood of innocence,
And flames shot through the crackling roofs of homes
Made desolate: from your snow-shrouded heights
That look o'er Leman's wave, Waldensian vales,
Or northward, where the broad and willowed Rhine,
Amidst its islands, shines in evening's sun,
Like to a river of heaven, Alsatian heights,
And Taunus faintly blue, skirted with vines,
Dark forests, peopled towns, and ample streams
Of Germany, where stalwart nations clasped
The truth of God; or, southward o'er the plains
Of Italy, and her historic fields,
Have ye not seen amid the centuries
The onward march of Christ's great militant host?
Have ye not seen the exalted spirit rise,
That treads beneath its feet death and its pains?
Have ye not seen the testimony given
From flaming piles, arenas, scaffolds red,
That counts truth paramount, and stands prepared
To die in attestations of its claims?
Like to the gloom of doubt, e'en as I muse,
The night has fallen, hiding you from gaze;
A pall of darkness covers this fair scene;
But from behind your peaks, the lightning's flash
With instantaneous blaze opens the night,
Reveals your shrouded forms, and forth ye stand,
Majestic in your awful grandeur shown;
While down the echoing colonnade of night
The long reverberating thunder rolls,

As if ye uttered in a voice sublime
Your attestation grand : " We testify ! "
   Had but Thy love, O Christ, been quenched in death
No exequies our sadness could show forth,
The bitterness extreme of such dread loss
And sore bereavement ; to serener skies
Thou mountedst by Thy blue aerial paths,
And reign'st invisible ; loved by Thy Church,
Thou lovest, and over all her destinies
Presiding, watchest with a jealous care.
Lingering on earth Thy love incarnated
Itself in those Thou lov'dst, in faithful breasts ;
Not from the dull inaction of the tomb,
The shackles of the tyranny of death,
Alone Thou winnest us : to our cold hearts
Thou teachest nobler, more enduring hopes ;
Called from earth's clinging damps, chill airs, low skies,
And fluttering autumn leaves, and hopes divine,
Thy Church, pure bride, dowered with Thy tenderness,
Must care for those to whom Thy love went forth,
Perpetual witness of the love divine.
   Rome now had reached the full meridian height,
The zenith of her power ; victorious,
Her arms had borne her proud triumphant name
From the parched deserts of the torrid south,
Northwards, to where Arcturus' chilly ray
Burned high above the Hercynian forests' gloom ;
From stormy islands in the western main
To Parthia. Empress of nations, throned
By lordly Tiber, the proud city rose
Magnificent, with temples, palaces,

Imperial mansions, columned porticoes,
Proud amphitheatres, worthy the realm.
Philosophy, had reached its manhood's prime,
And, with unfaltering voice, sought or to teach
Submission to th' inevitable stroke,
Or, with Epicurus, swiftly to seize
Th' immediate pleasures of the passing hour,
Envious of fate; to this the balance turned,
And luxury, that nicely crops the flower
And yet the thorn avoids, that wins the crown
And top of joy, present delight, made life
Indulgence, and the worthier powers obscured
With fumes of grosser pleasures, darkening hope.
Mansions of marble ceiled with fretted gold,
Ivory and cedar, light of precious gems,
And Seric robes woven in Coan looms,
Banquets with crowns of roses, unguents rare,
Massic, Setinum, and Falernian wines,
Obsequious slaves in stately retinue,
All that could minister to pomp and pride
Crowded life's day, till merciful death stepped in,
And closed the wearied pleasure-seeker's eyes:
Forth was he borne through the Capenian gate,
There proudly urned in marble sepulchre,
Silent companion of the historic dead,
The great Metelli, or the Scipios,
Or the Servilian house, or, where outspread
The Appian way, grim avenue of tombs,
That with its solemn marge curbed Rome's bright stream
Of varied life; chariots with prancing steeds,

The laurell'd cohort decked with glistening arms ;
The criminal by lictors led to die ;
The merchant, with his bales of silks and spice,
Fresh from the Adrian waves, or sailors swart ;
The gilded litter of the rich and great ;
Beauty and youth with equipages gay ;
Or gangs of slaves all sweltering in the sun,
Brown-handed peasants, wine carts, jingling mules,
Passed and repassed from morn to crimson eve.
  Scorned, disallowed, beneath the busy feet
Of all these thronging crowds, a people dwelt
That shrank from view in gloomy catacomb,
And subterranean vaults, a living grave,
Poor fugitives, 'mid darkness, hunger, fear,
And deprivation of life's chief delights,
Spending their days, bereft of home, love, friends,
Ease, good opinions, pleasant intercourse
With their compeers, worldly advancement, wealth,—
There cherishing in poverty and gloom
Sublimest hopes, confessing purest faith.
Strange fugitives ! Strange hiding-place for truth,
Destined for wide diffusion, future rule
Among the nations, foremost place to assume.
Between th' unthinking, powerful upper world,
Unconscious of the subtle influence,
The shadowy fingers that would mould the fate
Of the imperial realm, and those who crouched
Beneath their feet, antagonism had sprung ;
The armèd hand of Rome was 'gainst them turned.
Proud ignorance that would not deign to learn
Was theirs, injustice, source of cruelty

Prolific, and inveterate prejudice.
Affronted by the calm exclusiveness
Of this new creed, that silently dismissed
The august pantheon of the national faith,
Jove of the Capitol, Saturn, and Mars,
Bacchus with vine leaves crowned, and Terminus,
Lemures, lares of the sacred hearth,
As but mere dreams, a rabble crowd, unreal,
Mere baseless fancies sprung from mythic lore,
How reverenced, or by customary faith
Held venerable; resentment in them sprung.
Yet with a loftier philosophy
That in its ethic purpose, high intent,
O'erpassed man's dreams, Stoic, or Academic,
Socratic, Cynic, or the Italic sect,
These fanatics taught that to one Deity,
Supreme and only God, pure Spirit, of life
Th' essential life, Observer unobserved,
Omnipotent, was human fealty due :
That other worship was but mockery,
Or worse, dishonour to the King Supreme.
Though silently advanced, such tenets roused
Deepest resentment, unrelenting hate,
That sought full soon expression. None had seen
An altar that the Christian sect had reared,
Nor in their temples found image, nor shrine,
Statue, objective form. Hence rose the cry,
And accusation fierce of atheism :
And they who most had sought the rule supreme
T' acknowledge and t' obey, must now perforce
Confront a charge wounding their inmost souls.

Slander's envenomed tooth poisoned their fame.
Some recreants by torture driven, or fear,
Assailed their reputation with reports
Of immorality; slaves who had joined
In Christian worship, apprehending not
The sacramental mysteries, falsely told
Of Thyestæan feasts at midnight hour;
That, at their banquet dread of human flesh,
Was given to each a cup of human blood.
Maligned, treated as outcasts of their race,
And enemies of man, they shrank from view,
While holding forth as their apology
A blameless, pure, and heavenly-minded life.

There, at the midnight hour, when overhead
The city's busy crowds were hushed to rest,
Gathered a trembling few, gathered in fear,
Where the dark tunnel ways converging formed
Rude subterranean chapel, consecrate
By faith and bolder love, where timorous art
Not yet had ventured, there Christ's faithful few
Listened, as by the ruddy torch's light,
Their minister read from the sacred scrolls.
Then thought they of their dear and martyred Lord;
Thought of the crown to faith triumphant given,
And the bright world that lay behind the walls
Of sullen death, its liberty and peace,
Its gardens fair, and never-fading day,
With brightened eyes; and oft the whispered prayer
Arose for patience and confirming grace.
Oft as they sang their sacramental hymn
In tones subdued, with rapt uplifted face,

Resting their souls in confidence on God,
The persecutor's footfall smote the ear;
Then scattered they in darkness; soon was left
Silent and dark their oratory rude.
Not always thus the murderer's sword was balked :
Surprised, rudely dispersed, the wounded fled,
In dark and distant passages to die :
Thence borne by reverent hands to their last bed,
Hollowed from out the subterranean rock,
There, 'mid the faithful, were they sepulchred.
On their cold lips the kiss of peace was laid ;
Spices were piled within the narrow grave,
And, with the prayers of Christ's Church militant,
The sainted dust was to its slumber left,
Till the last trump shall call the dead. Thus grew,
As persecution's sickle reaped Christ's fields,
The martyred host. Upon the coffining rock
Were carved once cherished names, and laurel wreaths,
Rude crowns, emblems, and sacred monograms,
Mutely to tell of a yet nobler fame
Than that snatched from earth's noisy battle-fields.
  O death, thou sleep of peace! haven of rest,
With Thee these tempest-tossed and shattered barks
Have refuge found. Time's long and heavy night
Not yet has passed, fraught with disastrous deeds,
Events that shake the nations. O'er the heads
Of these calm sleepers have the tides of war
Swept and reswept with their destructive force :
Proud dynasties, legions invincible,
With glancing arms and fluttering pennons gay,
Hedging the mightiest thrones, have passed as dreams,

A silent unsubstantial pageant filed
Along death's dusty road; fierce battle-cries,
The tramp of armies, and the clash of war
Disturbed them not. Not yet the Lord has come;
And we, who dwell upon the golden edge
And margin of the dawn, are one with these
In the rich promise of the coming morn.
  The pangs victorious of Thy servants claim,
O Lord, my song: glories of martyrdom
Exalted strains demand, and loftier fire.
Countless Thy martyrs stand, true witnesses;
The sword, the axe, the consecrated cross,
Wild ocean waves, or hungry flames for them
No terrors bore: despite their violence,
A way they found through sorrow to the stars,
Gladly exchanging man's unreasoning hate
For the perpetual guerdon of Thy smile.
The voice of song has stirred the human heart
To rapture at the call of love, and struck
From harp-strings their divinest melodies.
Not of angelic symmetry of form,
Of coral blushing cheek, or tangled tress,
Tender low tones, and gentle blandishments,
But of sublimer passion, highest love,
Compulsive of man's energies I tell,
The upward drawing through this perilous world
Of hearts, smitten by love, rendering their all.
O Heavenly Bridegroom! bid us hear awhile
The awful music of triumphant souls,
Who, o'er the weakness of humanity
Uprose, mastering their agonies extreme.

Brave servants of our God! a happier lot
Has fallen on us in these the latter days,
Though one with you in love to our dear Lord.
Cradled in Christian homes from earliest years
Nourished in holy faith, parental care
Guided our infant thoughts till holy things,
Ere conscious knowledge of this life had dawned,
Familiar grown, another nature seemed.
The Christian faith ye held comes to our age
Not banned, proscribed, or illegitimate,
But national, august, most venerable,
Renowned, and richest heirloom of the past,
With all the highest glories of our land
Linked indissolubly. In our calm days,
When persecution seems a faint far dream,
Not easily we comprehend the stress
That on you lay in the rude days of old.
We sit at ease, not shrinking in the gloom
Of dreary catacomb, but, unrebuked,
Professing the dear faith for which ye died:
Yet must we think of you, O faithful ones!

   The summer sunlight broods in holy calm
Broad o'er the land; the whispering summer breeze
Quivers with mellow peals of Sabbath bells,
Ringing from ivied towers, 'mid village elms,
O'er field and wood, from hill-slope, vales remote,
Where but the tinkle of the sheep-bell sounds,
In cawing quiet of the country morn;
Brown homesteads buried 'mid their orchard trees,
Around the village church: beloved fane!
Lichened and gray, made sacred by the hopes,

And prayers of generations, sorrows, fears,
In silent passage of soft-breathing time;
Abode of Sabbath calm, where in the noon
The blue fly buzzes in the Gothic pane;
The mottled sunlight on the chancel floor,
That quivers through the pictured windows dim,
At play, like a pulsation comes and goes,
Restless mosaic, as the uncertain wind
Tosses the churchyard trees. As in a dream,
Twitter of birds among the churchyard elms
Is heard, rustle of leaves, soft organ tones.
How grateful is the holy Sabbath calm!
How absolute the peace that broods around!
Here, from the fulness of our privilege
Of you, O holy wrestlers in the past,
We think, whose dedication absolute,
And stern resolve counted all loss for Christ,
And life's supreme concerns. Amid the wreck
Of centuries, Rome's Coliseum stands,
Magnificence of ruin, gaunt, sublime,
As if itself the martyrs' monument,
Abiding trophy of heroic faith,
Enthusiasm's divinely-kindled fires,
More glorious than the spirit that subdued
Barbaric nations, or upreared vast piles
Of architecture towering to the skies.
Where the owl hoots and the blue moonlight streams,
Thousands once sat. Once more, tier upon tier,
I see them rise, till where the awning's marge
Edges the dazzling blue. From topmost rank,
To basement crowded with unnumbered throngs,

Whose laugh and jest and loud hilarious talk
Fill up the pauses of their holiday.
A mighty, varied, ever-moving crowd,
With flash of jewels, gleam of colour, arms,
Streamers, and bannerets, and carpets gay,
Silk canopies, bright clothing, waving plumes,
The charms of beauty, all the pomp and pride
Of the great city were collected there
To see our brethren die. And ere the hour,
Bright eyes are to th' arena turned to watch
Where stalks the gladiator in his pride,
Wielding with brawny arm the gleaming blade;
Or retiarii with deadly mesh;
Or flash the glittering spokes of chariot wheels.
There, in the basement cells, Christ's faithful ones
Await the crucial hour. Torn from their homes,
Half-scared, and fainting, through the unfriendly streets
By rude hands borne, hither they came to die.
Them wife and child, parent and friend besought,
With bitterest tears their faith to abjure, and fill
Again their darkened homes with welcome light:
In vain. The passionate kiss, bitterer than death,
Love's last request refused, the pleading light
In love's fond tearful eyes, the last embrace,
Cleft their poor hearts in twain. The Master's voice
Bade them be faithful even unto death,
The death of martyrdom. Now they await
Th' unbarring of the door between whose chinks
Glimpses of terraced crowds are caught, and cries
Of combatants in mortal struggle heard;
And ever and anon the hoarse, low growl

Of hungry lions that with flaming eye,
Claw their imprisoning bars with fruitless rage.
Now in this hour of expectation dread,
The captives raise their manacled hands in prayer.
Th' upholding power of faith is realised
If ever, now. Once more within their reach
Dear life, and all that makes life dear, are brought ;
Sweet liberty, and home, and love's caress,
And children's kisses, friendship, and the round
Of dear familiar life once more are theirs,
For one short word, for one submissive sign,
That may imply denial of their Lord.
Faithful they stand. The bolt is backward shot ;
Hailed by the jeers of the vast concourse, come
The trembling captives, come to bear for Christ
Their attestation glorious. For a while
They stand, as from their pallid quivering lips
Escapes the prayer for grace, when now the roar
Is heard, the flashing eyes of lions seen,
Loosed from their den and bounding o'er the sand ;
Upward the glance confidingly is turned,
The soul by one deliberate act resigned :
The dizzy brain grows faint ; the strength gives way :
This visible frame of mortal things all fades ;
One moment brief of awful agony,
The crisis dread is past ; eternity
Dawns on the faithful and victorious soul,
And the bright crown of martyrdom is won !
　　　The lingering thought unwilling to depart,
Tarries around the place now consecrate,
What time the crowds retire, and the day dies.

The silent amphitheatre is left
To echoes vague. Evil has done its worst.
The blood-stained sand is strewn with holy dead;
Night falls, and overhead glimmer the stars;
Then, through the dusk, the light of lions' eyes
Is dimly seen, and lean and swaying flanks
Scarce visible, slip past on cushioned paws,
And prowl among the dead, or, couching near,
Keep their grim watch. Now is faith's testing hour.
No vengeful whispers, no angelic forms
Girt for reprisals come, or, o'er the slain,
Vigil to keep; but silence, vacancy,
The steadfast shining of the distant stars,
The dread neutrality of brooding night:
And to the wondering mind the query comes,
What profit in such death, ruin complete,
Self-abnegation; where the merit lies
Of martyrdom? Reason, that clings to sense,
Balked with the visible defeat, is checked;
But faith takes up the challenge, firm entrenched
Amid God's promises, and looks with joy
To the reception of the martyr's soul
'Mid heaven's felicities. O martyr love!
That, in sublime forgetfulness of self,
Mounts to the heaven like some majestic peak
Of Alpine snow, piercing the noontide blue;
O martyr faith! more glorious than the roar
Of mountain torrent, or swift avalanche,
Whose noonday voice sounds like the voice of death,
Or lightning red flushing the cloud's dark heart
Like to a blossoming flower: O martyr trust!

Sweet confidence in God, that safely rests
In God's omnipotence, like the blue lake,
That, cradled in the mountains, calm reflects
The giant bastions towering all around :
Earth has no loftier, no sublimer sight,
Than the free mounting of th' ecstatic soul,
Faithful to God and loyal to His truth,
That spurns the pleasures brief of life's short day,
And makes of earth the stepping-stone to heaven.
  To you, O martyrs and confessors true,
I turn, and hail you, on your heights sublime,
Great army of our God! Rough was the path,
And difficult, ye found, to follow Christ,
Climbing the lofty heights whence now ye look
On our dwarfed lives, and by your dying teach
How we should live, and, by your sacrifice,
Your loss supreme, enriching our brief life,
And consecrating earth. The agony
The shame were yours, the anguish of rent ties,
And dread abandonment of life's delights ;
Ours the great benefit. Yet, when once past,
The crucial hour of your dire sufferings,
Ye won your glorious crown. How firm your faith,
How deeply bastioned in the living rock,
Anchored immovable, that could resist
The onslaught of the storm, and, bear unscathed,
The thunderbolts of hell ! Truth realised
Was yours, not lightly held, remote, and faint ;
We, balanced in contentment, hesitate,
And with the truths that mould the present life,
And make the next maintain but commerce scant,

Resistance slight but make; suffering false shame,
That fears the approaching footstep as a foe.
We have your dungeons still, gray ancient towers,
Weed-grown and ruined where ye lay for Christ
In darkness, weakness, loneliness, and cold.
The bolts that shackled your brave limbs remain,
The chains that robbed you once of liberty.
We point our children to the spot where once
Your holy blood crimsoned the cruel earth :
An age mechanical, irreverent,
And cold of heart, a church by faction torn,
Forget the lessons ye once nobly taught,
And emphasised with death. Yet, not in vain,
Your agonies, O martyred ones, nor vain
Your constancy. A base philosophy
May, in the name of science, pauperise
The race, and human duty analyse
To what may seem material elements,
Reduce the choicest products of the heart
To chemical formulæ, may teach man's love
Man's highest aspirations to be vain
And evanescent as the hedge-rose bloom,
Man's life the casual result of force,
To be resolved at death to nothingness ;
Yet on the horizon of the past ye stand,
Protesting witnesses, at once for God,
And for the dignity of man. Your lives
Ye counted not as dear, for ye had found
Yet better things than life could give, how cloaked,
Caparisoned with circumstance of wealth ;
Not yours dumb yielding to necessity,

Cheap virtues of spent souls emasculate,
Temptation's force being spent. Beneath, your feet
Treading earth's choicest gifts, ye patient climbed
The heavenward path, whence now on us ye look,
Rebuke our ease, and our ambition fire :
Potent your great example will remain,
Till from the peopled heavens the Lord shall call
Angels and men, the living and the dead ;
Before whose presence He will recompense
Those who relinquished home for Him, or friends,
Or life. Till then, look from your lofty seats,
Inflame our zeal and animate our fight,
Till we with you are by the Saviour crowned.

In vain the attempt, measures extreme or harsh,
The endeavour vain to break the fixed resolve,
Or cramp the Church's growing energies.
For still the holy flame of quenchless love
O'erleaped the bounds restrictive of man's hate ;
And, like a smouldering fire among the woods,
Which, in the calm, scarce visible token gives
Of life, if down the steep ravine the wind
Sweep in its course, the slumbering spark is caught,
And soon the mountain-side is wrapped in flame :
So grew the Church, from hidden sources fed,
Her fervour quickened by the very breath
That threatened her destruction ; by the storm
Upheld, and upward borne to loftier heights.
The fury of the persecutor swept,
Vexing the Church ; and many a darkened home
'Mid the Calabrian hills, the terraced vines
And tawny harvest plains of Syria,

Or the Bithynian woods, mourned for its dead
Triumphantly. Ten times the storm burst forth
Nero, Domitian, Diocletian,
Or, higher names, Aurelius, Hadrian,
Sought to eradicate Christ's sacred vine,
Branding with an undying infamy
Their names, and, foiled, desisting from th' attempt.
   Scarce had the storm of persecution ceased,
Which in its pitiless fury raged around
The infant Church ; scarce from the opening clouds
Had beamed the sunshine of prosperity,
Than the divine simplicity of truth
Was jeopardised. The worm of heresy
Fretted the clusters of Christ's chosen vine,
Indifference sicklied the once vigorous life.
Stately basilicas enriched with gems,
With porphyry, lapis lazuli agleam,
Marble and gold arose ; the catacombs,
The caverns, moor, and mountain solitudes,
And subterranean chambers whence had shrunk
Christ's faithful from the world's unfriendly gaze,—
Were now exchanged in the full face of day,
For golden smiles of power. No more proscribed,
Outlawed, discredited, the Church came forth
To find prosperity more perilous
Than persecution's dark and baleful hour,
The summer sun more withering than the frost.
Quick-growing seeds of heresy within
Demanded from the Church a vigilance,
And an intenser form of loyalty,
Not in the external militant act expressed,

But in the patience and humility
That seeks for truth, nor from the search desists
Till found, accounting it more dear than life.
To them Christ left the treasure of the truth,
Sacred deposit to enrich the world,
With an undying, uncorrupting wealth.
As from the marsh the pestilential breath,
Born of corruption rank, mephitic air,
Poisoning the salutary wind, is borne,
And creeps by unsuspected avenues
Into the home of health, past the fresh flowers,
The blossoming trees, and over velvet sward,
There misery and weakness to implant,
And lingering death ; so in the fair domain
Of Christ's own Church rank heresies arose,
And with them brought the bitterness of sect,
And internecine hatred, cruelty,
Blindness that will not see, dull bigotry,
False generosity that in the name
Of peace, will barter fundamental truth,
And by concession, part with all most dear.
Full well the apostle on Miletus' shore
The Ephesian elders warned, and prophesied
That grievous wolves should ravage Christ's fair flock.
The slow unrolling of the centuries
But verified the words prophetical.
From heated conclave, 'mid contention sharp,
Or from seclusion of the wilderness,
Or rocky cell, calm, earnest voices came
Of those who, testifying to God's truth
In its divine simplicity, rebuked

The heretic. Ye champions of the faith!
Stout-hearted shepherds, who through densest night
Of ignorance and vice, repulsed the wolves
That would attack the flock ; how deep the debt
To you we owe! To us the heirloom comes
Untarnished in the passage of the years,
In value undiminished, powerful still
T' enrich, illuminate, and strengthen life.
   The grand pacific march of Christ's great host
Amidst the nations now arrests the thoughts,
No empty spectacle, dazzling the eye
With blood-stained chariot and ensanguined sword,
But with high influence to bend the mind,
To fructify, exalt, enrich man's life,
Conquering the heart. From porch, or learned grove,
Oft had gone forth the secret power of thought
To rule the world. From Galilee's sacred hill,
Or Salem's room, by Pentecostal fires
Once consecrate, spread nobler influence.
The Magian star, chief in the Eastern sky,
Told of new dawn, new day, beneficent.
For Christ hath put new dignity on man,
Hath honoured him, and opened to his view
The boundless prospect of eternity.
Now poverty its bitterness hath lost,
Since truest wealth lies within reach of all ;
Exalted to a higher range, the soul
Finds freer sky and an unhampered flight.
   The liberties of nations then were born
When Christ was born, and, travailed to the birth
Strong peoples, with their high heroic deeds.

Pandects and codes justiciary were thrilled
By Christ's humanity, as wintry earth
Feels the spring sun. The dove of heavenly peace
Lighted upon the sceptre, and earth's kings
Learned clemency, their delegated power
Accepting as vicegerents of heaven's King.
Christ's gentler spirit to the battlefield
Went forth, and, 'mid the crossed and clashing swords,
Taught mercy to the vanquished, fixed the reins
Within the jaws of hot imperious lust,
Marshalled sweet peace and industry t' achieve
Their victories. Children have since been loved
With a new tenderness, the orphan found
Protection, and the destitute relief;
Woman to her true place is lifted, friend,
Most dear companion, not the slave of man;
The sick hears of immortal health, the serf
Of higher liberty; the aged smile
With thought of endless youth, vigour regained;
The poor, the wretched, find in Christ their friend;
For He hath ta'en the poor man's place, and taught
His people, when to parchèd lips they gave
The cooling draught, the hungry fed, or clad
The naked, to the prisoner pity showed,
That He Himself was the poor destitute,
That He accepted all as done for Him.
Art felt the glow, and sprang to nobler life;
For, better taught, no more the chill of fate
Palsied the cunning hand, since now the sky
Of heavenly beauty glowed with heavenly love;
While that the sense of beauty to the heart

Found easy way, and the expanding hopes,
The aspirations of ecstatic souls,
Blossomed in noble architectural piles,
Cathedrals, minsters old, enriched by art.

    Now to mine inmost ear there come the strains
From myriad souls exultant, thousand thousands.
Ten thousand told, who, of the benefits
Of Christ have known, sweeter than all the strains
Of summer's anthem, quiv'ring wind and stream,
Whisper of piny woods, hush of plumed fields,
The blush and glow, the sunshine, and the song,
All the sweet sounds enshrined in summer's noon ;
The lyric of the lark, the wood-dove's coo,
And the low tones from distant thunder-clouds ;
All sweetness of all sweetest, noblest sounds ;
So rises the great anthem of Christ's Church,
From hearts unnumbered gladdened, and from homes
Where sorrow has been soothed, and grief assuaged,
The lonely visited, the helpless cheered,
Where peace that passes knowledge, and where love
Have like a river flowed, deep, constant, full.

    Shall we not love Thee, O Thou tender Heart,
That felt for all and filled our world with joy,
That taught so grand a lesson, and that gave,
In Thine own death, example so sublime!
The ages were Thy tilth, and all abloom
They stand, with promise of maturing grain,
As ripens the great purpose of the world.

    O Book of God! the light, the lamp of life,
No light have we but that which thou dost give ;
Instructor grave, whose unimpassioned voice

Sounds through the generations; happy they
Who, guided by thy beam, direct their steps;
On either hand pitfalls and snares abound,
And those most perilous but ill observed,
Or not at all, till thou dost show the path;
Fountain of wisdom, from whose living source
Come life's best things; O salutary stream,
Cool and refreshing to the thirsty soul,
Garden of God's redeemed, new Paradise,
Where blooms the tree of life yielding its fruit,
With many a promise sweet as morning flowers,
And steadfast as the stars of midnight's sky;
The chart art thou for us poor voyagers
On life's wide ocean, o'er whose trackless depths
None safely find their unassisted way;
The guide of nations, churches, families,
To be consulted oft and heeded well.
Wrong are we if thy voice proclaims us wrong,
Though all the world applaud, and flattering vaunt
Our goodness to the skies, and right are we
If thy calm voice assurance gives of right,
Though with consentient voice millions condemn.
Sublime amid the shiftings of the world,
'Midst its impurities immaculate,
Rising, as in the morning's stainless blue
The snowy mountain peak uprears itself
Majestical, thou standest unimpaired
Amid all mortal fluctuation fixed.

 But now, far other scenes invite. Christ's love,
Whose all constraining power in holiest breasts
Meetest expression found, moved other hearts

Sincere, yet often to excesses led,
And of Christ's precepts and example mild,
Forgetful. Thus the Master taught His kingdom
Not of this world; and hence the sword forbade.
  With slow and stealthy foot, though surely, pass
The centuries, weighted with all their woe,
Unutterable; and as the Church kept watch,
Expecting the return of her dear Lord,
Deep sleep crept o'er her energies. Faith died.
Then came to prominence the engrossing thought
Intolerable, that o'er the Land of Christ,
Ruled the proud Saracen; the land whose hills,
Mountains, and lakes, and plains, were but the shrine
Of the Redeemer's life : this sacred land
Was by the Paynim held, the foe of Christ ;
And those most holy spots, identified
For ever with the wondrous history,
Bethlehem's manger, sad Gethsemane,
Or Calvary robed in awful mystery,
The Holy Tomb, and Bethany, where last
The Saviour's wounded feet pressed earth's green sod,—
That this fair land down-trodden should remain
By pagans, were a thought insufferable.
As seeds beneath the earth long time remain
Ungerminate, until the April sun
With friendly warmth give resurrection note,
While soft spring rains seek out the loitering life,
And call it to the fragrant glimpse of day,
So among Christendom desire had lain,
Waiting the clarion summons, which at length,
Was heard from fanatic lips. From altar steps,

Road-side, and market cross, where men most throng,
The hermit's voice spoke forth its clear reveille;
And as the summons through the nations rang
Men stood attent to hear; quarrels were healed;
The pleasures of the banquet lost their charm;
Hushed was the voice of song, the din of trade;
Through thick monastic walls its challenge passed,
Down echoing cloisters, yellow-lichened, gray
With sunny turf, where slumberous piety
Made friends with death; unchallenged passed the moat,
Summoning to arms. Then the proud baron doffed
His hunting gear, and his jessed falcons left,
Led forth his dancing cavalcade to war
In knightly armour cased, pennon and plume,
And banneret and spear, stern pilgrims bound
For Holy Sepulchre. His gauntlet hand
Resting upon his charger's mailed flank,
The warrior turned to look his last farewell.
Even the throne felt the advancing wave,
E'en kings put off their robes of sovereignty,
Visored and fenced in steel, not loath t' exchange
The cares of government, the peaceful charge,
And shepherding of men, to face grim death,
In sieges, sallies, and the clang of arms,
The incidents and chances of the field.

From various lands slow gathered, now set forth
In pomp of glorious all-glittering war
This great adventure to redeem Christ's land.
Proud war-steeds champing restlessly the bit,
And pawing as impatient for the strife;
With silken gonfalons whose rich, soft folds

Of crusted gold, courted the noon-day sun,
Jewelled caparisons, and saddle-cloths,
Morion and cuirass, battle-axe and sword,
And crests with gems aflame, and waving plumes,
With shining mail, embossed and chased in gold,
And shields emblazoned with devices quaint,
Heraldic purple, crimson, blue, and white,
With flying dragons in gold arabesque,
Lions, and eagles, and the savage pard;
While from th' unnumbered spears the noonday sun
Flashed like the meadow grass when every spire
Is with a dewdrop as a diamond tipped.
So swept the tide of war, with roll of drums,
And clarions shrill, and trumpets' angry blare,
Uttering high challenge to the foes of Christ.
 Proud was the burden the smooth ocean bore,
As eastward steered the cross-distinguished fleet;
Dromon, and buss, and galleys numberless,
That stirred with vigorous oars the ocean foam,
Gaily adorned with streamers, pennons, arms,
And brightly painted shields around their prows,
Were blown before the wind in cloudy pomp.
 But when the wished-for strand at length was reached,
The holy soil of Palestine, with tears
And earnest adjurations to their task
Did they betake themselves. By day the host
Marched onwards, broad displaying in their van
The cross, the symbol of their dearest hope;
And when the evening came, and evening's sun
Kissed with its reddening beams their banners' gold,
Softly enfolding with its purple mists

The wearied host, a herald through the camp
Exclaimed, " Help for the Holy Sepulchre ! '
And warrior voices echoed the glad cry,
And warrior hands smote on the hauberk's mail,
As registering afresh their holiest vow.
   Too often led by motives secular,
Love of adventure, or the love of fame,
The military instinct that would seek
For perilous risk, and glory snatch from death ;
Or influenced by grovelling avarice ;
Unworthy of the symbol that they bore,
Yet were there those whom loftier motives ruled.
High sense of duty, born of knightly vows,
Nerved many an arm, and many a hero fired
To deeds heroical ; and, higher yet,
True piety inflamed by heavenly zeal,
Expression sought for gratitude and love.
Richard of England, Lion-hearted King,
Who danger sought, and by his prowess gained
Endless renown ; Godfrey of Bouillon,
Tancred, and Baldwin, and ten thousand more
Of Europe's knightliest train whose names are lost,
Went forth for Christ. The sad Selesian wave
Quench'd the bright zeal in closing o'er the head
Of Barbarossa, bravest of his race,
Who, with proud confidence, though smit with age,
In single combat would the conflict bear,
Challenging the Saracen : never had death
Veiled purer eyes, never its anodyne
Had borne to heart more sorrowful. From life,
Of gentle piety St. Louis went,

Unfitted as the dove to meet the hawk,
Yet ready, in the holy ransoming,
To lay down life. On Dorylæum's field,
Entrenched by Antioch, or 'neath the walls
Of Tyre, or sacred Salem, in the heat
Of conflict, in the battle's din, or worn
By hunger, or by deadly fever smit,
Whole armies perished, perished as in vain.
For though they gained Jerusalem, its king
Declined the regal title, and refused
To wear a crown where Christ had worn His thorns;
The prize was held but with a feeble grasp.
As if the Master had again declared
His kingdom not from hence, disaster came
Redoubling on disaster, as to show
How vain the attempt to check God's purposes
Retributive. Down-trodden must the land
Remain until the fulness of the Gentiles :
And powerless as the mist against the rock
Was man's attempt t' arrest the avenging Hand.
Foiled though in purpose, yet the cross-led hosts
Gave proof of their devotedness to Christ.
Bootless ambition and unworthy views,
Inadequate conceptions of the Church,
And of Christ's spiritual rule, led them astray,
Yet lavish in their high chivalric deeds,
Profuse were they in sacrifice of love.
   From failure of man's loftiest schemes oft springs
Undreamed success. Through unseen ways God leads,
By secret providence the o'erflowing stream
Of human energy to irrigate

Remoter fields.   Orders of knighthood rose,
And the chivalric spirit that inspired
Crusading enterprise enshrined itself
In other forms, tinged with romantic hues,
Yet of the essence of the Christian life,
Self-sacrifice, ambitious purity,
Romantic tenderness, that sought to shield
The innocent, the helpless to befriend.
   Defenders of the pilgrims on their march,
The Hospitallers held the van ; the rear
Knights Templars, and on many a hard-fought field
Their flag was borne, their war-cry raised " Beau
   Seaint!"
Displaying oft their prowess terrible
Sprung of pure motive, winning rightfully
The guerdon of success; nor faintest blur,
Film of suspicion o'er their purity
Was cast.   Christ's soldiers bore the blood-red cross
Upon their mantles white, and standard spear,
Bright oriflamme, that, in the thickest fray,
Rallied their energies.   Such were they once,
In the first prime and lustre of their fame,
Their purest era ; but an age ensued
Degenerate, when from their height sublime,
Lured by the love of power, or listless ease,
Or siren voice of the enchantress fame,
Or greedy avarice, the curse of wealth,
Swerving from their high ends to lower grooves,
Their strength was spent.   In the fair Cyprian isle,
With regal state, lodging in palaces,
Lived they full sumptuously.   But luxury,

Sure foe to all or good or great in man,
Sapped their proud superstructure secretly;
Malignant calumny, of envy born,
Poisoned their fame. With accusation foul
They stood impeached; falling in one short day
To the chill dungeon's ignominious shame.
The rack extorted from unwilling lips
What recantation often soon denied,
Protesting to the last their innocence.
Before the towers of Notre Dame, slow fires
Consumed the sufferers. 'Midst his agony,
Their leader cited with his dying breath
Clement the Pope, Philip the King to appear
At the supreme tribunal, whither both
Followed ere one short year had filled its round.

   Yet not with these died the chivalric fire.
But in an age deep sunk in ignorance,
By violence o'ermastered, in the gloom,
Where the prolific energy of vice
Festering in darkness its dread mischief wrought,
Amid corruptions foul, like some fair flower,
The Christ-like spirit rose, and justified
Its presence by its native loveliness.
Not yet had come the hour when men would deem
Themselves the waifs of chance, mere withered leaves,
Like straws, and stems, swept on the turbid stream,
Uncounted in the universal wealth.

   True witnesses were found that to the age
Spake in its language, bodied in the forms
Best comprehended by the passing day,
The imperishable truth, forms strange and quaint;

Much we might reprehend, yet breathing still
The spirit of honour, quick to countervail
The turbulence of power, rapacity,
That made of many a proud baronial hold
A den of thieves; high duty recognised;
God's claim supreme on man's allegiance;
Rebuke of luxury, and manlier aim
Than the poor pleasures of the passing day;
Pleasures removed above the reach of chance,
Perpetual, worthy of man's rational frame.
 Manhood had scarcely thrown its deepening shade
Of thought across th' unwrinkled brow of youth,
Ere came the call to bear the knightly sword,
And through the world to quit himself as man.
There, in the darkened chancel all the night,
In silence and humility, the youth,
Kept his lone vigil, at the altar's foot
Laid down the unbraced and dedicated sword;
In dark and lonesome meditation mused
Of death, of life, and of the loyalty
Supreme to duty, till the morning dawned;
Then girt him on his sword, the knightly vows
Accepted, and went forth professedly
Christ's soldier, to defend the true and right,
The weak to champion, and th' oppressed to free.
Each age its own peculiar character,
Its type of the religious life produced,
Prosaic or romantic, while beneath
Flowed the unvarying stream of heavenly love.
Lightly we deem, in this mechanic age,
The quaint romantic figures of the past,

And quick dismiss the chargers, challenges,
The nodding plumes, the gay and gallant deeds
Of chivalry, forgetful that the Lord
Works out by ways obscure His purposes,
Distributing to each particular age
His gifts, as to the individual life,
And surely working out His sovereign will.
  As when fair odorous morn dripping with dew,
E'en to its nether skirts, comes from night's tent
And dusky tabernacle, for its work
Accinct and consecrate; the sky's aglow
With fervid trembling light o'er the fresh world;
The blue lake smiles as if a nether sky;
The climbing pines that fringe th' aspiring hills
Shake from their tasselled boughs their fragrance sweet;
On rapid twinkling wing the birds sweep by;
The bees are working 'mid the clover bolls,
And peace her sabbath keeps on all the hills;
The land is peace; reviving, pure, the air;
The torrent's voice sounds hushed, far off, at times
Inaudible, then like a whisper faint
Heard in a dream; the glistening of the scythe
Comes from the dewy swathe, while on the wind
The sound of voices tells of human toil;
So, in sweet silence, furtive beauty, stole
Christ's day among the nations, when that Thou,
O Sun of Righteousness divine, didst mount
Earth's lower sky to dissipate our gloom;
Beneficent to visit this dark earth,
And with Thy genial light and friendly warmth
Give endless summer to the souls of men.

Chief 'mid the Lord's behests remained the charge
To be the heralds of the world's great King,
Ambassadors of God in distant lands,
To bear the message that the angels bore
To startled Bethlehem, of a Saviour's love,
The many-sided message for all time.
The new divine philosophy appeared,
Rising like some tall peak amid the clouds,
'Mid doubts that brood above the sea of life,
And, towering, darken the clear face of day :
Vague philosophic systems, theories,
The dance atomic of Epicurus,
That weird and awful dream, vortex of fate,
Sweep of eternal motion, iron rule
Of passionless inexorable force ;
Systems deduced with patience infinite,
But baseless as the cloud-wreaths of the dawn.
The flame which burnt within the heart now fired
Christ's missioners with high enthusiasm
To win the world for Him. On, like the tide,
Swept their unlettered earnestness ! North, South,
East, West, their message sped. The forest aisles
Rang with glad echoes in their piny glooms ;
And sea-washed islands of the western main,
Shrouded in stormy mists, heard of Christ's peace ;
Upon the darkness of the savage mind
Dawned heaven's new light ; and, at the voice of truth,
The dim dread visions of the night like shades
Lifted and vanished. Woden, Frega, Thor,
Like spectres shrank, and in the savage deeds
Of their deformity stood at rebuke.

THE SONG OF THE MILITANT HOST.

Southward and Eastward, where the quivering palm
Faints in the torrid ray, the Orient strange,
Prolific mother of fantastic dreams,
Magic, and charms, and necromantic arts,
Where, in the credulous and primal age,
Fable and myth, like tropic undergrowth,
Each other choked with their fertility,
The simple tale of love was borne; the seed
Sown 'midst the jungle and forgotten oft,
And fruitless, as it seemed, yet not in vain,
Was by a later harvest justified.

In the obedience of Thy Church to Thee,
Fain would I trace Thy Church's love, O Lord.
Thy parting charge was to evangelise
The nations, true crusade to win men's souls
For Thee, from the heart's citadel to drive
Th' usurper, yielding Thee Thy blood-bought throne.
High theme for song! If all the glittering host,
And mechanism dread of savage war,
Can stir the pulses of the slumbering lyre,
The changing fortunes of the deadly field,
The ambitious stratagem, the alarm, the attack,
The stout resistance, the severe repulse,
The cries of victory, and large results
Of peace, security, and widening fame;
Yet worthier is this enterprise sublime,
To win the world for Christ, man's highest good
To ensure, to advance the interests of truth,
And freedom give to the born thralls of vice.
The pomp of bannered legions and the blast
Of trumpet told not of their going forth:

Silent and undemonstrative, yet sure
Of the inherent power of that they bore,
The presence of their King, and victory.
 So went the gospel like the mountain stream
That from the glacier steals, dallying awhile,
Now torn by jutting rock, or flung in foam
Down th' abrupt, till rockier channel reached,
Internal eddies, boulders interplaced,
Will lash its turbulent, hoarse-sounding waves
As if to agony, until at length
The torment of the foam is lost to view
In the dim silent pines, where, reaching now
The plain, its fertilising waters in the sun
Glitter and shine like as if molten gold.
 Each country has its witnesses to tell
Of those who for their Lord toiled, suffered, died,
Taught in the majesty of Christ's great name.
In Libyan Kephro, Dionysius,
Or, in Iberia, by Mount Caucasus,
The captive Nunia, by the power of prayer,
Brought souls to Christ. The Gallinarian monk,
Martin of Tours, led through Mid Gaul aflame
His fierce monastic host to wreck the fanes,
And break the idols of that pagan realm;
Or Ulphilas, who, 'mid the Gothic tribes
That on the frosty slope of Hæmus dwelt,
Or where blue Danube rolls its pictured flood,
Unfolded to their view the priceless Word.
Kindling his evening fire symbolical,
Patrick of Tara hailed the greater Light.
Columba, 'mid the savage Pictish tribes,

Lived Christ in saintliest life, till, worn by years,
At midnight, in Iona of the main,
Kneeling before the shrine, breathed forth his soul.
And, as the bees in summer swarm abroad,
Making new hives, so from the western isles,
Or Lindisfarne, new missioners went forth,
Virgilius, Columbanus, Kilian.
Augustine's band, led with uplifted cross,
Made Thanet and the Kentish Weald resound
With holy song. In the Thuringian wilds
The stalwart arm of Winfrid swung the axe
Defiantly, to smite the sacred oak
Of Thor, and his deluded followers won
'Neath milder heavens. The forest's dusk arcades,
As Sturm of Fulda urged his lonely way,
Heard his loud prayers for Christ's poor scattered flock.
The gentle Ansgar bore the glad good news
To Scandinavia and the chilly north,
Teaching the power of Christ-like gentleness.
The seed of truth to the Slavonic tribes
That bordered on the amber-bearing strand
Of Prussia and Livonia, by the blood
Of brave Adalbert was enfertilised;
While, 'neath the palms of torrid Africa,
The Balearic Raymund sought to win
The Saracen; there lived, and loved, and toiled;
Then died a martyr. Sancian's barren isle
Saw Xavier kneel a suppliant at the gates
Of China. Like a wasting flame, his soul
Burnt to the socket of his toil-worn frame,
And in his palm branch hut upon the strand

Hushed by the murmurous surges of the deep,
Folding his long and wasted hands, expired.
Prayer from the wigwam of the Indian rose,
As, down the cedar aisles and hemlock gloom
Of the American woods, there wandered forth
The silvery echoes of Christ's tale of love,
Sweeter than trill of bird or cascade's fall.
The blossoming prairies shone in newer light,
As Eliot's prayers subdued hard hearts to love.
Greenland's blue world of ice and dazzling snow,
And savage rocks up-piled, sterile and bleak,
Was by the heroic love of Hans Egede
And the Moravian band, a faithful few,
Invested with new lustre. Loving Christ,
There are who readily have sacrificed
For Him their all; for Him have wandered forth
To the most distant and degraded tribes
Under the cope of heaven, to tell His love;
Excluded from the world, to alien tribes
Consigned, alien pursuits and solitude:
Nor can the page historical present
Loftier devotion. Here, nor public stage,
Th' applause of multitudes, nor private gains,
Nor the rewards that crown th' adventurous toil
Of military prowess, could allure.
 Smit with Christ's tenderness, the Church has stretched
Her hands of love to the dense multitudes
Of eastern lands, to India's dusky throngs,
A continent of nations, or the expanse
Of China's fields, or palmy Africa,
Immersed in silence and obscurity.

Thither Christ's soldiers in their great campaign
With trust heroical, have bent their march ;
Thither as labourers but to find the field
By the thick growth of centuries matted o'er
With errors rooted deep, and prejudice,
Poisoning all wholesome life. Thither went forth,
In the first hour and dewy prime of youth,
The saintly Martyn, leaving all for Christ,
Attacked undauntedly the falsities,
The superstitions that o'ershadowing life
Had plagued the millions. Under Tanjore's palms
On the Carnatic, Schwartz, in earlier years
Had lived and taught, and, by the dignity
And uprightness of Christian life, compelled
The unwilling lips of enemies to break
Their silence in his praise. And Africa,
Teeming with unknown millions soon shall learn
New songs. By loving hands borne to his rest,
The pioneer of Christ's great army lies
In Westminster's proud abbey, who, consumed
By the fierce inward fires of holy zeal,
Had sought to win a continent for Christ ;
Looked on the swelling uplands and the plains,
Vast lakes, and shining streams of that wide land,
And coveted to bind in willing bonds
These dusky tribes of strange and foreign speech ;
Saw, through the coming years, till thence should
    rise,
Climbing to heaven, the incense cloud of praise ;
Restless to spread before his fellow men
The page unknown, and point the heavenly way.

THE MORNING SONG.

By toil exhausted, prematurely old,
Death found him kneeling in the act of prayer.
    East, West, North, South, the labourers have gone,
Amid the coral reefs of southern seas,
The peopled cities of the Eastern world,
America's vast plains and hunting fields.
India, and China, Africa, Japan,
Scattering the seed over the world's broad tilth,
With what results the future must disclose.
Now Christian hymns are heard, and Christian homes
Blossom already 'mid the heathen wilds,
And Christian churches in their first fond love
Unfold a promise of abundant fruit.
Since on the sward of Olivet Christ's feet
Rising have pressed, though centuries have passed
Slow toilsome centuries of bitterness,
Rancour and strife, calamities untold,
And the slow increment of knowledge won
Of slow research, yet through its long career
The initial love of Christ its victories
Has won. Yet greater far remain. We faint;
We fall; the work proceeds, and wins its way,
Widening, beneficent as light of morn,
Not on the individual life dependent,
And with none bound up. A clearer aim
Works through our purposes and animates,
Albeit unconsciously, our wavering thoughts;
A greater strength sustains our enterprise
Than aught we dream of, and our discord blends.
A glorious future comes. The word remains;
The kingdoms of this world shall yet become

The kingdoms of our Lord and of His Christ,
And He shall reign! Soon, through the gathering mists,
Christ's spiritual temple, built of living stones,
Unfinished now, shall lift its front sublime!
From walls of separation soon shall spring
The arch of union, and the common din
And noise of preparation shall die off
In the grand anthem of immortal praise.

BOOK THE NINTH

THE REQUIEM SONG

THE ARGUMENT.

The noon-day rest—Wherefore Heaven's gift?—Love enshrined—The Life-Giver's agency—The life of the world—Fragrance in the temple—The whispered fears—The testimony of the Word—The golden thread of hope—The world within the visible world—The quiet hour—Paradise of prayer—Death menaces—Yearnings and questionings—The soul's path—The further future—Love irradiating life—Requies æterna!—Earth's pleasures transitory—The summer of life past—Glimpses of future bliss—Echoes in the crypt—Earth's beauty pointing forward—Glorious hope of immortality—The marble effigy—Clouds o'er the future—Ruins of the past—The horoscope of nations—Conjectures as to the earth's future—Utterance of the Word—Safety of the redeemed—Heaven seen afar—Its beauties—The pleasant land—Glorious fellowship with saints and angels—The presence of Christ—"With Christ!"—Love has regained her own.

BOOK THE NINTH.

THE REQUIEM SONG.

S one, who toils along a mountain road,
Sunbaked and quivering in the glowing
   noon,
Comes to a deep ravine where winds his path
Amid the shade of whispering fragrant
   pines,
Sequestered, cool, and through the boughs deep-fringed
And lace-like tracery overhead discerns
Blue sky, or, downward through the underwood
And purple distance, glimpses of the lake
That slumbers far below, resting, well pleased,
Will pause and listen to the streamlet's fall,
Diminished now to a few silver threads,
That leap from rock to rock and fill the air
With dewy dampness of their rainbow dust,
Falling around upon the lush green ferns,
A gauzy veil; here, in the cool green light
He sits, and rests awhile, awhile drinks in

The grateful silence of the quivering noon ;
So travelling on this rough, hard road of life
We find a refuge in Thy love, O Christ,
Find deep delight ; the thought refreshment brings,
And quiet satisfaction and repose ;
Surprised at our own happiness, afraid
Lest the next moment should dispel the charm,
And bring again the hard prosaic facts,
The common places of our daily life.
We are, O Great Creator, in Thy hands,
And Thou, O Lord, art greater far than we ;
And Thou canst make the river of our peace
To flow with constant and o'erbrimming tide ;
And Thou canst make the harpstrings of our souls
Breathe to Thy breath divinest harmonies,
Responsive, and unutterably sweet.
Made for Thyself, alone in Thee, we find
Our happiness. Glad as a bird at dawn,
My heart rejoices thus to sing Thy love ;
To tell th' enshrinement of that precious gem,
Pearl of uncounted price, in truth revealed,
Provisions for the spiritual good of man,
Religious forms in their simplicity
August, expressive of our deepest hopes.
 Gift of the Father's love, Thee first and chief,
O Christ, we celebrate! Auguster theme
Nor human nor seraphic joy e'er stirred.
Amidst earth's broken lights these discords harsh,
And windy storms of doubt, this tangled maze
We turn, we look to Thee, and doubt no more.
Immaculate, Thou stand'st, O gracious One,

THE REQUIEM SONG.

And with divinest tenderness endowed,
To ratify our else too daring hopes:
Yet not, O Christ, for mere display Thou camest;
Not on the azure dome of heaven, Thy hand
Wrote its evangel, or the emerald earth;
Hadst thou so chosen every wind that blows,
Freighted with joy, might have the message borne,
Each wave of restless ocean found a tongue,
Till all creation with consentient voice
Had joined in singing of so grand a psalm,
To show Thy love. Thou might'st have strewn life's path
With jewels, laden every tree with fruit
Ambrosial, from the golden sky rained wealth
Upon the neediness of man : Thou gavest
What most he needed, though he knew it not,
Nor felt his want, that worst of poverty.
As Saviour of the lost Thou camest, true Friend:
Blest Friend! to effect what none could e'er attempt,
And in this function absolute of love
Thee would we recognise, Thee glad accept;
And hold Thine honour tenderer than life.
When tempted most t' attach our mortal lot
With blame, in lonely miserable thoughts,
Counting ourselves but waifs of destiny,
There shines against the darkness of the past
The form divine with arms around a child,
Pathetic rendering of God's shielding love!
Emblem of God's protecting tenderness;
Thy voice sounds like a brother's in the mist.
Long o'er the story of Thy wondrous life
We muse! Love there finds voice in every line,

Finds sacrifice of self in every act,
And when we see Thee give on Calvary
Thyself, out of pure sympathy for man
We wondering ask, Wherefore the awful gift?
 O mystery of the unknown Christ! That Thou,
Heaven's best beloved, the King of kings, shouldst stoop,
Shouldst silently assume a place 'midst men,
And the small functions of our mortal life
Meekly discharge! to each succeeding age
That Thou shouldst come, and to each separate soul
Present Thyself, with all the benefits
Of Thy pure life, Thine agonies unknown:
And Thou art not perceived! Thy locks are wet,
O Bridegroom of the soul, with dews of night,
As patiently Thou knockest at the door,
Where wrapped in drowsy slumbers of sin's night
The obdurate lies, nor hears Thy kindly voice.
And all is love; for through the opened door,
Of the awakened and believing heart,
Stooping to its low portal, Thou dost come
To second incarnation; Thou dost bring
The infinite peace, and there enshrined, O Christ,
Thou dwellest, making Sabbath in the soul,
With a perpetual sunshine; Thy approach,
Thy coming, Thy indwelling, all is love.
 Would we behold the evidence of love?
In the forgiveness of the penitent
Most clearly is it shown. Unseen man's sin,
Unrealised, until the inward sight
Is from on high illumined; then the abyss
Yawns deep and vast beneath the yielding foot;

As when the lightning in the midnight storm
Reveals the jutty and precipitous heights
That rise from misty depths of cloud and gloom,
A mountain mast scaling the very heavens.
The love that in forgiveness lies enshrined
Is priceless, offered with such tenderness,
Such forms that must subdue the loftiest pride,
The heart most obdurate. This paves the way
For future intercourse, opens the path
To everlasting bliss; initial act
That in the abyss of its own tenderness
Engulfs past accusation, as the morn
Rising in gentleness above the waves
Engulfs the night. Pardon embodied holds
An everlasting all-enduring love,
Real though not obvious; mere sentiment
Were like the pomp of clouds that fill the heavens,
Which, at the touch of the sun's wizard beam,
Melting, dissolves in boundless azure depths.
For love upon foundations deep erects
Religion's pillars twain, of faith and love,
Of true belief and true obedience.
Were not Almighty justice there involved
And satisfaction of the eternal pact,
Quittance direct, our peace might baseless rest,
And at the mercy lie of each dread shaft
Hurled in temptation's hour. God's pardoning love
Springs from the fountain of redeeming love.
Christ for the sinner died, supremest pledge
Of love, that in its earnestness would burst
The chains of death. Thus ran the covenant;

The substitute came forth, to bear man's guilt,
And on the milk-white page of His pure soul
Were written all sin's accusations dark,
Counted His own, accepted, by His death
Piacular.   Love stooped to suffer, bleed,
And in the place of the belovèd, die.
   Like when the thunder-storm long time has raged,
And in its fury lashed the tortured boughs,
Drenching the swimming pane, as from the sky
The gale flings forth the slanting sheeted rain ;
Then comes a pause ; a cleft amid the clouds,
A patch of blue like to a smile appears,
The clouds divide, the rains trail their dark skirts
Along the mountain-side, with rainbow hues
All richly dappled o'er, the sun comes forth.
Now from the dripping coppice near at hand
Jewelled with rain-drops from its ev'ry thorn,
A solitary bird begins his song ;
The flute-like melody wakes other strains
From many a grove and glistening hedgerow near,
Of sweet-concerted music.   Now the sun
Makes the fresh landscape glad, and the blue sky
Breathes heavenlier peace and fresher glory wears.
So from the gloom of penitence the soul
Emerging rises to the life renewed
Of God's forgiving love.   The storm is passed :
How fair, how pleasant, the familiar life ;
How beautiful the world that God has made,
Place of brief sojourning, not final home ;
How full of interest the daily task !
'Tis life to live beneath the smile of God ;

Essential love its most essential life,
The power of love, with bliss ineffable,
And God-ward turning of this heart of dust
From a poor world of shadows, dreams, and husks,
And unsubstantial joys that mock the soul,
To the enduring substance, best of things;
The power life's duties to discharge, and make
The daily path an avenue of heaven.
Now to the soul new-born, offspring of love,
Old things are passed away, all things are new.
Habits, by long indulgence vigorous grown
As the gnarled oak, at length relax their grasp.
The past is past; no more it drags the soul
With shadowy hand the dreaded nether path;
But as an eagle shakes a serpent free
That round its talons has entwined itself,
Hindering its flight, and to the zenith mounts,
The soul delivered from the serpent twine,
The serpent fangs of sin, exultant rises,
And in the empyrean spreads bold wing.

 As in some Gothic fane, hoary with age,
The streaming light of centuries will rob
In its slow passage all the fresh bright tints
From eastern windows filled with glass rich stained,
Till in the gloom antique the taper's ray
Is necessary, even though without
Shines the effulgence of the noon-day sun;
So the plain gospel truths, plain with intent
Divine, as suiting best this rude rough world,
Where the great crowd must needs have simple truth
Or none at all, may be obscured by rites,

By o'erwrought symbolism, or hollowness,
That eats the heart of fruitful piety.
Oft in the secret individual life,
Familiarity with truth deprives
The truth of all its vivifying power,
Till darkness finds a home within the light.
   Thee too we celebrate, Spirit Divine,
O Holy Comforter, the Paraclete!
Too scant our reverence, too slow are we
In this Thy world to yield Thee Thy due place,
To recognise Thy functions; deeming Thee
But the faint effluence of divinity,
The channel of activities divine;
Not personal God. These are Thy mighty works
O Mighty One! Upholder Thou of earth,
Wrapped round with wondrous living tapestry,
That from the loom of life comes ever forth,
Mystic and beautiful, a changing web
Of loveliness, colour with colour blent:
Thine is the fair broad day, the sapphire sky,
And the serene magnificence of night,
The balanced moon 'mid the clear blue abyss,
The fire's wild fringe, and the white wings of light,
The purple amphitheatre of hills,
And distant mountains on the horizon's line;
The world is full of Thee, Life-maker, Fount,
And never-failing Spring of energy,
From deity's abysmal depths e'er fed,
The breathing of the low soft summer wind,
The forest's dappled shade, the sunlight's gold,
The glistening insect buzzing on the wing,

Wild woodland melodies of answ'ring birds,
Plumed field flowers blossoming, uprising streams
Of fragrance from innumerable spires
Invisible, all life, variety,
Are Thine; the ceaseless changes, endless forms
Commingling of earth's never-resting life,
Bent ever to remoter excellence:
And in our human world, Sovereign Divine,
Thine agency appears, dark world, unformed,
Or slowly rising from th' enshrouding clouds
Chaotic, over which, O Spirit of life,
Thou hoverest, and their potencies obscure
Renderest prolific, calling thence a world
Of ordered beauty indefeasible.
Mysterious agency, whose work oft lies
Beyond the compass of our feeble thoughts,
Evolving life from death, prosperity,
From what to us adversity appears,
Thine is it, O reviving Breath of God,
To breathe upon the slain, armies to call
To light and life from their low bed of dust.
Thou shedd'st Thy friendly light, as on the road
Which erst Thy chosen through the desert trod:
T' instruct the reason and support the will,
But more, with manna of the heavenly love
To feed, and from the smitten spiritual Rock
To give to drink; to nourish secretly
The mystic bush of life, as Moses' thorn;
Filling the heart, Thou fillest this fair world
Till all things speak of Thee. Truth to disclose
Is Thine, O Blessed One, and truth t' apply;

To take the things of Christ, rich treasury,
Most precious things, and show them unto us,
Else dark, though needed, and with pining sought,
On the blest page by inspiration penned,
Itself Thy gift, to throw the inward light,
Perception give and apprehension clear,
Unseen, unfelt beside. There Christ is seen,
Christ in the sweetness of His character,
Christ imaged, symbolised, or plainly read;
For as the priest entering the temple swung
His golden censer till the fragrant clouds
Rising aloft filled the whole edifice,
So Thou, O Spirit of holiness, dost come,
And entering the mean temple of our hearts
Sheddest the love of God, fragrance untold!
More sweet than myrrh, or storax of the hills,
Or desert frankincense from eastern lands;
That the blest soul may shed rich perfumes round
Its daily path of holy love and hope.
But chiefly, O Thou utterance divine,
In this great ministry of love Thou show'st,
And testifiest to the sons of God
Their sonship; giving them assurance glad
Of pardon and acceptance through the blood.
Bold in the confidence inspired, the soul
Rises to own and tremblingly to claim
The privilege, and with its prayer draws near
Pleading with child-like trust; then comest Thou,
And all unseen, the utterance of faith
And new-born love Thou tak'st, and with Thine
  own

THE REQUIEM SONG.

Most potent intercession dost present
Before the throne of Majesty Divine.
  But as the eye, in some cathedral old,
Notes how the piety of centuries past
Enshrined itself in generous, lavish gifts,
Withholding nought that deft and cunning hands
And minds alive with thought sublime could do;
The towering column and th' aspiring arch,
Windows of richest hues, marble and gold,
Bosses, and capitals, and lines recessed,
Vastness with glorious symmetry combined;
Proofs everywhere of pious ends in view,
Desire to honour God, of thoughts devout
And the aspiring hopes of human kind,
Pathetic, mute expressions of deep faith;
So in the structure of the truth revealed,
This noblest fane of thought upreared by love,
Firm seated as the hills, whose glories fair
Outshine earth's fairest, o'er whose mystic charm
Time has no power to sift sepulchral dust,
Or rob its beauty of one particle,
The good news of God's love is sweetly told.
  O God, to Thee we tell our dreary fears:
Changelings of destiny, poor counters we
In this vast system of created things,
Vortex of being in its ceaseless whirls,
Uncounted items in the total vast,
And unconsidered. From its troubled depths
The desolate soul, lonely, cries out for light,
Cries out to Thee. For thus the drear thought comes;
We are as nothing, and no friendly hand

Is through the darkness stretched to shield life's flame,
Flickering, defenceless, or no friendly eye
Observes ; and when we lapse in death we drop
Into the vast abyss of nothingness,
Whence we at first emerged, and leave behind
Of all our trouble and our endless care
But a few bubbles on the moving wave,
To tell that once we were. Voices are heard,
Misleading voices, whispering through the gloom
That we are but electric mockeries,
The outcome of the elemental strife,
And victims. Like the fringing northern lights
That in the freezing starlight dance a while,
And then relapse to a profounder gloom ;
Awhile we stay, then are for ever lost.
    Far other is the utterance of Thy Word!
By golden links the soul redeemed is bound
In new relationships, and, by the blood
That consecrates the bonds, a citizen made
Of heavenly Zion, city of the skies.
O city of our God, home of the soul,
Whose glories rise above the heights of time
In their sublime undying loveliness ;
Visions of sunset, or the sanguine dusk
Of the awakening dawn, earth's noblest scenes
Of towered capitals, with colonnades
Withdrawn, spacious and stately halls, and spires,
That with their fretted pinnacles sublime,
Dare the aerial blue.; or natural scenes,
Far distant headlands smit by slanting beams,
And shining summer seas, blue hills remote,

THE REQUIEM SONG.

And golden pastures sleeping in the sun,
Red harvests quivering in the hazy noon,
Or dusky woodlands gay with foxglove spires,
The gorgeous vesture of the ample light,
Across whose airy woof the sunbeam's warp
Weaves ever-changing loveliness; still lakes
Where hawking swallows dip and leave their rings,
Or where the early stars mirror their gold:
Earth's fairest scenes suggest thy lovelier charms.
Dreams come to us immured in this dull life,
Along whose miry ways with weary steps
We trudge our daily march, glimpses far off;
Even in the world of sleep the sick desire
Broods o'er thy beauty, city of our God,
And on the sullen black expanse of night
Paints its bright hopes in hues too fugitive.
One with the saints, of that bright company
We dream, earth's perfected and virgin souls,
Whose love, fidelity, and holiness,
Made round their daily path a little heaven.
Of you we muse, ye servants of our God,
And of your high pursuits, bliss that remains
At God's right hand, yet strive we still in vain
To image forth the glad surprise of death,
Curbing our eager and too restless hopes.
Christ's soldiers militant we lift our hearts
And bless our God, and bless the bond most dear
That links us to your glorious company.
Assured Thou wilt, O Lord, make good the word
In which Thou causedst us to put our trust,
Secure we build, smile at misfortune's storm,

And wait impatiently the dawning day,
Courting the future, deeming it to hide
Priceless advantage, treasure manifold;
Impatient as the prodigal in rags,
For the best robes wherewith the son is dressed.
The kiss we have, the reconciling kiss,
And through eternity must cherish still
The memory of forgiveness; yet we wait
The investment of the wedding garment fair,
With which arrayed at heaven's high festival
We may appear unblamed. What human love
In its sweet peace and tenderness can do
We partly know, and find contained therein
The promise and the pledge of endless life.

Hope is the golden thread whose brightness runs
Through life's vicissitudes, bringing its peace,
E'en when despondency with sullen gloom
Bows down the soul, or the fierce doubt besets
That we are waifs, abandoned of the skies.
One with the family of God! the fact
Waits not until its force be realised
To yield its benefits. We play with truth,
But dimly apprehending at the best
Its deep significance. God's purposes
Lie far beyond the reach of mortal ken.
By virtue of this golden link the soul
Access now finds, and with the voice of prayer,
In confidence serene, makes known its wants.

There is a world within this visible world,
Real and undreamed of, life within this life,
Whose freshness, peace, and beauty are untold;

The life of holy love, where God sole reigns,
And with His peace unspeakable, the heart
Safe garrisons. No dream fanatical,
Dim vision of some weak disordered brain,
That gathering up its wrecked and broken hopes,
A refuge from its own distraction builds ;
A world where reason humble, reverent, finds
Life's infinite mysteries around it spread,
And rests beneath the shadow of the night ;
A world where love, unmenaced now by death,
Seeks her lost treasures confident to find,
And cheerful goes to meet the infinite love.
Eye hath not seen this world, nor ear hath heard
Its sweet and deep-infolding harmonies ;
Where, entering by the door of prayer, we find
Stillness and refuge from the worrying crowd
Of earthly cares, with hunger unappeased ;
Thence from the presence chamber, come refreshed,
Strengthened and armed for this our earthly fight.
Blest privilege ! in this rude world to find
Refuge so near, and sympathy so blest,
And in such form conveyed that the dumb heart
Speaks but in tears ; oft lacerated sore,
Oft burdened heavily, and with its load
O'erwhelmed, ashamed of self, of effort past
Rejectful, yearning still for better things.
Prayer breathes upon the spirit sabbath peace,
Stills with the tide of love care's babbling streams,
Heals deepest wounds and ebbing strength recalls.
   Fair paradise art thou, O quiet hour,
To which we flee, and from the tree of life,

Pluck the ripe clusters, there enjoy repose,
While listening to the flow of time's great flood,
And hearing unalarmed the voice of God.
For, in that silent hour, the soul draws near,
And with its Maker high communion holds.
Thou art, O God, our good; in Thee we find
True happiness, as Thou dost give Thyself.
Birds in the element of air rejoice,
Diving and tossing with uplifted wings,
Ocean's blue depths to glistening shoals afford
Capacious home, while in the sunshine basks
Th' exultant insect on his jewelled wings;
Thy favour is our element, O God!
Our sun, our air, our all-supporting main,
And in the sunshine of Thy love alone
Blooms to perfection the fair flower of man;
For man is fair when Thou dost make him so.
Drawn near, accepted in the Well Beloved,
As the condition of Thy love, life wears
Value supreme, for then alone we live,
And, with that glad experience satisfied,
Might on extinction smile. The chaliced heart
Thou fillest with Thy sacramental love,
Not for our passive joy, but to ensure
The swift discharge of life's entrusted powers,
And earnest diligent spending of ourselves.

 Red morning sun shines from the crimsoned east
On dewy pasture and well-cultured field,
Blue haze of grain waiting the ripening beam,
That o'er the landscape makes its fervour felt,
Gilding the tree-tops of the mounded woods,

Until the brooklet seems to run with gold.
The piercing stimulating ray matures,
Refreshes, strengthens ; with its golden wand,
Beneath the matted leaves of last year's fall,
The withered twigs and cones, touches the earth,
Silent and slumbering, bidding it awake ;
So, from celestial love, comes all that makes
Man useful, good, or great, stirring the will
To reach the highest use of all his powers.

As children when returning home at eve,
Stand at the entrance to the forest depths,
When day is darkening and the storm abroad,
Doubtful, alarmed, uncertain of their road,
Down where the woodpath leads to thickening gloom,
Look wistfully, and wish and yearn for home ;
So we, Thy children, Lord, wandering and lost,
Amid the awful lone immensities,
Cling to each other with pathetic grasp,
Whispering our doubts, and fearful of our hopes ;
The mind though fortified, fully matured
By the calm teachings of philosophy,
Stands balked, doubtful of what may yet remain
Behind the veil of death ; for though our fears
May fail to verify themselves, times come
When the reluctant soul must leave its best,
Finding its loftiest most ambitious schemes
Thwarted, as o'er some precipice abrupt,
The mountain stream leaps from some rocky height
To wave in mist upon the gusty wind.
Life casual seems, disjointed in its parts ;
Then comes the fear lest that the future hold

Unseen contingencies, disasters new;
So tarry we th' unrolling of the years.
The assurance yet abides that He who made,
Who led from infancy to this quick hour,
Knows all, and looking from perfection's height
Sees where the life stream flows and whither tends,
Torn with what rapids, bosomed in what gloom,
Or by what shelving steps to spend itself
On the wide glimmering strand where ocean lies,
The low waste foreshores of advancing age.
Frail as the moth upon the evening wind,
Soon broken, in the hand of God alone
Safety is found and guardianship divine.
We cannot deem our life fortuitous,
Reasoning on human duty, nor can think
The human soul as irresponsible
As is the lightning of the summer clouds,
Or shimmering ignis-fatuus of the marsh.

 As one who wandering in the night's dark shade,
Perplexed and hesitating often turns,
Now to the dun sky looks, scarce visible,
Or darker earth, nor knows where one false step
May lead, what danger unsuspected lie
Close to the path, doubts of his every step;
If but the moon behind the eastern hills
Emerge, like some broad golden shield, and throw
Her placid light o'er the black tangled scene,
His heart revives: against the illumined sky
In bold relief stands forth each tree, till where
The foliage veils the moon's bright mottled disc,
But not conceals, rendering each branch distinct,

Each separate twig and leaf in outline clear;
His path the traveller sees, discerns the cliff,
And hearing unalarmed the torrent's voice,
Renews with confidence the homeward path.
So doubts no longer the illumined soul,
When once the love of God serenely shines
About life's path, but through the wilderness
Pursues its way; no child of destiny,
Offspring of chance, where life's main problems seem
But doubtful, in an unresponsive world,
Where to the soul that on the good alone
Determines, nature speaks with low soft voice,
Unheard, unheeded by th' unwilling heart,
And lends its guidance to th' imperilled hope
By chances numberless surrounded, armed
With fullest powers to slay our loftiest aims,
In one brief moment, with enduring gloom
To obscure the future, through the up-pointing spears
Of dangers passing, and to that exposed
Which reason justly fears, self-degradation,
And by disuse impoverishment of powers,
Or sapping of our faith, by slow approach,
And the entrenchment in the citadel
Of unbelief, the agnostic's cheerless creed.

Perplexed, full oft, how life is to be spent,
The motive wanting that with high constraint
Would marshal forth the concentrated powers
To attempt a high deliberate aim of life;
Like mariners at sea, without or port
Or object of their voyage. Or, to merge,
Counting these higher yearnings as but vain,

Into the natural world, to recognise
The essential oneness in essential things
Of man and nature, cease this weary strife
And vain attempt to bear the heavy load
Of this vast, dumb, and inarticulate world,
Or understand the mystic frame of things,
One with the lichened tree moved in the wind,
Or sharded insect twinkling in the grass,
Birds' voices in the woods, the distant moan
Of thunder long prolonged among the hills,
Like inarticulate utterance of a soul,
That found but disappointment, where it hoped
For pleasure ; listening to these voices faint,
To yield the vantage ground of reason's height,
Content the individual self to lose,
And onward drift with time's resistless flow ;
Or, to retire, taking our patient stand
In the distinctiveness of rational life,
And vainly wrestle with life's problems vast
That mock our feebleness, and in the cave
Of meditation, quiet divine of thought,
Blaspheming voices hear, unguarded, rash,
O'erweening speculations ; dismal choice,
To still the inward cry for sympathy,
Hardening the sentiment, compelled to accept
A blind fatality, forget the past,
And from the future nothing hope, but drift
Unquestioning, whither the current bears,
To primal gloom, blank of unconsciousness
Whence we emerged, slowly to know ourselves
And know we were, darkness intense, unmoved,

A darkness in whose all-encircling gloom
The light of life wasting upon its wick
At last expires, nor re-illuming knows.
   Whither shall this poor anxious spirit glide
What time the soul, like some white sail, shall round
Death's mighty promontory, silent, dusk,
And to the ocean of eternity
Head its lone prow, on unknown voyage bound?
Will then the conscious sentient life prolonged,
Incorporal, more sensitive become,
The organs of sensation being removed,
And to a more immediate contact brought
With the substratum and essential life
Of natural things, with clearer vision see?
The tenant of the grave! ah! dreadful thought,
Conscious of its dark prison and the worm;
Or, haunting still earth's dear familiar scenes,
Unrecognised, observant, in the gleams,
Moments transitional, or shadows dim
Of twilight, or unheard, with footfall light,
Treading night's portico of sullen gloom;
Or habiting, mayhap, some shadowy realm,
With its faint echoes of this thrilling life,
This tangible frame of things, to live again
The pleasures, joys, pursuits, or hopes, or fears,
Of this material world in semblance dim.
   And, of the further future, more remote,
Awful abyss and dread engulfing void,
Where plunges to its rest time's mighty stream;
What strange developments await the soul,
What new experiences, mutations new,

Puzzle the mind, and tire the restless thought.
Hath man undying flames, that, like the bush
In Edom's wilderness, burn undestroyed?
That when the earth by slow consuming fires,
Erosions of its elemental strife,
Grown aged shall expire, or its firm bands
Relapsed, upon the eddying whirls of space
Its vast solidity be scattered wide;
Or, when the sun's high-leaping fires shall fall,
And on their ashes slowly flickering die,
Shall man still live, and, living, in what sphere,
Environed by what circumstance, swept through
The infinite void mere prey of destiny,
Abandoned, bodied in some form undreamed,
Borne on the whisperings of the summer breeze,
In the light flutter of the summer leaves,
Careering in the tempest that o'er leagues
Of sheeted hissing foam sweeps its dread path,
Or, harnessed to the incessant lightning's blaze
Shimmering around the world, or, to the depths
Unfathomed flung, e'er falling through the abyss,
To wander through the azure starry depths,
Pathways of worlds unmarked, or, pausing watch
The world with its dimensions vast sweep by,
Balanced on nothing, sorrow-laden, dim,
With spotted silvery disc, mountains or seas,
Diminish in the distance to bright speck;
Or, in the underworld imprisoned fast,
Dungeoned in solid rock, restrained, reduced
To utter exiguity of being,
The lowest ebb of barest consciousness,

That ever hovers on the brink of pain ;
Or, at the mercy of the elements,
Now denizened ten thousand fathoms deep
In ocean's caverns, 'mid the ooze and slime,
Where dwell unearthly forms with staring eyes,
And giant serpent shapes that twine and glide
Through glassy depths profound.   And this how long ?
    Thus questions this poor child of man, O Lord,
Forgetful of Thy Word and will revealed,
Thus frets his mortal hour, afraid of self,
And timid of existence, with the sense
Of strangeness of this life, and its conditions
And beaten by the task, like weak-winged bird
That, hastening from the storm, attempts to cross
A mountain ridge whose lofty rampart hides
Serener skies, but helpless falls again,
Too weak to rise.   And we are children, Lord,
Poor ignorant children, yet, too oft, without
The childlike spirit, and too confident
Upon forbidden ground to walk, to wrest
By dint of intellect, the mysteries
Thy mercy hides.   Yet, humbled, when we yield
To the sweet invitation of Thy love,
And humbly seeking Thee in patient faith
Find Thee in Christ, and prove all things made new ;
Yea, life itself a higher nobler thing,
And full of music as a summer's morn ;
New voices now are heard when Thou dost speak ;
The wind's fresh breath, the mottled shade of clouds,
The sunshine red, the pleasant face of day,
The beauty and the fragrance of our earth,

Perfumed with breath of flowers, by quiring birds
Filled with melodious echoes, give new charms,
As the responsive soul thrills with delight
To know its God. This is Thy world, O God,
And all its beauty seems marks of Thy favour,
Its pleasures charged with messages of love.
We are Thy servants, Lord, unwilling oft,
Oft blind, yet ours the happy privilege
To fill each little day with happy toil;
O happy day, too short to tell the love
That makes a pleasure of each weary step,
To show in willing deeds the gratitude
Of a forgiven soul. O happy life
In such sweet service spent, to work, to wait,
To serve so kind, so good, so true a Lord,
So condescending to accept the gifts
That mortal frailty brings. O happy world,
Irradiated by the love divine,
Become the secret banquet house of love,
Within whose chambers hang proofs ever new
Of the great love wherewith our souls are loved;
Adventurers no more on life's rough sea,
Freighted with destiny, exposed to loss
And ruin irretrievable, that fate
And envious time may bring. The days are linked
With golden bands; purpose divine gives life
Its unity, its object, and its peace;
Made willing, and in acquiescence glad,
One with the system of the universe,
Content with what the Power Supreme adjudge
To be our lot, desiring but to merge

Our frail and erring wills in His, and know
None other law. To live, to work, to rest,
To suffer, or to die, these all are His
T' appoint or to deny, ours to submit ;
And from this secret spiritual harmony
Springs peace, our peace with God, and with ourselves.
Nor longer now the eager need to clutch
Life's opportunities of happiness,
Nor stand defensive as if nature armed
Menaced the faithful ; now an unseen shield
Surrounds them, and how long, how short, how vast,
Or how obscure and insignificant,
The task assigned, until the work be done
We live : then turn from earth and homeward go.
God hath all uses for His instruments,
Known and unknown, yet in the readiness
We manifest to do His sacred will,
He manifests His purposes. With this,
Supreme all-comprehensive fact, will come
The blending of the discords of our life,
Its inner harmony, from thence proceed
Its sweetest cadences. Oft in the gloom
Profound of grief the star of hope shines forth ;
Oft from low valleys of humility
Rises the life to a sublimer height
Of snowy purity else unattained.
To recognise God's hand, to own His power,
To trust Him, though in darkness, and to love
Unseen, though richly seen in loving gifts,
This the grand lesson, this the privilege
Of mortal life. Whither our life-stream tends

We faintly guess, or fondly vainly hope;
As when one walking in the moonlight clear,
The vast dusk velvet landscape dimly seen,
In shadowy outline sloping far below,
Hears how the torrent down the steep ravine
Falls to the restful stillness of the lake,
Hears, but sees not, till onward a few steps
Advanced, discerns below the silvery thread
On which the moonlight strikes, winding its way
To its near resting-place : glimpses we have,
And know that rest awaits our restlessness,
And peace at length will heaviest trouble lull.
   Were this but all, this were enough to give
The Christian life value unique. But more,
And higher far, remain. The evening dressed
In the rich promise hues of crimson cloud,
Forms but the prelude to eternal day.
Stripped of the blessed hope that gilds death's gloom,
Though with the background of oblivion dark,
The Christian life would even then present
The highest style, the happiest mode of life.
The Gospel, the divine philosophy,
Gives armour against fate, prepares the soul
To meet with magnanimity, unblenched,
Th' inevitable, to endure the petty stings,
The thorns and vexing troubles of this life,
With equanimity ; to crop the flower
Of pleasure and avoid its sting, bereaved,
To find in hours of loneliness and pain
Companionship, and consolation deep,
As ne'er the academic grove could teach ;

Sweet honey of truth, sweeter than Hybla's store;
These have we; but yet more, the blessed hope
Of new developments of love unknown
Lifts our glad hearts and stirs our energies.
Now through the lattice of this mortal life
Glimpses we catch of the delightsome land,
The future of our hopes, God's paradise.
Earth's music falls and dying fainter grows,
But to faith's ear a loftier anthem comes;
The seen, the tangible drift off like clouds;
The eternal, the invisible remain.
Hope's better and enduring substance grows
As earth decays, draws near as earth recedes,
And with an ever brightening lustre shines.
  "Rest! rest! O Lord, eternal rest!" so cry
Thy wearied ones, while stretching forth to Thee
Imploring hands; for Thou alone canst give
The satisfaction craved: for Thou alone
Canst smooth the wrinkles from the furrowed brow,
And breathe upon the soul Sabbatic peace.
Cares, like a red-mouthed hurrying pack, have driven
The hunted soul, till, like a tired stag
That seeks with lagging limbs some glade to rest,
Or pool deep-shadowed where to lave its flanks,
It refuge seeks in these inspiring hopes.
The restless life craves rest. Now the spent wave
Folds its smooth curve upon the peaceful shore,
The rack drifts from the clearing evening sky;
And all the storm tints drear and cold now blend
In crimson promise of a summer morn;
Bright on the toilers' faces as they come,

Returning homewards, shines the evening sun.
Welcome, O peaceful eve! welcome the star
Ushering the solemn splendours of the night,
Dark archway to the dawn, all studded thick
With constellations, like night's avenue
Leading to endless day. What is there here
To daunt the flight, or clog the nimble step?
Ambition waits the glad release of death.
 Thy will be done, O Lord, not ours; Thy will
Our will shall be. Here, in this battlefield,
Thy people stand. Some wield the sword for Thee,
Defenders some, some sentinels to guard,
And pace the weary hours of darkness through.
Thou art our Captain, and at Thy command
We come, we go, we stand, we stay. Wanting
Death's consecration, if unmeet, forgive
The half-concealed desire, should it appear
Disloyal, or to lack submission true;
Suffering unblamed our frailty to indulge
The glad anticipation of a hope,
That, like the smile of morning, gentle breaks
Over the dark forbidding face of death.
 Bright eye of youth, elastic step, quick pulse,
The fulness and the freshness of life's morn
Pass like the early dews, nor know recall.
The spring time comes brightening the spiritless earth,
Covering the hedgerows, orchards, groves, with gauze
Of snowy odorous blossoms, earth's fair veil,
Bringing the chirp of birds among the trees,
New decked with opening leaves of liveliest green;
Making it seem a new-created world.

Yet like a dream its brightness passes by.
Life's pleasures in the using perish ; cheat
The jaded appetite, mocking the mind
That stoops to make its home in meaner things
Than are provided in its proper range.
Home joys are sweet, yet transient as the gleam
That gilds the passing ripple on the lake.
The mother's voice no more is heard, the ring
Of children's laughter, while on floor and stairs
Patter of little feet grows strangely still,
And in the drowsy lonely silence dies.
The well of knowledge inexhaustible
Appears ; the well is deep, the strength is small.
The ardour which in earlier days impelled
To self-repression and self-sacrifice,
That suffering smiled, now flags. The heart grows old.
Yet like some hidden spring whose waters run
Below the parching sands, the quivering breath
Of torrid noon, so, deep below the change,
And dull familiarities of life,
Rise living waters, secret sure supplies.
Though faded now the blossoms that were strewn
Over life's earlier steps, the open air
Still breathes its gentle blessings, Nature speaks
In graver tones, answering the inward thoughts.
And when the solemn noon of life is passed
Few flowers are scattered o'er the traveller's road
But those that in the paradise regained
Of God's own word have bloomed. Apart from Thee,
Apart from Thee, apart from light and love,

Great spring of joy! how poor are earth's delights,
How quickly fading, and how mixed with pain ;
Dull repetition with decreased desire,
Handfuls of chaff and dust. Youth scarce has passed,
Before we find the emptiness of life ;
To get us gold, to win a fleeting name,
To beat with weary foot the same dull tramp,
Or pleasure seek in sensual delights,
And ministering cloyed appetite in vain,
Unworthy seems. The soul seeks freer range,
And like an eagle mewed and moping sits,
With bright eye glancing through its prison bars
To the blue sky or lofty mountain-tops,
Longing to spread its wing and heavenward soar.
  How beautiful the summer plat abloom,
With dew-washed roses sleeping in the sun ;
The sisterhood of flowers, carnations, pinks,
White lilies breathing out their beauty sweet,
Embodied thoughts of spotless purity.
The trumpet honeysuckle on the wind
Its perfume blows, the jessamine's white stars,
Or modest mignonette, pour fragrance forth
Like grateful prayer ; all interlocked they stand
With clasping tendril, overshadowing leaves,
As if they loved each other's company.
Bees come and go at buzzing hour of noon ;
The lark is in the sky; the misty hills
Seem distant, dreamlike ; brooding silence reigns.
Days come, days go ; then autumn's voice is heard,
Hoarse in its anger, shrieking in loud gales ;
Choke-full the brook, swirling the red leaves round ;

The sward is sodden, and the ways all mire.
The flowers are gone. Ah me! our flowers have gone,
And taken summer with them; loved too well,
Too fondly clasped, too soon, alas! removed.
The dear ones slumber 'neath the mossy turf,
White marble glimmers, and the chirp of birds
Is heard, and early violets steal, where lie
Hopes fondly cherished, and affections deep:
Now musing mouldering time greens their low bed.
Death breaks our links, the closest links that bind
Dear kindred souls, and carries to the skies
Our best belovèd to allure us there.

As on some foreign shore, perchance, one hears
The tolling of a solemn deep-toned bell
From ancient tower, that calls the soul away
To thoughts above the differences of men;
A sound with which the deepest hopes have blent
Of unknown thousands in the unknown past,
The tongue of time, joy, grief, devotion's call:
So in thought's silent hour religion's claims
Waken suggestions of most solemn things,
Of human life in bare simplicity,
The fundamental duties of our lot,
Nature's demands, God's claims, no austere Judge
And the great world of things outside man's life:
For round us are suggestions manifold,
That lure the watchful hope; analogies,
Inwoven in this visible frame of things;
Like crimson clouds of sunset, foreign, far,
As if belonging to another world,
That lift the rapt beholder out of self,

With sense of vacancy, with thoughts of things,
And distant worlds far different from our own.
As those who wander in the gloomy crypt
Of some cathedral pile hearing stray sounds,
Snatches of blended song, deep organ tones,
In solemn sweetly-dying cadences,
Faintly vibrating through the charnel vaults,
Echoes of worship rising overhead,
If never seen, but faintly could conceive
The lofty aisle, the many-coloured light,
The white-robed priests, the chanting choristers,
And exaltation of the worshipping throng;
So, in this crypt-like earth, we dimly dream
Of the all-glorious worship of the skies.

Without Thee, Lord, life seems a dread abyss,
And utter loneliness! Without Thy love
Time is a dreary ever-widening waste,
An enigma unsolvable, a maze
Bewildering, a tale soon told but full
Of pathos infinite. For Thou dost give
Those seeking Thee fresh interest in life,
Gilding their earthly work with heavenly aim;
To stem the tide of sin, earnest to stand
As witnesses for God, or reaching forth
With Christ-like tenderness t' assuage the ills,
The sorrows mitigate of man, or bind
The broken heart and stanch the bitter tear,
Befits us well, becomes our noblest powers.

Time's shadows lengthen with the closing day,
And evening comes, the wished-for peaceful eve.
Hushed are earth's noisy echoes, faint and far,

Dying away. No more the chiding voice
Of blame unmerited is heard, harsh words
Of fierce disparagement, or insult rude.
Now false applause, detraction's ceaseless bark,
The sting of self-dissatisfaction, or
The hiss of envy, biting though it dies,
Passion's constraint, temptation's dangerous lure,
The clamour and the turmoil of the crowd,
And all the noisy goings on of life,
All merge ; then break as billows on the shore
Of the eternal silence. Trouble ends.

As one who through the fields delighted roams
In golden glory of the summer's day,
Beguiled from step to step with prospects new,
Along mossed wood-paths dim where foxgloves blow,
In the green quiet of the woods, with hush
Of drowsy trees above the dappled fern,
If through the opening of the hillside boughs
He catch a glimpse of meadow, field, and town,
Or far off river shining in the sun,
Yet all subdued by distance, till they seem
Parts of some heavenly landscape bathed in light,
Anon he turns, indulging the charmed gaze,
Well pleased to listen to the wood dove's coo,
The trill of linnet, or the blackbird's note ;
Before him like a dream a lake expands,
Bosomed in trees, poplar or silvery birch
Responsive to the wind ; no ripple breaks
The mirrored calm, in tender light subdued,
Of the smooth wave; peace reigns, and calms the soul:
So, through the dim and shadowy things of earth,

Hard and prosaic, with restricted view,
The eye of faith looks forth to heavenly things.
 To thee, O land of bliss, O future home,
Insensibly we turn, quickened by hope,
And restless with desire. Earth's beauty points
To beauties unconceived, a widening range
That upward slopes, passing our mortal ken.
Ah! beautiful is earth; th' aspiring thought
Of art, delighting in the beautiful,
Mounts ceaselessly, endeavouring to grasp
These fleeting forms of earthly loveliness,
And fix them in its rapt and silent world;
Yet the great stream of beauty ever flows;
Fresh faces, graceful forms, and colour gleams,
Expressiveness that ever waits the eye
Observant, forming one vast moving scene
Of varying loveliness, beneath, around,
Above, the broad and sapphire sky of day,
Imperial dome of night; the emerald earth
Enamelled fair, or ocean fathomless,
Dim waste of quivering blue with ceaseless plaint.
Like some great scroll unrolled before our eyes,
With combination strange and novel grace,
New pictures are disclosed, pleasing or drear.
All that is in the earth, fecundity,
Beauty, forgetfulness, and kindliness,
The generous hand, that, to the giver gives
A hundredfold; dark wondrous caves of power,
Whence issue, vested in their loveliness,
Snowdrop, or hyacinth of fragrant breath,
The primrose meek, or dancing daffodil,

THE REQUIEM SONG.

Or lurking violet, with gentle lore
To instruct, admonish, and encourage man;
Earth's beauty is unsung; poets have dreamed,
Rendering their glorious vision in high song,
Always inadequate, full oft far short
Of that which thrilled within th' ecstatic breast,
Snatched earth's brief dream of beauty ere the veil
Of blindness fell, or death's oblivious gloom
Darkened the stage, as apprehensive lest
There were no better things beyond the tomb:
Then vanished in the all-surrounding dark,
And, unexhausted left the brimming fount.

  Yet is earth's beauty marred. Beneath her shades
Death menaces with awful brow, malignant.
The lightning flashing from the angry sky
Gleams like the sword of guarding cherubim,
Death is there in the sun, mildew in shower,
Ravage in fulness, and corruption rank
In mere quiescence, on perfection's marge
Hideous deformity and slack decay,
Tarnish and rust, the sickle keen of time,
The feebleness of age, and over all
The spell of change. Nature's imperial pall,
Crusted with gems and stiff with cloth of gold,
Like regal mantle cast about a tomb,
Conceals the crawling worm, defacement, dust.
Like to some ancient proud domain, once trim,
Its lord long absent, fallen to decay,
Forlorn misuse, neglect, and barrenness;
The flowers run wild, the arbours pleached with care,
Or shady avenues, fruit-gardens rich,

Grown ruinous; the hold baronial tressed
With weeds forlorn, where once the banner waved
Defiance to the foe, now feebly plumed
By yellow wall-flowers fluttering in the wind;
Towers ivy-mantled, rusted gates, and moat
Dry, or with scum of vegetation rank.
Thus seems our earth, from its original height
Run down, and working in a lower groove,
Beneath its powers. If human care may raise
The wildings of the thicket till they yield
Rich juicy fruits, or fragrance new impart
With glowing colours to the wayside flower,
What potencies in nature may remain
Waiting the summons of the Will Divine.
Built of few elements this wondrous frame,
Material, might assume far other forms;
And He, who, in the ocean's caves remote,
Tints the bright shell and hides the lustrous pearl,
Lavishing beauty where no human eye
Observes, may well display in larger scenes
A loveliness and glory now undreamed.
  O glorious hope of immortality,
Whose music floats about our dull, cold world,
As angel music, sweet but faintly heard;
Even in the blank untuneful hours of life,
With lowering troubled sky, near view, unrest,
And hard environment, through which the soul
Finds no escape, your soft sweet strains will rise;
Yet are there hearts insensible and dead,
Unheeding as the marble effigy,
Warrior, or maiden, or anointed king,

Belted and crowned in stone, or palmer, worn
With pilgrimage to holy soil, now lying
In the cathedral aisle, clasping its hands
In prayer, where fall the many-coloured hues,
Rich beams of rainbow light from pictured pane;
Stirring the solemn silence, music comes,
With its sweet pathos, winning gentleness,
The plaintive human voice thrilling the heart,
With the grand harmony and swelling peal,
Melodious thunder of the organ's tone;
The music dies, the statue slumbers still.
Weak human nature with its purposes
Oft crossed unwillingly, its instincts blind,
Its highest aims, persistent energies
By unsuspected influences warped
To fell ambition, and its virtues high
Basely transmuted by the touch of earth
To selfishness, or unsuspected pride,
Twice deaf to disregard the voice of love,
Twice blind to turn aside from love's own hand.
 Then rise, fond heart, in contemplation high
Survey in thought so fair a realm of hope,
This heritage divine. See from afar
The beauteous light of heaven's eternal day;
No effluence of the sun, nor moon's blue ray;
God is its light; serene and mild the flood
Of radiance that fills heaven's dome sublime.
O sky, more tender than spring's tenderest blue,
O'erarching, all-embracing as the love
Divine, where tempests never sweep, nor storms
Yelling with fury through the vast concave,

Distracted, thunder-driven, can strew with rack,
Nor fading eve, nor sable night shall drape
In dusk serenity. The luminous tide,
Like to a summer sea of glory, broods
Over the land. Shall Eden be adorned
With foliage deep and verdant meads and glades,
And pleasant rivers sparkling in the sun,
Moist dells, or shady nooks, or sunny slopes,
Where flowers up-spring, as if the earth had smiled,
And tuneful birds their sweetest carols pour,
Where perfumes breathe from odoriferous groves,
And bounteous nature spreads her golden fruits,
Shall nought more beautiful than this exist?
This the spent effort of creative will?
Nay; adumbrations faint are these; dim types
Of heaven's realities. New flowers there bloom,
Mayhap, of undreamed beauty, fragrance rare,
And unimagined forms, not as on earth,
Rare visitants, spring's gentle harbingers,
Summer's gay crown, and autumn's pomp and pride,
Frailest of earth's frail things, perennial there,
As promises of fruitage unconceived,
Fruits that may spring from out the exuberance
Of generosity divine, new modes
Now unimagined, yet endowed to lure
And satisfy celestial appetites.
New and strange forms of life we may conceive
Existing there, and with new loveliness,
New creatures, rational, intelligent,
Who have attained by other paths than ours,
Earth's ways of sorrow, heaven's high eminence,

Kindred with us in sympathy or form,
Gifted with other powers. The mind, well pleased,
Broods o'er the possibilities, where love
Will lavish its choice treasures to enrich
The home of the redeemed. What glad surprise
Shall wake the sleeper from death's heavy dream,
With ravishing prospects of those sunny plains
Of Sabbath rest, and occupations new,
Pleasures disguised in sweet variety,
When from this narrow world of sight and sound
The soul shall pass, entering a world unknown,
Escaped from sin's alluring perilous dreams,
Finding delights, pleasures more exquisite
Than aught that earth affords. Drawn nearer now
The central Fount of being, heightened sense,
May gain more intimate and fuller view
Into the inward mystery of life,
Far ampler knowledge, closer intercourse.

    Clouds o'er the future hang, a darkness deep
Shrouds the fast coming years with sombre pall.
On through its orbit whirls the unquiet earth,
Bearing throughout the deep and sounding void
Its mass of woe, its mingled joys and griefs;
Veil the great orb of sorrow, O ye clouds,
With all its breaking hearts, its broken ties,
With all its desolate homes and ruined lives,
And graves deep-trenched; ye infinite depths of space,
Bury earth's miserere, dismal plaint,
That like the moan of morning constantly
Circles our globe. Change upon change succeeds;
Good slowly grows; new forms of vice upspring,

Entangling with a fell perversity
The ardent footsteps of the coming age.
The mystery of sin, dread mystery,
Appals the soul, this second deluge vast,
That lifts its horrid and engulfing waves
In awful clamour, threatening to drown
In woes remediless the souls of men.
And in the picture dark few gleams appear;
There are dumb yearnings, instincts of the race,
A leaning and a growing to the light,
Broadening of view and general advance;
Then comes a backward movement as the tide,
With reinforcement of the hindward wave,
Swirls its huge mass again to ocean depths.
The national spirit stirs, the national strength
Stretches its growing limbs, and forward sets
To ventures high, yet round its ardent steps
The dogs of hell, rapine, and avarice,
Ambition, lust, will ever sniff and slink,
Ready for their dread work, ready to check
These nobler movements of the human race;
And all the fondest dreams of largest minds,
Peace, reverence of truth, humanity,
A great uplifting of the general life,
Are in one moment dashed to utter wreck.
Yet through the drifting and unquiet clouds
Ring on the Christmas bells, as if Christ's church,
Patient through prescience, with a heaven-born trust,
Clings to a hope so priceless to the world.
New systems of philosophy will rise
To mock their predecessors, then in turn

Betake themselves to dark oblivion's paths.
New waves of thought will sweep the human world,
New movements and new masters of the race
Rule their brief hour: new victims yet unborn,
Suffering, shall curse their fate and yearn for death.
Nations shall rise and fall. The world is full
Of ruins, and each ruin mutely stands
A prophecy to all that dominates
The present, how commanding, strong, or brave.
In halls of state the savage lioness
Suckles her tawny whelps; the asp up-coils;
The bittern and the jackal haunt and prowl
Where crowds once dwelt by the Euphrates' stream;
And desert sands rustle o'er marble floors
Where royalty in perfumed pride once passed;
Gaunt ruin, hollow-eyed, possession claims
Of palaces, and owls now hoot and mope
Where kings once reigned. Heaps, pools, and shapeless mounds,
Alone remain to tell of capitals
Of mightiest name; Susa, Persepolis,
Or Babylon, Thebes midst Egypt's palms,
Or Tyre upon its melancholy strand,
Where now the surge breaks over columns prone,
Palmyra of the desert, or the crowd
Of nameless cities 'neath forgotten mounds
Cumbering the earth, silent of their great past:
And many a proud and thronging capital,
Now world-renowned, whose peopled streets are filled
With busy crowds, shall desolate become:
Where navies ride the solitary loon

Shall in the rushes lurk; the wild swan fish
Rivers alive with commerce of a world;
Low lies the architrave; the ambitious dust
Crowns the wreathed capital, while, on the plinth,
Basks the mute lizard in the noon-day sun;
And o'er the broken arch of busy mart
Or echoing council halls, the wild brier throws
Its matted thorny veil, as if to hide
Mortal humiliation. Yet may rise
New nations of new name and language new.
We know not what awaits, nor how the earth
Will to its future speed; if changes yet
Will mark its history, and epochs make,
Oceans upheaved, and continents new born.
Science may don her robe prophetical,
And, with vaticination ominous,
Cast the world's horoscope, of cataclysms,
Collision with some mighty wandering orb,
Or, of the sun's retracted forces dream,
When its diminished fires at length withdraw
Their kindly heat till the capacious earth
Shall sweep its ever-narrowing circles round,
And in the flaming vortex drawn at length
Rush to destruction swift; in wider view
See the whole universe of circling worlds
Convulsed in spasm of universal death,
Contracted from its wide extended shores,
Extinct and dead, in one huge frozen mass,
Suspended in dark lone immensity.

Conjectures, vaguest speculations all!
Airy and baseless; for more surely led

By warrant of God's word we surely look
For the Redeemer's advent, long delayed,
Long wished for ; day of tribulation sore,
Sudden, unheralded, snaring the nations.
So shall it come. What mighty storms shall rise,
To shake the stars from out the fixèd heavens,
Cast like untimely figs, what sudden gloom
Shall this great world envelop, sudden dread
Palsying familiar life, when the Great Judge
Shall with His retinue in heaven appear,
No mortal tongue may tell. The piercing blast
Of the archangel's trumpet, dreadful sound,
Terrific, thund'ring through the earth and sea
Shall wake the dead, and summon them to judgment!
Assail the walls of this great world, and throw
To crumbling ruins their solidity ;
Call from their lowly graves, earth's dust, from piles
Of masonry deep laid and leaden bound,
Or cells where the red fire its victims hid,
Or ocean's caverns vast, call the great crowds,
Unnumbered multitudes. Dread spectacle !
The peopled heavens above, earth's concourse dense,
Vast sea of upturned faces pale with fear,
The living and the dead, now dead no more ;
While from the aspect terrible of Him
Who sits upon the throne, the guilty earth,
As conscience-smitten, shrinks and quakes with fear.
Mountain and rock their solid basements yield
At the dread sight. The sinner's piteous plea
For refuge, hopeless plea, is now rejected,
For e'en the stony-hearted cliffs he sues,

Falling, refuse concealment: dreadful lot!
To be exposed to all the pelting storm.
O spectacle of majesty and dread!
The crash of falling worlds, nature's dismay,
Darkness and tempest and the voice of words,
And more than midnight gloom, with lightning cleft,
Convulsive throes of earthquake, echoes dread,
Of an expiring world, sights terrible,
Appalling sounds, from which the thought shrinks
    back;
For now is seen the Judge upon the throne!
The mind o'erwhelmed sinks at the prospect dread,
Though but the forecast of the awful scene,
And instant refuge seeks; with penitence,
Self-accusation, and with bitterness,
Rejecting its imperfect sin-stained past,
Clinging to Christ with utter confidence
And His atoning work on Calvary wrought.
   Yet, resting in the covenant of love,
No fears distress. Robed in Christ's righteousness,
The spirit views e'en an expiring world,
Safe in divine protection; as the eye
Notes the spent tempest, moving from the sky,
Retreating thunderstorm, that, as it goes,
Blazes with voiceless lightning, till the clouds,
High piled in all their formidable pomp,
Fringed and pulsating with their lessening fires,
Drop o'er the horizon's edge, and leave the expanse
Of innocent heaven a perfect spotless blue.
For love assurance gives of victory,
Victory o'er death! for in that hour extreme,

Wrestling with doubt, e'en then love's voice is heard,
And the triumphant soul shall in the hour
Of its dread agony, from out the pains
Of dissolution rise, and conqueror prove.
The righteous nought can harm ; no hand can pluck
Their souls from out their Great Redeemer's care.

    The mailed Crusader hailed with rapturous joy
Blest Salem's towers, while the unbidden tear
Rushed to his eyes. Jerusalem divine,
Fair haven of our thoughts, thou city dear,
Zion, beloved of God, by fondest names
Most fondly cherished, most delightsome, hail!
Christ's faithful turn to thee their longing eyes,
For thou dost hold enthroned their glorious King,
And loved Redeemer. Oft their wistful gaze
Turns from the murky clouds and gathering shades
Of earth, eager to catch one glimpse, though faint,
Of thy celestial splendours. Mortal eye
Those jasper battlements, like summer clouds,
Sun-shot, in lofty grandeur piled, suffused
With hues ensanguined, fringed with foamy white,
Hath never seen, nor ranged the golden vision :
Streets, palaces, and bastions, gates of pearl,
Within whose glorious ramparts, ever safe,
Walk Christ's redeemed, the holy, white-robed throng.
O beatific vision ! glorious home
Of ransomed souls, how do our spirits long
As those who watch till that the night be past
And morning dawn. Immured within these walls
Of sad mortality, here prisoners pent,
Reluctant witnesses of sin's dread power,

Foul shapes beset us, avarice and lust,
Detested tyranny ; here pain is seen
With her dark face convulsed and trembling mouth,
Bosomed on feeble human sympathy,
Woe with her reddened eyelids, hopelessness
Staring all moodily, and livid death,
And blank despair, man's last iniquity :
For thee we yearn, and fondly dream our dream
Of promised blessedness, and fondly look
For the unclosing of the jealous dark.

  May we not dream that in the land of God
Mountains far loftier rise than those of earth
Whose snows are reddened with each setting sun ;
Rivers that flash and sparkle in the light
Of an eternal noon. Canaan's fair hills
With flocks were clothed, her vales stood thick with corn ;
The grapes of Eshcol hung in clusters deep,
And Sharon's rose its fragrance shook abroad
Upon the breeze that made the lilies dance.
There many a prospect spread, there many a nook
Of secret loveliness concealed itself ;
Glimpses were there of the far-shimmering sea,
The snows of Lebanon, or Gilead's heights,
Judea's terraced vines, or Bashan's glades ;
Cedar clad slopes, and cliffs precipitous ;
Vineyards were there and cornlands of the plain,
Round many a home of peacefulness and rest,
Bosomed in trees, or, basking in the sun :
Fair prototype of scenes surpassing fair !
The glorious world by love for love prepared :
By love prepared, th' unfathomed love of Christ.

His are creation's works. His quickening voice
Spoke into being this wide universe,
Devising and effecting earth's vast frame,
With all its treasured wealth, or wonderful
Or beautiful. His the broad summer land
Of whispering trees and odour-breathing flowers,
The sea is His, with its unfathomed depths,
Its treasure-house fast locked of buried wealth.
Again hath Christ put forth creative might
Not for unfallen man ; for His redeemed,
Hath He prepared the chosen land of bliss.
Hither from life's sore battlefield they come,
With piercèd hearts, conquered though conquerors,
Crowned with the thorns of mockery, full oft,
Bleeding and footsore from affliction's paths,
The shards of poverty, the pangs of grief.
If streams, deep shades, bright flowers, ambrosial fruits
Were for the parents of our race prepared
In Paradise, what welcome shall await
Christ's own redeemed? Theirs were His latest thoughts
While here He tarried ; His last offices
To wash their feet, to give them holy bread,
And cheer them with His holy mystic wine ;
And when they come from their death-chamber faint,
Shall not refreshment wait them, ministerings
Of angel hands, voices of gentle love ?
O Friend within the veil! wilt Thou not give
The bread of heaven, wilt Thou not to their lips
Present the chalice of Thy royal wine ?
This Thou didst promise, and with this, yet more,
Thine approbation, seal of faithful life !

And we will trust Thee, O Thou best of friends!
And through the darkness go to seek Thy love,
Bright jewel of eternal blessedness!
　Love is the quick and cunning architect,
Ample provider, servant swift of foot;
And love has decked the land to which we go.
O blissful scenes, bright 'neath your cloudless skies,
Unfading trees in ever-during spring,
Rivers whose glitter hides no snares of death,
And sunny fields of lasting pleasantness,
Fresh balmy air with gently-breathing winds,
Fair light that never fades from out the sky;
Ye flowers, in all your undreamed loveliness,
Untainted by decay or smell of mould,
Whose odour sweet above the towering hills,
The battlements of jasper, never blows,
How do your beauties lure our shrinking hopes?
Imagination in so vast a field
May roam unchecked, even in its loftiest flights.
Pleasant the land where darkness never comes,
Nor age decays, disease, nor withering death
Unpins the body's tabernacle frail,
Where sorrows ne'er befall, nor pains are felt,
Nor tears steal forth, nor sighs nor groans are heard,
Sorrow's sad music being for ever stilled.
Pleasant the land where it is always spring,
Where blossoms hide the ripe and blushing fruit,
Genial and calm the day, nor sun's hot ray,
Nor baleful smiting of the moon by night,
Is felt; no rushing winds, no frost-bound sod,
No tempest in its fury, earthquake's shock,

Terror by day, nor pestilence by night.
Pleasant where friends meet their lost friends once more,
Not in the ruddy firelight round the hearth
Awhile, then all too soon to part, to wave
The tender signal from the lessening shore,
Tear-blinded, and with sorrowing boding hearts;
Now never more to part; for love regains
Her treasures: and dear kindred souls are loved
With love that never more may know excess.

Like the poor bird belated, his co-mates
In summer's festival southward long fled,
That spreading its drenched wings through fog and rain,
And bitter cold of this bleak northern clime,
Escapes, to find, within a few short hours,
Bland skies and sunshine of a southern land,
Orange and citron groves, and breath of flowers:
So, from the storm and tempest of this life,
The soul makes its escape to find in heaven
True rest; flies from a sick and dying frame,
To health perpetual, and perpetual youth,
Flies to th' eternal house not made with hands;
Escapes from life's probation to the assured
And absolute security of heaven;
From sorrow to the joy unspeakable,
From pain to pleasure, and from death to life.

Blest saints of God! for your bright company
We yearn. There, crowned with everlasting bliss,
Earth's noblest stand; prophets and patriarchs,
Martyrs and saints in number numberless;
Brave speakers, noble doers of God's truth.
True manhood there in purity and strength,

Loved womanhood in all its tenderness,
Matrons and virgins chaste, as lilies fair
Against the golden sky, children's sweet forms,
Earth's loveliest, all we call fair, or bright,
Beloved, or beautiful, or true, or good,
There fairer far, most loved, most beautiful;
Perfection's height attained, nor lurking fear
Of sad decadence. Grander far their song
Than earth's sublimest strains, the quiring wind,
Or waves deep-voiced, surging on rock-bound coast,
Commingling with the roar of pathless woods,
Full blended harmonies, true worship there.
And, intermingled with that company,
Angelic forms; rare visitants on earth,
But now perpetual companions.
Oft through life's rugged ways their kindly hands
Had reached, extending friendly sympathies,
For round life's path these angels ministrant
On each believer wait; to mortal eye
Unseen, undreamed, pouring celestial balm
Into the spirit's wounds, and with their strength
Upholding tenderly the feeble frame;
Nor lot so dreary, suffering so dark,
Nor life so lonely, but their help is given.
No rustling leaf, no whispers faint betray
The angelic presence, but the heart is cheered
Not knowing how, and cheerfully again
The daily cross uplifts; but now brought near,
Benignant spirits! passing sweet the hope
Friendships angelical to form, to learn
The secrets treasured in seraphic breasts,

With heavenly love inflamed, ecstatic joy,
To catch the gleam that from the shielded ranks
Of mighty cherubim, shines proudly forth,
True loyalty unstained as virgin snow ;
In your bright company to spend the hours
Of the eternal day, day without night,
In high pursuit of knowledge, there undimmed,
Or learning your proud spirit of loyalty.
  "With Christ." So runs the Word. Not rapt in sleep
Oblivious, with suspension bare of life
Poised o'er its elements, or lost in dreams,
But in the presence of its loving Lord ;
Banished all doubt, misgiving banished now,
In the first glimpse of that most blessed Face.
Evil is past, conflict and weary toil
In death's great Sabbath, and e'en bitterest woes
Hushed in the ocean vast of endless love ;
There rest the righteous till the trump shall sound
Through earth and sea waking the slumberers,
And in the sky the Judge enthroned appear,
To all men visible, with throngs begirt,
Of holy angels and the blessed dead
Innumerable, with rapturous acclaim,
The welcome of the living Church caught up
To meet Him in the air. Then when is passed
Judgment's great session, shall the gates unfold
Celestial, and mortal vision fails
In the bright glories of eternity.
Nor know we more. " For ever with the Lord,"
In unimagined bliss. Then shall the King
Be seen, arrayed in beauty, not obscured,

Like the pale winter sun, dim seen through clouds,
But in the splendour of the summer noon;
Nor, as on earth, in His humility
Disguised, but crowned, enthroned. So runs our hope.
  Then sons of God indeed, and like the Son,
Then will the endeavour of the daily life,
Wish nearest to the faithful Christian heart,
The Gospel's aim be fully realised,
For the believer shall be like his Lord:
Like Him in body; for at length shall Christ
Fashion this body of humility
Like to His own; in spirit like; in power,
In holiness, and in unbounded love.
The circuit is at length complete. The love
From which we sprang, creative love, has reached
Its object ultimate. The golden clue
That through the labyrinth of life conducts
The willing soul, is needed now no more.
Love has regained her own. The mortal will
Blends with the will Supreme in life's great end.
Then, in a language lisped but feebly here,
But dimly traced amidst earth's mysteries,
The human love merged in the love Divine,
God's saints shall comprehend, shall fully know,
That greatest of all mysteries, "God is love."

THE END.

www.ingramcontent.com/pod-product-compliance
Lightning Source LLC
Chambersburg PA
CBHW020304240426
43673CB00039B/695